About The Au

Ewan Morrison is the author of a trilogy of n
(Jonathan Cape / Vintage) and of the collec...
Other Stories (Chroma). He has been short-listed for the Le Prince Maurice
Literary Award and is the winner of a Royal Television Society Award. His
novel *Close Your Eyes* will be released in 2012. The film adaptation of his novel
Swung is being made by Sigma Films.

Praise For Tales From The Mall And Ewan Morrison

"Morrison continues Ballard's tradition of locating menace beneath
the sleekness and shine of postindustrial life. You also learn a lot along
the way. A truly interesting book."
-Douglas Coupland, author of 'Generation X'

"Tales From the Mall is a great book. It's touching and emotional
and part of a new form of literary storytelling. It's worth reading,
worth loving."
-James Frey, author of a Million Little Pieces

"Ewan Morrison captures beautifully the point at which anecdote
becomes urban myth and reportage slides into fiction. A really
important new form has emerged."
-Claire Armitstead, Books Editor, The Guardian.

"A wonderful and important book that does the most difficult thing:
laying bare the overlooked everyday world in which we live. The dark
dreams and lightweight fantasies of shopping malls and those within
them are exposed with incredible acuity and great tenderness."
Catherine O'Flynn, author of 'What Was Lost'

"The most groundbreaking and moving book to come out of Britain
in years. A dazzling book about everyday peple trying to find heart in a
heartless place. Morrison is so far ahead of the zeitgeist it's frightening."
-Doug Johnstone, author & journalist

"A precocious literary talent."
-The Sunday Times

"A writer of serious intent and prodigious talent."
-The Times

"The fictional passages, where Morrison all too convincingly shows how Mall culture affects the behaviour of his characters, are where the book becomes really terrifying. Tales from the Mall is a highly convincing argument that our current retail models, based on a false premise of infinite expansion, are damaging our culture and ourselves. It's well researched, and well written, but its real strength is that it has a force to it which comes straight from the convictions of the author, not to mention the abundance of evidence his case draws on."
-Keir Hind, The Skinny

"'A definitive expedition into the alternative universe death-star environment of the mall. Sure-footed, smart and necessary. Morrison unpicks security barriers between genres, documenting his fictions, and smacking us with real-world retrievals."
-Iain Sinclair, writer and filmmaker. author of 'Ghost Milk'

TALES
FROM
THE
MALL

EWAN MORRISON

CARGO
publishing

"Tales From The Mall"
Ewan Morrison
First Published 2012
Published by Cargo Publishing
SC376700
978-1908885012
Bic Code-FA Modern & Contemporary Fiction
FYB Short Stories

Produced with assistance from:
Creative Scotland

Also available as:
Ebook
Kindle ebook
Enhanced ebook
App for iphone/ipad

Printed & Bound by CPI Group (UK) Ltd, Croydon, CR0 4YY
Cover design by Craig Lamont

www.cargopublishing.com

All you'll ever need, under one roof.

WELCOME TO THE MALL

THE MALL has over 50 stories and facts under one roof, including short fiction and true-tales-retold from 100 interviews in shopping malls. Inside you will find fictions with all your favourite brand names and many tantalising images. THE MALL is also the perfect place for family fun, with 'things to do' and 'play n' learn areas'. Follow the site map to find historical and sociological information. THE MALL has more than you'll ever need, and no matter where you are, it's never far away.

DISCLAIMER / RECLAIMER

Tales from the Mall is a collection of short stories intercut with (1) facts about the history and global spread of shopping malls and (2) stories I've been told by people who work and shop within malls, in my home country, Scotland, and in the United States. These reported 'incidents' were originally recounted to me as anecdotes and urban folklore. Here, I attempt to retell the tales in the most simple, transparent, language, to let the people and their stories speak for themselves.

Historically, there have been many attempts to save authentic local histories from extinction. Of note in international terms, was the forty-year-long project conducted by the School of Scottish Studies in Edinburgh University; a vast archive of folklore, stories and songs of the Scots and the 'travelling people'.

What has this to do with malls, you might ask, and rightly so. Aren't malls precisely the kind of homogenising modern phenomenon that are forcing indigenous cultures into decline? Am I being ironic, or nihilistic, or just plain ignorant in trying to document the folk culture of the mall?

Not in the slightest. The mallification of my country is an historic event, as important as the Jacobite Rebellion or the Highland Clearances. Those that do not believe this could do with asking themselves why most of the clothes they wear are manufactured in China and most of the culture they consume is made in America; why most of their population now works in retail. *Tales from the Mall* is an attempt to discover what has survived the levelling of consumerism and has potential resistance within my country as it becomes part of the globalised economy.

A question has bothered me in the course of my research: **Why are there so few books about malls?** After all, do we not live in a time in which global consumerism invades all aspects of our lives; in which the mantra of 4% consumer growth dictates every government policy in our countries? Countries that look ever more the same.

Most troublingly, I've noted a dominant trend in culture – in fiction in particular – towards nostalgia. It is, as critic Fredric Jameson noted, that the more we head towards a globally-homogenised future, the less we are able to talk about the present; we tend instead to dig out our old 'authenticities' and celebrate the parochial pasts that existed before the advent of consumerism. As a result of this epidemic of nostalgia, the historical obligation to document our passing lives and the conditions we live under, for future generations, is being forfeited. A hundred years from now, our grandchildren will ask: what was life like in your time? And we will only be able to reply that we spent our time fantasising of other times, and perhaps, shamefacedly: shopping.

This may be because our era has no narrative; all that we require from a story – the struggle of the individual against all odds, towards a greater goal – is increasingly hard to envisage in an economy that undermines the lifelong project and in its place offers only quick fixes. It may be that consumerism and the struggle for daily survival in a deregulated job market of all-against-all has reduced our lives to short-term personal goals without a broader collective narrative. If so, then it is understandable that the stories we tell ourselves should be about a more wholesome, epic and engaging past, and this might explain the question – **why are there so few books about shopping malls?**

There have been mall-based novels written by such respected authors as JG Ballard, Eric Bogosian and Catherine O'Flynn, but these all portray something else *occurring* in a mall. The mall in these is a location, as if in a film – a backdrop. Within the thirty books set in malls that I've read there is without exception a murder or a madman on the loose with a gun. This clearly does not depict our daily experience. Perhaps the dream of genocide in the mall is the guilty conscience of the happy consumer, half-aware that mall shopping is based on some abstract exploitation.

Tales from the Mall is not an overarching critique of malls. I want, simply, to talk about the impact that such a culture has on our lives, given that the very city I live in – Glasgow, Scotland – has turned itself around from a city in post-industrial decline to become a leading consumer centre – Buchanan street, with one mall at the top and another at the bottom, is now the seventh largest *retail avenue* in the world.

The literature of my country is vehemently opposed to what it sees as a takeover of our national identity by multi-national forces; but at the same time, most of our revered writers take the stance that the best form of defending a more authentic past is retreat into it. I remain convinced that the non-story of a country in the hands of modern global consumerism still has to be told, banal as that may seem. When I set out to write this book, I wanted to find out if, in the heart of the anonymous international shopping mall, there were indigenous stories worth protecting and celebrating. I discovered that there were many.

There are, however, obstacles in retelling such stories. Not least of all is branding law. Each of the corporations within a typical mall police the use of their brand name by others. The author and the reader are then faced with the absurd demand that no real corporation or product names can be used in the depiction of a mall.

The legal advice I received before publication was – 'take out or change all the brand names'. But imagine a book about a mall in which every store and product had its name deleted. For example:

'Joe decided to stop off in DELETED for a quick DELETED, before heading over to DELETED to buy a DELETED for his girlfriend's birthday.'

This would become still more absurd if the author had to come up with new names for products and brands, to conceal what these really were, while, at the same time, attempting to imply what they had been before they had been edited out.

'Joe decided to stop off in BURGER PRINCE for a quick HIPSI-COLA, before heading over to JENNIFER'S DISCRETION to buy a WUNDER BRASSIERE for his girlfriend's birthday.'

Not only would this be a waste of any writer's energy, but the reader would become distracted by attempting to decode what the fictional brand names might have been before the change. After all, branding is an important socio-historic fact and a multi-billion dollar industry; real brand identities have been created and tested

11

by thousand of advertisers over many decades. Furthermore, renaming say, PEPSI as HIPSI, would be a misrepresentation of the status PEPSI has achieved in the world. Surely it is important, sociohistorically, that a character called Ahmed is drinking Pepsi in Afghanistan or a person called Ivan is wearing Nikes in Siberia, or that I might use Virgin for my phone, air flights, train travel, music, home and life insurance. Ironically, if Virgin or Nike, for example, were to remove their names from a text, they would also be losing the opportunity to demonstrate how ubiquitous their brand has become; how our lives have come to depend on them.

The fact that corporations have the power to delete any use of their brand name they do not deem to be 'on message' is a form of censorship that extends well beyond the rights of any democracy. If representations of the world as-it-is are deleted from the page then they will be deleted from our minds, eventually crippling our ability to build a true picture of the world we live in. The paradox is that this censorship is occurring at the same time that the very brands of-which-we-cannot-speak are consuming ever-more space in our streets and towns, our media, our culture, and our minds.

A little foresight shows that if branding censorship continues its trajectory, we will soon arrive at a point where storytelling will have to reconcile itself to the limited task of re-depicting the worlds that existed before multinational corporations existed. Perhaps we have already arrived at this point.

The legal system that protects corporations from having their brands named was one established in the US. It regards corporations and their brands as having the same status as 'individuals': therefore any mention of a corporation can be viewed as libellous, according to the same laws that protect persons. Corporations are clearly not individuals, but until this law is repealed, the simple naming of corporations, even as backgrounds to a human fiction, is potentially litigious.

However, although America first spawned such corporations, there are also legal safeguards in the states that can protect authors from their power. The first amendment law of freedom of speech allows for negotiation. So it is that Bret Easton Ellis in *American Psycho* could name the brands which his serial killer obsessed over and upon which he built his personality; these included Armani and Hugo Boss. No such law protects British writers, and American corporations regularly exploit the lack of constitutional protection for freedom of speech in the UK to bring cases against those who have mentioned their brand names in printed material in the US. This is a loophole, an artefact of a legal system developed before modern copyright law. A ball and chain around the British author.

My aim has not been to defame or criticise any corporations specifically; I simply wish to depict the real and recognisable world in which such brands exist and to do so without deletions or redactions. For this reason I have used the true names of companies whenever I have deemed that a tale (true or fictional) has required that information for verification or in the interests of verisimilitude. There is only one instance in the book where a brand name has been redacted and that is for poetic rather than political reasons. In every other case I have kept the brand names as they are and the only names I have modified are those of specific malls and individuals. I have done this to protect my sources, as many of the anecdotes I have been told were humorous and confessional, and certain mall workers wished to protect their identities by remaining anonymous. It could be said that, here, I do not extend the same rights to corporations as I do to individuals, and that is in fact the case. Individuals exist in one place only, while brands are transnational; it is simply impossible for an individual to have the same power and influence – in many countries at the same time – that the corporation does today. That corporations are granted 'personhood', is an historic error, which many across the political spectrum are actively seeking to rectify.

I ask that my use of real brand names be considered an exercise in free speech and as part of our 'cultural commons'. Brands are as ubiquitous, globally, as the landscape itself; to have to delete them from our picture would be like having to describe the countryside with the word 'trees' deleted. In a world filled with brand names, we must surely have the right to repeat brand names in print, and to acknowledge the importance they have in our lives. Otherwise this book will have 867 words deleted, and will be no picture of a modern mall at all. The deleted will become the bigger and more pressing story that will still need to be told.

Welcome to the mall.

Ewan Morrison, 2012

Every ten days – the rate at which a new mall opened in the US during the heyday of 'infinite retail expansion' (1966–1981).

Every five weeks – the rate at which a mall closed in the US due to bankruptcy and market saturation (2004–2011).

While the mall is in steady decline in the US, the US mall model for economic growth and the inevitable entropy it carries within it has now been exported to the rest of the world. From 2007–2010, a new mall opened on non-US soil (former 'Soviet' Countries, 'The East' and 'developing' countries) **every seventy-two hours**.

STORE / STORY GUIDE

All of the following areas contain true stories or information.

CAR PARK

CUSTOMER INFORMATION

 **SECURITY**

 SHOPMOBILITY AND DISABLED ACCESS

M **MALL OFFICE**

STAFF AREAS – RESTRICTED

The Unfortunate Tale of Victor Gruen

If you have ever entered a shopping mall with the intention of purchasing, say, a pair of shoes, and have left with a hairdryer, four bars of chocolate and a flight to New York, then you've probably been a victim of 'The Gruen Transfer'. This is the name psychologists use to describe the process whereby consumers respond unwittingly to stimuli in the retail environment – lighting, layout, sounds, smells – all of which have been designed to create disorientation, leading you (the customer) to lose all sense of direction and purpose, opening you to irrational desires and 'impulse buys'.

Victor Gruen (1903-1980) – who the condition was named after – did not consent to having his name borrowed or his life cast in this mould. He started out with a rather different set of goals.

Gruen was an Austrian-born architect who fled to the USA from Nazi Vienna in 1938. He famously arrived in New York with 'only $8, an architect's degree and no English'. Gruen disliked much of America; the suburbs, automobiles, and even shopping. He believed that a stop had to be put to the sprawl and the destruction of communities that had been unleashed by the proliferation of strip malls – strip malls being unregulated development by retailers, along freeways between towns and cities, which led to American roadsides, in the 40s, becoming dominated by cheaply built stores and huge glaring advertisements which stretched on for hundreds of miles, obscuring the landscape beyond.

Gruen was concerned by the fact that suburban Americans knew nothing of their neighbours and drove tens of miles to shop for essentials while still never encountering each other. He wanted to call a stop to this newly emerging lifestyle before it resulted in social atomisation and the dissolution of community life.

His alternative and radical ideal was the construction of a focal centre; a 'crystallisation point for suburbia's community life' – a concept he likened to the ancient Greek 'Agora' or marketplace where goods and ideas were traded. Gruen was a committed socialist and subscribed to the utopian, modernist belief that bold new architecture could literally lay a foundation for a better society; his vision was that of constructing a social gathering space, which coupled modern commerce with a celebratory, communal ethic: it would have fountains, clocks, trees, playing and strolling areas, it would host live music, talks and public events. Such a place would be styled after the great civic parks in Washington, Boston and London, and like them it would take the name: Mall.

Gruen was vehemently opposed to any forces, political or economic, which sought to covertly manipulate the individual, but History had its fun with Victor Gruen. He went on to become the most influential commercial architect of the 20th century, and his designs became the international template for the modern mall, laying down a blueprint for the homogenous retail architecture and consumer-based city planning that followed; facilitating the spread of transnational capitalism. Against his better intentions, his designs contributed to an acceleration of the social fragmentation he spent a lifetime trying to prevent, and to the destruction of many city centres, towns, rural areas, communities, and, some would argue, entire national economies.

In later life, shocked by the 'bastardisation' of his ideals, Gruen returned to Vienna and lived out his last days in a country retreat, far from the modern world. In a 1978 speech, he recalled visiting one of his old malls, where he swooned in horror at 'the ugliness... of the land-wasting seas of parking' and the 'soul-killing sprawl beyond.' He died on his private estate two years later.

Next time you leave a mall with a new pair of shoes, when you only went in for a sandwich, please consider the unfortunate tale of Victor Gruen.

Victor Gruen is to the right demonstrating his model for a new mall. 1952. Image from the film The Gruen Effect via derStandard.

FOOD COURT

Mother

This is not her, this shrillness of voice, these schedules and rules, these flashes. She shouts at the traffic, at her children. She's in the Subaru, checking time. Sixteen minutes till the first time she has seen him since *he* ran, one month before, February the 12th. She has protected the children from as much as she could, the separation agreement has been counter-signed, his things boxed, ready for removal, but now she must face his face, as law demands. Rights of visitation.

They are driving to *a mall* – this is what he has reduced them to. Joshy is twittering excitedly in the back, *Will Daddy get me a Xmas present?* Claire, the little madam is tutting, *Jeeso, it's practically Easter – get a frickin' calendar, retard!*

Language, young lady. This is how she talks now. Policer of words.

Other 'newly separateds' have used similar locations, her lawyer said; a mall is a neutral space without prior emotional associations, not her place or his, but halfway between. They also have high security, thus reducing the chances of abduction.

No one can be trusted, she sees that now. The sex and drugs on the streets, on the net. Josh is allowed only one hour of Xbox per day. Claire is banned from Facebook. Since *he* left she has had no choice but to do this. Toxins are everywhere; she has put the children on a macrobiotic diet, although she worries that this is why Josh has started hiding things under his bed: crisps and adverts torn from her magazines. Images of women eating ice-creams and posing in bikinis. She must search the entire house. She must take her son to a child psychologist. This is what he has done to them.

She's swearing at the parking space, then apologising. She's saying *This is our new arrangement, your father is very busy right now.* Her daughter tuts. *For Godsake, will you stop that nonsense animal sound, young lady!* She must not shout, must retain some control, if only of herself. She's running through the list of rules with them. *Call me immediately if he smells of alcohol – if he is with another woman. Absolutely no fast food or gifts. Remember, one hour, then be ready to leave, I'll be at my pilates class.* And that is not true, and she has never lied to her children before. *If you're late, if he makes you late, I'm calling the whole thing off.* This is not her voice, this is some other woman.

Claire

Oh My Actual God – the place is jam-packed with scummers from Inverhales, like Sheila McGovern and Debra Mackay. She's texing Fi – *OMAG, it's soooo Zombie central LOL!!!* She's trying to joke this whole saddo Daddo scenario away but it's shiver-making when she sees him, down the bottom of the escalator by H&M – like this scrawny version of himself, like *Skeletor* or whoever. And totally cringe-central –like how he's on the ground floor and they've come in on the first floor, and Momsee might actually have said, *C'mon, let's go down to his level.*

Then it's a major *You've Been Framed* experience cos doofus Daddo's coming up the up-escalator just as they're heading down-the-down. Then he's waving as they pass by; giving it *I'll come back down when I get to the top.* And blubber-boy Joshy is trying to climb over the moving railing, giving it *Daddy, Daddy.* Then at the bottom Momsee's giving Daddo hand signals, mouthing *WE COME TO YOU – YOU STAY THERE – STAY,* like he's a frickin' dog. Jeeso. Claire's big re-union with sad ole Daddo, trashed by escalator embarrassment. She texts him so he'll get the message.

The next bit is the worst and Claire is so trying not to tut. But Daddo's giving it the big cheesies: *Hey kids, how's it going? Great to see you again.* And Momsee giving him her totally autistics: *One hour, don't leave the building. I will pick them up here. This spot, exactly.* Then there's the solemns and Momsee's silent threats as she waves goodbye. And as soon as she's out of earshot, like on cue, Daddo's giving it: *OK rascals, my treat, anything you want.* And Joshy shouting *MacDonald's, MacDonald's!* And Daddo saying, *Well Josh, I don't think there's one here.*

Burger King! Joshy's shouting. The frickin' pig-belly. And Daddo's doin' his change of subject routine, *OK, so how about we… get a…*

Build-a-bear, Build-a-bear, Joshy's shouting. He has like ten bears already.

Claire lets them drag her along and texts Fi – *Daddo is majorly tryin 2 buy his way back in. Wot a LOSER!!* And that goddamn store. There's fairy bears and army bears, even goddamn Darth Vader bears. She's thinking what's next? Porno bears, or like cryogenically frozen Michael Jackson Bears! And, of course, Daddo has to let fatzoid pick the biggest, and there's all these uber-brats standing in line clutching their bear skins and this fluff-stuffing machine that fills the skins. She texts Fi – *OMAG, its like a durex jobby-bag! Euwww!!* And fatboy's whining, *Daddy, can I get a spaceman costume, too?* That's when it hits her, the divorce is final. Claire runs to the toilet and sticks her fingers down her throat.

But on the way back, who does she spy? Who indeed but frickin' Momsee! It's like forty, forty-five mins to go and there's freako-mom pretending to be shopping, for Chrissakes. Claire susses it: Pilates never frickin' existed. Momsee probably sat in the car for no more than five before creeping back in for some major surveillance.

She could shout out *Hi Mom*! but decides to turn the tables and spy on the spy. Total LOL. Momsee keeping her distance, hiding behind this fake palm tree, then trying to merge with this group of girlies and making like she's looking in the windows of Ben and Jerry's. Claire texts the whole story to Fi. Fi texts back, *OMAG. LOL!! U shld totally film her!!!! XXXX*

Claire goes back to Daddo and Joshy and this frickin' forty-pound spaceman bear and she can totally tell that even before time is up Momsee would be waiting at the escalators. And she is – Kerching! Plus Momsee even accuses Daddo of being late and lays into him on the bear-front, I thought you said you didn't have any money, presents aren't going to make up for... Jeeso, maybe if the freako actually watched some soaps once in a while she wouldn't end up like being one. Loser.

Daddo says his sad goodbyes, all cinematically lost-for-words and Claire figures he'll probably be running off to 'drown his sorrows'. Momsee ushers her and bear-boy back to the safety of the Subaru and Claire has to endure even more of the smiley-faced-crap.

So, what did you get up to with your father?

We drank blood and raped a virgin, Claire could have said, but Momsee confiscated her mobile last time she said that. She takes her time and thinks of the worst thing possible. *We went to Burger King*, she says.

Don't you start lying to me, Madam!

How do you know we didn't, Mom? I thought you went to your 'Pilates Class'.

Young lady, I'll have less of that language!

Then Joshy makes-up one of his dorky two-word songs and sings it all the way home, Burger King, Burger King, lah de dah, and that drives Momsee nuts and Claire has to hide major sniggers.

Back, self-locked in her room, Claire IMs Fi the whole saga. *U shld have seen her face. OMAG. Joshy soooo rocked! I cld just eat him up – mind u – I'd prolly barf.*

Fi IMs back. *OMAG. U shld totally go to BK nxt time – it wld totally kill her! LOL. x*

Father

Every day now, he comes to the mall and takes the escalators to the fourth floor food court at 2.00 p.m. exactly. He never before enjoyed either shopping malls or fast food, but his time is his own, now that he is without work. He orders his meal from Burger King because it's cheap and they have a new Healthier Options Menu. He goes there because he cannot eat unless he is surrounded by people. He fears returning to his empty flat and cooking a meal for one. He finds the silence overpowering. He gets panic attacks, dizziness, nausea. Before he started eating in Burger King, over four months ago, he had lost three stone in weight.

His National Health Service psychiatrist said this was maybe because of the separation, because he was once the family chef. His Bolognese had been famous at dinner parties. He cooked an impressive roast sea bass with green salsa; he followed recipes from the *River Café* cookbook and entertained many guests and their children.

The only times he could cook and eat alone was when he was drunk. In the first month he melted an aluminium pan to the hob when he fell asleep after a can of beans and a half of Jack. He went dry then and so could not eat.

The doctor was concerned and warned of irreversible damage unless he got over his fear of eating alone. It was suggested that he try to eat in public places, cafes, railways stations, even the canteen in the local hospital. The mall was not on the list, but he found that in the half hour after seeing the kids, in the empty hour after hand-over, he could eat without the panic or fear or vomiting.

Since eating in the mall he started to regain his strength. He would love to share what he eats with his children, but their mother has them on a strict health food diet and he must not make things more difficult. As a result, his daily Burger King meals are a closely kept secret. Before meeting his ex-wife, he scrubs his hands and lips in the toilets and chews mints and antacids to hide the smell of fast food, as once before he had done with cigarettes, with alcohol.

Over the months he has learned that there are other regulars in the food court. They are not there to shop, only to eat. They are old men. They never learned how to cook, perhaps, and have now lost their wives, to cancer, to old age, to things unspeakable. They sometimes nod their heads to him, as they eat, as if they know.

Sometimes there are women, young women in the food court, and he catches himself thinking, he could sidle up, start to chat. But then again, such behavior was what started all this in the first place.

Some days he sits there, gazing up at the glass ceiling, with a bloated happy feeling, licking the ketchup and mayonnaise from his fingers, grateful for this simple meal that years ago he would have scorned. Sometimes he laughs, to, or maybe at himself.

He looks forward to the day when he can eat like a normal person in his own home with his children. In the meantime, his favourite meal is: The BK Flame Grilled Chicken Salad Burger – *which includes crispy lettuce, red ripe tomatoes, crunchy carrot, cabbage and sweet corn, wearing the latest designer dressing.*

Mother

She feels cracks on her surface. Sandra says resentment can age the skin. She gave her a book called *The Whole Self. Get a babysitter*, she said, *stop blaming, start dating*. Sandra has lined up three dates for her with eligibles. But she is unsure, has enough time passed? It is almost six months after *he* left and she must stop saying *he*. Not all men are as *he* is. There is one from work, Dan, and he is different, he is in the same boat. She must stop making rules or she will become brittle and break.

The motorway tunnel was jammed; there was no way she could make it on time. She had started driving around for the hour when he had them, in ever-wider arcs, circling the city, but she had mis-timed it. Road works and only the lanes in the opposite direction flowing. He'd texted her – *Where R U? We R waiting*. She'd called and told him and he'd said *Easier if I bring them back to you. OK?* She did a U-turn and went home, waited by the window. That was a mistake.

She couldn't help herself – *You're twelve minutes late*. Then other things, a raising of the voice, a cracking around its edges, *You need to get Joshy a car seat, I can't believe you let him sit there with no car seat*. And every word stupid because she didn't want him driving Joshy anywhere, ever.

Then he was at the door, sorrying, calling her by her name, and Josh was trying to drag him inside, to show him his bear castle. And the tantrum because she was saying *No, no, now Joshy, your father has to go – he's a very busy man*. Her daughter's eyes drawing pictures of her in negative; her son, wailing, kicking her shins, screaming Daddy!

Not here again, this was a mistake.

Well, how about, I take them to mine from now on, he'd said, smiling and that smile had no right. And the thought of it, this other place called his, the mess there, the smell, the meat, the drink, the students, the music, the other woman, the years stolen. No, no, we have to keep it to the mall, she yelled over the screaming. *Same time next week at the mall.*

Father

The video game store, the play-pen, Mothercare, Gap, the Nike place, Ben and Jerry's and time is being killed, his credit card cutting a hole in his pocket. He has tried to keep them from the food court but Josh has led him by the hand up to the escalator toward the smells. Why, time and time again, do they want this?

Now Joshy, he says, *you know what Mummy says.*

But Claire has tutted and muttered, he thinks – *Kiss-ass.*

What did you say madam?

She tuts – *Kids-pass. You can get like an eat-till-you-puke party pass for groups of under-tens. See,* and she points at a sign. BK KIDS. Balloons, party hats.

Kiss-ass. As usual, she has a point. The mother and the world are mad with control. Obese kids are being taken from the parents by the powers-that-be; diet is the new surveillance; a girl was arrested for eating chips on the subway. To hell with it. *OK, fine. Just this once*, he says, *Consider it a holiday from your mother's value system.* He hoped that would make his daughter smile.

Claire

She had this whole thing planned out, like how she was going to have a major biatch. Tell him, *Momsee can't even boil a frickin' egg. Can't you just come back and cook for us?* She was gonna hit him with the inside info, like how she's totally sure Momsee is seeing some guy, cos she's bought heels and all this anti-wrinkle shit and was checking her texts, like every ten mins, and how she goes out to so-called-Pilates till like eleven at night, wearing perfume and the aforementioned flirty-footwear, and of course the biaaatch dumps her with total crap-loads of babysitting.

But BK is no place for a heart 2 heart, and she's grossed out by the tacky gloopy ketchupy tabletop and the fart smells of the great unwashed. Then Daddo's goin' retard, holding up the menu, getting Joshy to read it out aloud, like this was frickin' Sesame Street.

And Joshy's like *The sum... sum... feet.*

And Daddo's like *The Summer Feast, well done Josh.*

Then they're like – together *Tuh... tuh tuh... tum... tom....*

And Daddo's like: *Tomato – well done Josh.*

It's so heavy on cringe factor she just has to text Fi. But then he's like – *Young lady, will you please put that infernal technology away and give us the pleasure of your exquisite company!*

She couldn't help but kind of smile, cos of that silly ole voice of his.

She tried to start the biatchin' but Joshy was barging in with this order of supersize fries and a Coke and they call it the *Caribbean Glory* – like for how, for why? Does it like come with a goddamn banana, for chrissakes. So Claire has to go through this whole order ordeal and there are some scratch-your-fingernails-down-a-blackboard moments when he's asking about her weight with his

34

'concerned face'.

Jesus, well maybe I'd eat like normal person if I came from a normal frickin' family. She doesn't say this, but her face or something must have set him off, cos then he's doing this whole rap about how he knows Burger King had a bad rep in the past, but, really, they've cleaned up their act. And actually, the chicken salad, he says, is made with 100% fresh British breast, and the veggie patty is sourced from local veg and how the world isn't so bad and people can change, and if she wants she can order the new *Healthy Options Spanish Feast, with real Chorizo, rich tomato sauce and Batavia lettuce all in a chive-topped oval-split toasted organic brown bun.*

And Claire's like, *Errr, Dad, do you like work here or something?*

And he's like, *Errr, or you could just have... a salad.*

And she's like: *Wait, wait, wait – How come you've like memorised the whole Goddamn menu? Have you got... like... autism or something?*

And he sort of leans over and whispers, *OK, kiddo, between you and me; I eat here quite a lot.* These are like major food revelations, but then he must have realised Joshy might have heard cos he was backtracking, *Shhh, Never mind, forget it. OK?*

Tell me dad, tell me!!!

But Joshy is totally begging for his Dead-hoof Surprise, so then Daddo's up and away and at the counter. When he gets back she's going to make him spill the beans. But this waiting and staring at Daddo in his beaten-up overcoat, going through his pockets, like he's a few pennies short of a supersize, and my God there's no way our species was designed to be having these kinds of feelings for their parents.

Father

He has returned with the burgers and so they sit. But already it is too much for him. His daughter has intuited this. She has taken her iPod and placed it over the ears of his son to protect him from what she insists must be divulged. Claire. His good little rebel-child always trying so hard to be bad. It is her he worries for more than the mother and son. And the weight she has lost. She does not touch her salad and he cannot face his food. He had not realised that simply sitting down to eat with them would trigger this again.

Seriously, eating this shit? That's weird, like how often we talking?

How can he tell her that he has already eaten here today and will do so again tomorrow? That he knows the names of all the staff and cleaners. That the old man over there – Tom – lost his son six months back.

And the sight of his own son's face gorged in ketchup and mayonnaise, the child's ears deaf with music. Her hand reaches for his just as he is about to stand and she has not done that for so long, not since she was little. He has to hide his face.

Oh My God, she says, her hand to her mouth – *You totally live here!*

Claire

Trust fatboy to spoil everything, always. Daddo's in major panic stations, whispering *Shhh, not a word to your mother* but Joshy's got his headphones in his hand asking *What about Mom?*

Maybe you ate it a bit fast, Daddo's saying to Joshy, then frantic, muttering to himself, *I shouldn't have taken you here… I'll tell her, I don't want you to lie on my behalf… Damn, I'm such an idiot. You OK, son, shall we go to the toilet?*

Daddo's losing it so Claire seizes fatboy by the hand, *Dad, it's fine, I'll sort this out.* Plus Joshy does actually look like he's actually going to barf. *Come on dear chubster, let's go to the little boy's room!* She pulls Joshy away fast around a corner, past the muffin place, and she says in her scariest-whisper-voice, *Right Pigs-ville, were you spying on me and Dad? What did you hear?*

Nothing.

Cross your heart? And he nods, nods, like he could bubble.

OK, OK, so we tell Mom we had a snack. OK, vegetarian, from Holland and Barrett, or M&S, OK. Some nuts, that's all, we didn't come here. OK!

Joshy's pointing at the muffin place, like reaching out to get one – Jeeso.

For frickssake pigster, concentrate! I swear, if you tell Momsee we went to Burger King, I'm never going to speak to you ever-ever again, and I'm gonna tear up your goddamn build-a-bear! OK! Promise? I'm totally serious – cross your heart Joshy.

He crosses his little heart, and Claire's majorly relieved. But then Pigsy must be confused again, cos he wants a muffin and he's throwing a huff and not moving an inch. Jeeso, what can you do? She says the only words she knows that work every time you want to get Joshy to do anything. Like if you say *c'mon* or *move it*, or please, he won't budge for shit, but if you say *Race you* he gets totally caught in the grips of some magical malignant force and just forgets everything and runs and runs. *Race you back to Dad. Marks get set go…*

Mother

She parks the Subaru in the parents-and-children parking bay, and checks her mascara in the mirror.

Err, are we on a loop? We totally came here like yesterday! Hello? The madam is protesting. *Are we gonna see Dad?* Joshy is asking.

No, actually, for once, we're just doing a bit of shopping, she says, *Funny, I rather like this place now.*

Lies, and how do they start and when do they stop?

The divorce was not final, the papers not yet signed. She was still, technically, married, and wanted to feel what it felt like. To see if it offered any answers as to why, to put herself in *his* place and see how it felt from inside. Something urgent and necessary, surely, some quickening of the pulse, some gorging need, something elemental, some secret about the sexes. It wasn't revenge.

Dan had been charming on their first date, cautious on their second. His wife had left him two years before and he had a son, of a similar age to Josh. He wanted to meet her children before they took it further.

As she fixes her lippy, the little madam beside her is tutting and texting.

OK, she says, *No rules today, just this once, you can have anything you want.*

Claire

Claire is majorly sensing shit afoot and seriously crapping it in case Daddo's there doing his saddo chow-down in BK. So she's trying to direct attention away from the food court and at-the-same-time texting – *RU here?* She deletes it then writes it in proper words cos he doesn't get it if you do it the text way. *Are you at Burger King?*

Momsee has them in Gap for some shorts for Joshy and Claire hates that goddamn place, and she's picturing this whole movie of when Momsee bumps into Daddo and she says *What on earth are you doing here?* And he confesses or maybe lies, then Joshy'll spill the beans. OMG! Claire checks her mobey but no reply.

As usual blubber-boy wants to stuff his cheeks, so Momsee leads them to Holland & Barrett. Momsee's phone rings and her face is illuminated with so much girlee laughter Claire could barf. Momsee's like covering the mouthpiece and giving it, *You two go inside and get something nice.* It's like – totally portentous.

Claire tries ringing Daddo cos the situ is way too complex to explain in a text. It rings out, so she leaves a message, *If UR here, then please don't come down, OK? This is majorly weird… Soz, explain later.*

Oh hello, what are you doing here? This is Momsee talking. Claire looks up and there's this total square-chino-hunk-guy with this major-minor brat in hand.

What a coincidence, Momsee's saying and she can't act for shit. She's like, *fancy bumping into you.* Blah de Blah.

This guy is like one of those major saddos that's totally balding and was probably good at sports in school, he's probably even Momsee's divorce lawyer or something with ironed creases in his chinos. And this mini-moron in tow. Seriously, wearing a *High School Musical* T-shirt.

Children, Momsee's saying, *this is my friend Dan.*

Joshy is like cowering. And poor high school musical is doing the same. Claire's in this slo-mo, thinking Momsee and Chino must have spent nights working out all the dialogue, maybe Momsee did it in a mirror, maybe in her sleep, maybe this is like her dream. *Joshy, this is Dan, Dan this is Joshy, and this is Hamish.* And Chino is hands-out-to-shake, and *I've heard so much about you*, which totally exposes the lie. Plus his hand is kind of wet and testosteroney. And Momsee gives it – *Quelle surprise*, for like the third time. All these bods passing them by and Claire's gagging at Momsee's femme-show – playing with the hair.

Then her mobey beeps and, shit, it's Daddo. *Am in Burger King, is your mother here? Should I come and say hello? Where are you?*

No, bad idea. Sorree. XXX. Then – *Dad, major bad time!! Can U just go away? Pleez. Explain later.*

And Momsee's totally having to resist touching Chino's big frickin' shoulders, and laughing like a slapper and he's not even said a joke. And he's giving it *Wow, Hamish loves Build-a-Bear too,* cos Josh has his stupid spaceman bear with him, like frickin' always. *Hey, maybe we could hook up for a play-date sometime.*

So, Claire, he says, bending in, *have you bought anything today?*

And his eyes hover somewhere below her neck.

She's thinking of Daddo, up there alone in Burger King. Maybe she's a saddo like her Daddo – and a baddo too, cos this evil plan comes to her and she's picturing it unfolding. She whispers to Joshy. *Hey, you wanna burger?* He's nodding and turns to the escalator and it's like his feet are already revving up. He knows where he's headed, he could run it in like one minute. She holds him back and whispers: *Race you.*

Mother

She turns from Dan and shudders, as if her breath has been stolen.

Claire, where's Josh?

The madam tuts, shrugs.

Oh God. Dan, did you see him? Can't you. Oh God.

I'm sure he's just a few feet away, come on let's look for him together.

Didn't you see? We were just, I was… she's calling out *JOSH, JOSHY!* Then the man is calling out her son's name and he has no right. It was his fault. *His.*

We'll call security, he says, *look why don't I go and get someone. This happens all the time… they shut the doors, don't worry, they have a system.*

A system! She has seen mothers interviewed on TV before: the pleading, the lashing out, the begging for witnesses. She's screaming – *Joshy! Josh!* She's running now, animal, not caring who sees, past shops and shoppers, a blur of panic, searching for those eyes, that little head of gold. *She* is to blame.

He has followed and takes her arm, this man, this Dan, this goodnight kiss on a date, in a safe location. She shouts, *My God, will you fucking just…*

He raises his hand, *Marjorie, please, be calm, stay still, I'm getting Security, right now, OK? Stay here.* And he leaves her there. Fuck, she's shouting Fuck, fuck, fuck. And she will not be told what to do by some any-man and she is running off in the opposite direction past Mothercare and Gap, feeling it in veins, the need, ancestral, the blood. *JOSH! JOSHY!*

Talking to herself now, retracing it – *I was standing there talking, he was behind Claire, I just… it must only have been a few seconds… I must have…*

A hand on her shoulder, she swipes round.

Mom, it says, her daughter, the foolish girl.

What! What?

Mom… eh… maybe he's just gone for some… like… food.

Food? My God, she's screaming, *Ohmigod, what have I done!*

The man called Dan is there with a security guard, who's telling her, *This happens all the time,* saying *Foxtrot, Alpha, come in.*

She's screaming, *This is my child!* The man's saying *OK madam, try to remain calm.* This Dan's hand on her shoulder – *Don't worry*

Marjorie, he says. And she's shouting *Go, leave me alone!*

Mom, Mom, it's OK... maybe he just went to Burger King.

Her daughter pawing at her arm, saying, as if in echo. *What are you talking about, why on earth would anyone...*

The security man is saying, *How old is the child, I need a physical description, what was he wearing?*

Wearing? Wearing? I don't know, I... She cannot focus, she cannot picture, she is a terrible mother, she will never see her child again. *Claire,* she's saying – *Help me please, what was Joshy wearing? Claire?* But her daughter too has vanished.

Claire

So she's running up the escalator and out of breath and has to stop and it just keeps on moving, like creepy, like all these faces grinning like doofuses at her, and the smiley-spooky music, and she gets this sickly sixth-sense, what with the slo-mo escalator, like one of those reveal shots in movies, like when someone's supposed to be there and they're not, or like the cops are waiting, or like an axe murderer, and she's trying to kill the picture and, like, imagining, for once, the best possible movie scenario. It's so corny cos in it she'll find Daddo then they'll run and find Josh, and she can't believe she's even thinking this, but if it doesn't happen then she just knows that her and Daddo and Momsee and Joshy are gonna be in different movies, forever.

Up at Burger King Daddo is totally alone and there's no Josh, so then she just breaks down or something about how evil she is, like how she wanted this to happen. And Daddo's not freaked, he's cool, he's taking her hand and saying *OK, where is your mother?* And she's like *Dad, I'm so not sure that's a good idea.* And he's like,

Claire, don't worry, I won't tell her, we just have to be practical… now where's your mother?

And on the way down the escalator she gets this major clinging thing and has to, like, hold his hand or something and she's totally dreading the whole predictable screaming match that's gonna ensue.

But, like, at the bottom, Daddo, is all striding up to Momsee and these three frickin' security guys around her, and Chino and the kid, Haggis, or whatever his name is – and this is the weirdest, she's not even asking *What the hell are you doing here?* She's not even bawling him out or anything, she's like *David*, calling him by his name, and he's like *Marjorie, it'll be fine, he's done this before, remember the play-park?* And it's like, in some way, who knows, she knows, maybe she always kinda knew, in some subconscious fricked-up way he'd be, like everywhere, like it or not, you know – till death do us part.

And Daddo doesn't even turn to Chino Guy and say *Who the frick is this?* Or *Begone ye impostor.* He's like, totally, in control.

So Claire lets him take her hand again and they run, and he's saying *Quite a bloody mess you've made here, madam.* And she's hundreds of sorries as they scan faces and shops. *C'mon*, he says, t*hink, think… where else could he be?* And it comes to her and she looks at Daddo and her words come right out his mouth:

Build-a-Bear!

They're sprinting and it's like one of those shots, when the camera zooms in, and there's the star in the middle of frame, and there's Josh, totally standing by the Build-a-Bear, staring at the goddamn bears. And totally like nothing has even happened and he just turns and says *Daddy can we get a Darth Vader bear?* And Daddo picks him up, majorly out-of-breath and calls him Rascal, ruffles his hair, says *Gave us quite a fright there*. And carries him on his shoulders.

And on the way back she's giving it more sorries but he whispers, *It's fine Claire, but best not tell your mother about your little intrigue, though*. Then he's actually asking her to use her mobile for once – *Call her now, tell her we're coming*.

For once Claire and Fi are actually talking on the phone cos Fi wants all the gory details. She's like *Oh my actual God!! So what… are your mum and dad like 'getting back together' again?* and Claire's like, *Blagghhh! I dunno, it's like a major embarrassment, cos I'll have to un-tell everyone at school about the D.I.V.O.R. et cetera – they're like downstairs, you know, doing 'the talking', like in our actual house. I dunno, even if they do they'll probably split up again. It soooo sucks.*

It soooo rocks, says Fi, *your Dad is like a total king or something*.

Yeah, says Claire, *like, frickin' king of nothing*.

Nah, nah, like… like king of… burgers.

Yeah, totally… Burger King!

And they laugh out loud. But not like 'LOL', cos Claire is so over LOL now, and even 'Oh My God' and 'Oh My Actual God' and shops and families and pretty much everything for that frickin' matter.

Incident in a Mall # 6

The Price of Life (as told by Pope Jim)

One day you visit Scotland's largest mall and buy some clothes. You pay for your parking ticket and drive to the exit. The machine takes your ticket but the barrier does not rise. A queue of frustrated drivers starts to form behind you. You push the help button and speak to the parking attendant. The intercom voice instructs you to come to the payment booth immediately to resolve the issue. As the cars behind rev their engines and faces swear through windscreens you follow the signs and fight your way through the fume-clogged air. You are furious that some little man can humiliate you in this way, implying as he has, that you are a liar, a thief or an imbecile. By the time you finally locate the tiny payment booth, you are ready to scream at this idiot behind glass, who has not even turned to face you; who seems, in fact, to be laughing with some colleague beyond your line of vision, maybe even laughing about you.

Now Sir, he says, with a thick Irish drawl, what seems to be the problem? He has a disarming smile; but you do not want to be disarmed. There are now twelve cars parked behind yours, all hitting their horns.

Look, you shout, I need to speak to your superior!

He pauses for a second, Well, apart from God almighty, he says, I'm the one next in charge down here. A minute later, after he has taken your ticket and smoothed out the crease that was causing the scanner fault, joked with you and told you that you are not alone in this predicament and God knows what idiot created such a stupid system in the first place, you find yourself apologising profusely to the lovely man for the inconvenience you have caused him.

This is Jim – forty-nine years old, the father of three sons and a daughter, who he proudly boasts is the first in the family to ever make it to university. His nickname is Pope Jim, or just Pope, but he has never declared any faith and has not been to a church since he was twelve. The nickname, he claims, came about because his ticket booth looks a bit like a confession box, with its little circular window. Jim has more than once said things to customers, like:

That'll be fifty pence and three Hail Marys.

Or it may be because some of the other staff are true blue royalists; they dislike Jim and his chirpy tone, and see Pope as an insult. All of this is just water off a duck's back to Jim, who enjoys a joke, even at his own expense.

And may the Lord be with you, he mutters after the people who call him idiot, moron, spastic and cunt. And may the Lord be with you.

If you can spare him the time Jim will be grateful for the company; he'll even invite you into his booth for a cup of tea and to hear his stories (he is the tale-teller of the mall). So it is that you find yourself here, now, sitting with Jim, your car parked across the way. He promises you a great story about a guy who tried to kill himself, up on level five. But first he reels you in with cheerier tales.

Thelma and Louise, Jim says, let me tell you about Thelma and Louise. It was a fine sunny day in June, and two old ladies were stuck in a red fiat Panda at the barrier. A large queue formed behind them as they tried to reverse, then do a U-turn. And no matter how much he waved at them, they'd failed to notice the help button and the intercom and the chaos they'd unleashed, as they reversed into four different vehicles and the car alarms started screaming. Jim ran towards them and was knocked to the ground when they accelerated straight for the barrier. They crashed through, snapping it in half, then speared their car on the security bollards. The security bollards, Jim says, three feet high! You should have seen it, the back wheels of the Panda stuck in the air and still the old dears revving their engine, like it was the indie 500, smoke blasting out the exhaust. When Jim knocked on their window he saw two of the primmest, nicest, little old ladies smiling back with no trace of apology or distress, Don't worry about us officer, the plump one said, we're just on our way. Thelma and Louise, Jim calls them. Thelma and Louise. Wheels spinning in the air. Thelma and Louise.

The old folk. Jim feels sorry for them. They used to have a town centre and a social club, he says. Now they come here, wander about by themselves, like little lost sheep, buy endless cups of tea, and read their newspapers in the public toilets. It's not right. It's not right.

There was an old skinny bloke he came across, up on level four; standing there, in his socks, no sign of shoes, the old fella didn't even have a shopping bag. Standing there by the down-ramp, not even on the pedestrian walkway, and a dangerous spot too, the cars racing down from the top level. Jim had gone up and asked, Can I help you, sir?

Mind yer own bloody business, the old man yelled, I'm waiting for ma bus.

Waiting for ma bus, Jim repeats, that's a good one, You have to laugh eh, or you'd weep. Stocking soles on the fourth floor, eh? Waiting for ma bus, waiting for ma bus.

Jim repeats himself a lot, which is understandable, given the nature of his work. Also, storytelling breaks his day into events with beginnings, middles and ends, and saves him from the constant cyclic onslaught which never progresses. People often ask him – Why the hell do you do this job? And for so long? He's been here since the mall opened, twelve years before; people in this kind of work usually leave after a year.

Well, I used to be a prison officer and before that I was an undertaker, he grins. I don't know, I suppose I'm a people person.

You laugh and sense that he's trying to keep you longer in his booth. If you don't hear the story soon, you'll have to go. Perhaps sensing that, he begins.

It is a day in October and this guy has come to his window; this would be a year back; he's respectable looking, mid thirties, bald-headed, smart dressed.

Now, Sir, Jim says to him, What seems to be the problem? The choice of the word 'seems' is crucial – it defuses blame on both sides, and it is always 'the problem', not 'your problem'. Jim digresses again and tells you he's done three different anger and conflict-management courses; and as for the Irish accent, yes, he came from the south originally but he finds that people are less aggressive when he hams it up. There are reasons for this, that he'd rather not go into, which came from a documentary he saw on how African-American slaves used outwit their masters.

So, the guy is brandishing his parking ticket, shouting that the barrier won't open, that the screen says Ticket Not Valid. And protesting that his ticket is bloody well valid cos he only paid for it five minutes ago.

Jim checks the time and the ticket and the guy paid for it twenty minutes back. Jim waits for a gap in the rant and points this out.

You saying I'm lying, the man's shouting, you saying I'm a fucking...

Jim quietly shows him the printed time on the ticket – Paid: 11.04. And while the guy yells over and over No, no, you, you listen to me, Jim explains that car parking is by the hour, so if you park from ten till eleven, that's one pound twenty and if two hours then two pounds forty, but the guy is yelling, You fucking people, this is a dictatorship, you miserable little fucks, draggin' us all down to your fucking level.

Jim maintains a state of calm and explains to the man that since he took so long to find his car, twenty minutes in fact, he has entered the new hour and so a further payment of one pound twenty pence will be required to clear the outstanding balance.

So, if I stand here another hour, taking this shit, I'm gonna have to pay more to get out? Right? Are you fuckin' kiddin'? Are you listening to me, you're not listening, fuckin' listen man!!

And Jim hates to say it, but it's the only back-up he has, and it's an old thing called The Truth. In these cases you just have to repeat it, even though it makes them angrier – what else can you do?

I'm sorry sir, those are the rules, he says. There's nothing more I can do.

No, course not, ya fuckin' moron, you're fuckin' dead, man!

And the man punches the wall beside Jim's window and runs off. And Jim falls silent. Is that it? You ask. I thought you said it was a suicide story.

And here Jim digresses again. Anger and frustration, he says, are built into the very stones of the mall car park. As it is the cheapest parking in the centre of town, the demand for space always exceeds availability. The developers, when they gained planning permission, didn't properly assess the 'environmental impact' on the local road system, and hugely underestimated, or perhaps misrepresented the pressure it would place on the inner city. The city planners, urgent to push through the multi-million pound development deal, must have turned a blind eye, so, as a result, queues for the car park spill out onto the main streets, turning the entire city centre into a huge traffic jam. The idiots! There's also no sure way of telling when the car park is full. An average of forty cars a day end up scouring the many floors and leaving without having found a space, having to either pay for their non-park or fight with Jim.

Every day they scream to be let out – they will write to the government – they will hire a killer to do him in. One time a guy screamed, I've got my pregnant sister here, open the barrier. She's going into labour! and when Jim went to the car he saw that there was no pregnancy, not even a sister. Then there are those who've lost their tickets, and when they're informed that they have to pay for a whole day's parking, which comes to twenty-four pounds, they throw away their keys; those who can't find their car and insist it has been moved without their permission; and those who storm out in a rage only to return days later, shamefaced, to pick up their cars.

Oh yes, Jim has been spat at, punched, and had a wide variety of objects thrown at his reinforced glass window, including cans of Irn-Bru, pre-packed sandwiches and, on one occasion, a dirty disposable nappy. His day is, in fact, nothing much more than the long hours waiting for precisely such incidents to occur.

So what happened to the bald man? You ask.

Well, after he ran off, Jim thought nothing of it and sat himself back down. He looked out and was surprised to see that the man's car, a VW Passat, was still parked nearby and the guy no-where to be seen. He stared at his monitor and at his tea, which was now cold. He stuck it in the microwave and waited.

And? So?

Well, there was nothing else to do so he thought he'd scan the floors to try and find the guy; he could be up to no good, taking a piss behind a pillar, scratching a car with his keys, these things had happened before. So he's on the CCTV, toggling the camera and there he finds him. Up on Level Five. He couldn't believe it – standing on a tiny ledge, it wasn't even a proper ledge, just ornamentation, his arms behind himself, gripping the concrete.

Well of course, Jim called Security. And here Jim puts on the voices of himself and the security guys talking through their walkie talkies.

This is Charlie Papa, which means Car Park by the way, we have a Delta Fifteen, Area Five, come in, over.

And here's another thing, Jim says, we always get a few a year. It's the height you see, and the only place in the city you can get onto a rooftop without anyone asking any questions. Or maybe folk like the spectacle of it, the crowds gathering beneath, maybe even a camera. Four jumpers we had last year, five the year before. Only one of them died – in '98 I think. When *I* do it, Jim says, It'll be off a cliff, and no one'll see me.

So he lived? You ask, What did you do?

Well, says Jim. If I was a catholic I'd have prayed, but I'm a practical man. You don't want to run up on these folk and startle them over the edge. So I had my tea and waited.

You did nothing?

I watched him on my tellies and after a while, standing there, thinking about jumping, he started swaying. And just in the nick of time, Security came, and the police, and they talked him down and wrapped him in a blanket. I watched it all on my tellies. It must have been a whole two hours. They brought him back to his car and patted his back and sent him on his way.

And there I was thinking, Jim says, Ah yes, but he's still not paid for his parking ticket, has he? And he won't get out of here till he does, and I'm damned if we're going to have to do this all over again.

Now, I'm not a stickler for rules, Jim says, so I pay the money myself. I walks up to guy, as he's looking through his pockets for his ticket, and I say, You're lucky. And he nods his head, thinking I'm talking about the fall and all.

I paid it for you, Jim says. One pound twenty… Actually, it was four pounds eighty, as you've been here three extra hours, but I'm no stickler for rules. I'll let you off this time.

And the guy says sorry and thank you, thank you so much, and he gives Jim a tip, twenty quid, and actually hugs him, like it was Jim that saved his life. Then he gets in his car and off he goes, through the barrier.

I'll let you off this time, Jim repeats. Can you believe that? One pound twenty – the price of a life, eh? I'll let you off this time. Jim laughs till tears come to his eyes. The poor bugger. You know if it'd been twelve years back, it'd have been fifty pence, that was the price for an hour. Kill yourself for fifty pence, eh?

Jim seems emptied after the laughter and telling his best story and now it's time for you to go. But Jim won't hear of it. You want another one? I've got lots more, he shouts. Have another cuppa and I'll tell you about another suicide – Rena the Cleana, what a story that is.

You promise one day you will come back to hear the story. And so you go.

Jim calls after you. That'll be another two pounds forty, you've been in here for two extra hours.

As you go into your pockets to pay, he laughs.

I'm only joking, off you go. I'll let you off this time. I'll let you off this time.

The Barbell, the Crucifix, and the Anchor

The perception of shopping malls as generic 'boxes' is reductive, inaccurate and prejudiced. Historically, malls have two essential architectural structures, which are ingenious in their union of function and form and which conjure almost poetic imagery. They are the 'Crucifix' and the 'Barbell'.

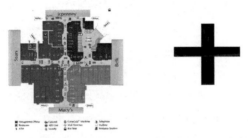

Cross Creek Mall, NC, showing crucifix-form with four anchor stores – North, South, East and West.

Broadway Plaza, Walnut Creek, CA, presenting classic Barbell-form with two anchors at either end of the walkway.

Although the barbell shape has rather negative parallels architecturally (it was the model for the infamous H-Block political prisons in Northern Ireland) and the crucifix is the structure of most cathedrals and churches, it would be erroneous to infer any symbolic significance from such coincidences of form. Malls are neither *prisons of the modern soul*, nor are they in any simple sense *temples of consumerism*. The reason for the adoption of these essential forms is practical and based on a single socioeconomic fact: Malls, from the very first designs (Gruen), were based upon the presence of two or more 'Anchor' stores.

Anchors are so called because for the construction of any mall to take place it is essential that major stores invest in the financial underwriting of development costs and of ambitious construction; that they 'anchor' the financial foundations of a mall. Any and every mall that has ever been built has required at least two large stores to commit, contractually, to occupancy. Traditionally, these anchors have been department stores – Sears, Bloomingdales and Macy's in the US; John Lewis, BHS, M&S and Debenhams in the UK. Anchors generally have their rents heavily discounted, and may even receive cash inducements from the mall developers to maintain their commitment. In physical configuration, anchor stores are normally located as far from each other as possible to maximise the amount of traffic from one anchor to another. As *enemies kept apart*, they typify the cold war era in which they were first constructed. The space between both is then filled with smaller retail outlets who are drawn to the consumer traffic that both anchors guarantee. This is what creates the 'barbell' shape – two large stores with a line between. The crucifix is simply a double barbell – it has four anchors.

Since the slow decline of the national department store in the late 1980s, the duality model of one department store facing another as the basis for mall architecture has been outgrown. The concept of the two anchors has been superseded by using one 'Mega-supermarket' as an anchor, or by having a larger number of reliable multinational chain stores replacing the anchors completely

(Gap, H&M, La Senza, Starbucks). As a result, the architectural form then had to change shape. The form that best accommodates this new 'plural' arrangement of 'life without anchors' is the semi-circle, or 'half moon'. Here, many competitors can co-exist in the mall without the old two-ends face-off, and also without one retailer seeming to have dominance. Many new malls, built in the post-anchor era, utilise such curvilinear forms.

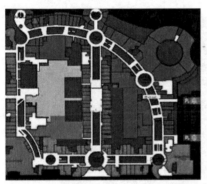

The massive Dubai Mall (opened 2008) with its celebrated 'arc'.

The Glasgow Fort, UK, (opened 2004) has no roof and apes the shape of an old village street.

It was the night after the conference, and Joe was sitting in the hotel bar long after he should have been, thinking about the old town, the road north and how little time it would take to drive there. Tomorrow he'd be home in Chicago and it could be years till he'd be back in the UK again. He must have been staring at the contours of the barman's back because the barman turned.

So which one of these guys d'you work for, if you don't mind me asking?

A store, Joe replied, a big one... a very, very big one. Double entendres were an old habit he should have shaken off by now. Sorry I can't tell you which one, confidentiality clauses and what have you, Joe added, then regretted it immediately, as withholding information could imply an interest in certain acts which would require discretion on a strictly no-names, no-repercussions basis. In truth, he'd intended no intrigue at all, and was quite simply not at liberty to discuss the workings of one of the world's leading discount, outlet and supermarket chains. In trying to quietly explain this, however, he became conscious that the barman was watching his lips.

The barman nodded at his empty glass.

Bar's closing now. If ye fancy anither one you could order it on room service an' I could bring it up tae ye.

Joe smiled, charmed at the proposition and the accent. He shook his head and set a few notes on the counter. Goodnight, he said, Have a good one. For a second he wondered whether the 'one' in question was a night or a lover or a life.

Joe flicked through some TV channels then sipped an Evian from the mini-bar as he stared out the window at the old familiar signs illuminating the freeway: Shell, Office World, TK Maxx, Tesco. You see one mall, you've seen the mall, Juan had once joked. Or had it been Dom? Eight hours on a plane and you haven't moved a mile.

He closed his eyes to summon senses: the smell of the sea, the sounds of gulls circling, the old bike sheds, the high school play-yard, the long grass. Once again he was running, jumping over fences, clambering over wires, his pulse bursting in his lungs, clawing for breath as they pursued him.

Skype was beeping. He should've called Ted two hours ago. Ole Teddy Bear.

Hey hun, how's 'Bannie Scatland?' I won't nag about making me wait this long, I'm sure you have an alibi. What time's your flight get in anyway?

Joe took a moment to work out how to tell Ted of his plan. Just one more day, a slight detour, that was all.

Are you insane? Those rednecks'll skin you alive this time! You wanna end up under the ground, or back in therapy? You know, you should have sued their asses —you could have bought a yacht with all that money. Hey, wait, why don't we call it a holiday? I'll fly to you, we could do a loch! My God! Hold on, are you alone, or is there some kilted thing hiding in your closet?

Joe laughed, and gently reassured Ted that nothing exciting was happening at all. Adding it all up, he said, he'd only be delayed for a day, and after a gentle drive north to say goodbye to the old place, he could put all the old demons to rest.

OK, OK, well I won't sleep a wink till you're back, I'll be calling every minute. Don't you dare turn me off, I know you will. OK, I forgive you. Oh, and bring me back some shortbread and whisky and shit. Actually, skip the shortbread... and the shit.

The Mercedes is free with the air miles on his company card. It has power steering and cruise control. Joe has chosen a stick-shift, not an automatic, so as to make the experience more real. Mountains, castles and villages speed by as if they're an advert for the car itself. He tries to add a soundtrack with the radio but the songs are generic and American. The GPS has a human voice; she sounds like a robotic Kathryn Hepburn.

The freeway too is anonymous, so he turns off the GPS and improvises; taking the B roads, zoning in to the changing rhythms of the road. He has trouble changing the gears on the steep inclines and this adds a degree of pleasurable engagement. As he gets closer, only twenty miles to go, he thinks there should have been fear, some sense of dread at least.

Images flit before him, then fill the emptying landscape. Ridiculous cinematic scenarios.

He sees himself driving into town and parking the big fat car where everyone can see it, outside Woolworths perhaps. Like some gangster, he'll push down the automatic window and, from behind his mirrored Ray Bans, he'll ask the scared-looking locals – D'you know where I can find a man called Jimbo?

And one will turn and run and the other will stammer that Jimbo works at the butchers. And that will make him laugh. How apt. And he'll take his time then, driving past McGovern's men's outfitters and the town hall and Doris's corner shop and Johnson the baker's – the names have not escaped him – through the old cobblestone streets, past the harbour and the hundreds of boats to St.Clair's the butchers.

Jimbo will be bald now, spattered with blood and bone, serving some old ladies perhaps – pork chops and hash beef. Joe will loiter and start to whisper – Jimbo, Jimbo. And Jimbo will look up and recognise the little scar on his lip. Jimbo will drop his knife, as Joe whispers the words: You're dead, ya fucking poof.

Then he will walk away.

He laughs to himself as he drives. Poofter, Jessie, Lassie, White Settler. Strange how being foreign implied some gender or racial mix-up in their minds. Ted thought the trauma had been formative in Joe's sexuality. Poof didn't even begin to cover it. Everything about you is bi, Ted said, bipolar, ambidextrous, ambiguous, ambivalent, you're like a switch, on/off, love/hate, utterly untrustworthy and totally gorgeous. Just don't tell me about your international affairs OK, men or women, I don't want to know, and don't bring back any foreign bodies!

Funny, he'd been faithful to Ted for almost a year. But still there was the blockage, the fear of gentle touch.

Joe passes a row of old abandoned crofts. Sheep grazing on a hillside. It will only be minutes now till the loch and the line of pylons, and then over the brow of the hill the town will reveal its spires. There is weariness in his eyes from the drive, but there should be more. You never let yourself feel anything, do you? Glen had said, You run away before things get too deep... you're so fucking superficial. And that stupid grin of yours. What secret horror have you Americans committed that necessitates such smiling?

Laney. Laney Mackay.

She would be the hardest to find. Perhaps she would be a hairdresser or a secretary now. He would find her in a down-at-heel bar. The nightclub by the harbour. What had they called it? Sparkles. Yes.

He'll walk in and take his time, gloating at the sight of

her: the make-up shovelled on, the wrinkled breasts on full display, the peroxide blonde with grey roots, as she wipes the sweat from her brow with hands muscled like a man's from twenty years of hard labour. Every last bit last bit of feminine allure will have gone. She'll be divorced, her body wrecked from childrearing, from drinking. She'll have been fucked and fucked over by all the guys in the town; suffered the revenge small towns have on pretty girls. He'll stand there staring, till she starts to sweat. Then he'll walk out.

No, he'll walk up to the bar. He'll flash his Amex card, he'll buy drinks for the locals, he'll tell her that he works in an executive position for a multinational, and that, most probably, she's wearing clothes entirely from his store, and the food she eats probably comes from there too; though of course he can't say the name of the brand.

He'll make her laugh and flatter her. He'll wait till the bar closes and say You wanna go for a walk? By the harbour perhaps. Yes, long shimmering lights across the water. And he'll ask, What was it like growing up here? Do you have kids? Are they happy? He'll take her hand and stroke her thumb as they stroll and she'll confess to the great dullness of her shit little life. And as the late night taxis pass and the waves lap by the pier, he'll say, It's so beautiful here, let's keep walking, to the edge of town. Maybe her heels would be hurting her feet, maybe she'd take them off and walk barefoot. What's your name, she'd ask. But he'd keep her waiting.

He would lead her then along the path where they chased him. Past the old hospital, through the housing scheme to the field that stretched for a mile to the abandoned airport. He'd pick up a fallen branch and play with it in his hands. He'd climb through the fence with her and stop before the old bunker and, just when she thought he was about to kiss her, he would raise the branch and tell her his name.

Joe laughs. He's out of practice; he's not pictured this for maybe ten years. He has to focus on the road. The incline is dangerous now, he rides the brow of the hill and expects to see the cliff-edge and the tiny winding road, but there is a new bridge where none had been before. He cruises along its gentle slope and such ease feels inappropriate. A mile on he passes a sign for the freeway. He can't recall it having come this far north before. He refuses to join it and follows its side along a winding B-road. He turns off down a single track, deciding to enter the town from the back road.

And Tommy. He will find Tommy at the welfare office. No, perhaps pushing a baby buggy. No, on his knees in the garden of a tiny prefabricated bungalow. Yes, there will be a generic budget Toys R Us Wendy hut and yellow, red and blue toys scattered on the grass. Tommy will have put on a lot of weight. He'll be tending to a rabbit in a hutch, hiding his cigarette from his three children as they run around with water pistols, screaming, spraying him. Joe will sit across the street in the SUV watching as Tommy's obese wife comes to the door and shouts at him, relishing the sight of Tommy cowering like an obedient dog. He will walk into their garden and speak very clearly; he will say, If you don't come with me now, I will tell your wife what you did to me.

And Tommy will beg. What do you want? Tell me, please, God, anything, you want money? And seeing Tommy on his knees among his plastic toys – it might be enough. He might walk away. He might say, Have a good one.

He slows as the hills become familiar and it comes to him that perhaps the locals had been scared of his family. It was a small, insular community after all, fearful of invaders. His father had worked at the NATO airbase in the 80s and the old airport had been used by the US military during the cold war. His dad used to stride around town, flashing his cash. Maybe he even had a mistress there, some poor local hooker. Maybe it was the mother of Tommy or Laney, maybe that was why.

Yankie poof.

Funny how the local kids put on American accents when they played their games, shooting imaginary guns, pretending they were in *The Six Million Dollar Man* and *Charlie's Angels*. The beatings were usually more severe, the day after a big movie had been on TV. *Dirty Harry* was the worst.

Pick up the stick, Jimbo had said, Go on Punk, make my day!

They'd called him Yankie Poof and they wore Levis. Their mothers sang along to Dolly Parton and Elvis, and muttered Yanks Go Home when they passed. One morning Joe woke to find those words scraped along the side of his father's car.

The town appears on the horizon like a model of itself, church spires and chimneys. The buildings are so much smaller than memory. Incidents are maybe amplified in a child's mind. To mark the occasion Joe takes a breath as he passes the Welcome sign. He passes the old cemetery and the houses on the outskirts, trying to recall the name of a girl who lived in the big house with the tree swing. It's still there. Elise, Eliza, Elsie?

He drives down the main street, expecting a hundred faces, but the sidewalks are deserted. A group of three old ladies stand silent at a bus stop. A seagull picks at something in the middle of the road. He passes the old grey town hall. The police station is still as it was. The report was never filed. His parents divorced after the incident and his mother ran with him, back to the States.

He stops at the new pedestrian lights; the lights change although there is no one crossing. The big hotel over the bridge has a sign outside saying *Riverside Rest Home*. He gazes through the windows. Framed by frilly chintz curtains are twenty geriatrics, all watching TV. He drives on and Woolworths is boarded up; he takes a left onto the cobblestones and has to steer carefully around the ancient bends. *For Lease* and *For Sale* signs line the tiny alleyways. Where Mackay's Fashions used to be there is a pound shop. McGovern's men's outfitters has gone. The window of Doris's corner shop is smashed. Johnson the baker's is boarded up. A solitary teenager with a baby buggy passes him by. In the distance, the sound of a car alarm.

He heads out towards the harbour. Where Sparkles nightclub should have been there is a Job Centre. The harbour is empty, only two boats now. The old dry dock is closed, no hulks on the high risers. There are cars though, parked everywhere. It is as if the townsfolk have turned into vehicles. He drives on, searching for faces and finds only two old men smoking outside a pub. No trace of anyone his age. The old fish and tackle shop has gone. The harbour café has a *For Lease* sign. The town is a ghost. No revenge he could have dreamed of could have been so violent.

In his professional mind he looks for reasons, changes in demographic, rural depopulation, the death of the fishing industry. It's clear now that there will be no meeting with Laney, Tommy or Jimbo. And he is a fool, full of fantasies. He should turn around and head back.

But to leave with nothing.

His phone beeps. He looks at the screen and it's Ted. Ted

will want the running commentary, the blow by blow, to joke about it all. With his one free hand he turns off the phone. Maybe he should leave Ted, another violent betrayal, then run.

He drives to the school. It is still there; grey, Victorian, obstinate. He slowly retraces the track of his run, along the river, past the bushes, through the back streets. On his right, in its expected place, he sees the old hospital. A signs says *Luxury Apartments, Reduced Rates*. A BMW and a Hyundai in the car park.

He parks at the edge of the housing scheme where the path ends and the grass begins. He sits with his heating system on waiting for some intense feeling to arrive, some epiphany. Maybe Glen was right, maybe he'd become too superficial. Ted would have laughed at the folly of it all.

Joe flicks the hazard lights on and steps out. He breathes. He stands in the middle of the road and feels like some actor in a western. Two cars pass, leaving town. Maybe they're watching him, laughing, asking why the freak is standing there. Fucking tourist.

The road is now empty in both directions; he looks back at the town, not a sound. Maybe it has been bypassed by the freeway. It happens, it would explain things. Even the road signs seem neglected.

The plan is to retrace the steps, walk the mile through the grass, over the hill to the old airport. To find the bunker, to locate the exact spot, to wait for the moment, to maybe touch the ground, or weep, to maybe write his name on the wall, to carve out a piece of concrete and take it home. He will know what to do when he gets there.

He steps onto the overgrown verge and begins.

He looks for traces as he wades through the tall grass. A crisp packet blows by, an abandoned car tyre lies rusted, a can of

Pepsi. In the distance a seagull circles. Wind through grass. A tune is playing in his head, something about boyfriends and girlfriends. Yes, he is so superficial.

He tries to recall running. Yes, a car passed by and he turned and tried to wave for help as he ran. A mistake as it had slowed him. Tommy was sprinting after him, stick in hand. He had headed to the airport because he knew they'd outrun him if he kept on over the fields. He'd thought maybe he could hide in the hanger, that maybe they'd be scared off by the signs that said *Danger Keep Out.*

Beneath his feet the texture changes, there is concrete beneath grass, rubble, rubbish. To his left are trees where none should be. Past them he discovers a path worn through the grass. He follows.

The bunker had been a mistake; they found him hiding in a dark corner. After they'd made him strip and got bored of whipping him, they said 'close your fuckin' eyes', they said 'don't move or we'll kill ya'. He heard them run off, laughing, but he cowered there till the counting of breaths was lost in repetition. Craning for every sound, the birds, the wind; fearful that a movement might trigger their return. He focused on the pains, the gashes on his back, buttocks and genitals. After a while the body spoke. It said, if I die here, no one will find me. He found some of his things amongst the grass and broken glass, but not his jeans. Wearing only his sneakers and underpants he walked in the dark along the edge of the road towards the town.

Joe looks back, towards the housing estate, and he is not alone. Two tiny silhouettes are walking towards him through the tall grass. His breath starts to race as his feet trip forward. He runs, checking their distance from him. It couldn't be Laney or Jimbo, he tells himself, but the visual illusion fuels the fantasy. He tears across the grass and makes it to the brow of the hill. He stops to catch his breath and to look down on the old airport.

It has gone. In its place is a large, flat-walled, windowless white building with a shining metallic roof. The sound of many cars and the sight of the road beyond complete the picture. It is a mall. Of course, it makes sense. Four towns within twenty miles. Regional catchment. A roundabout and link to the freeway.

Joe can't double back without having to cross paths with the grass people. He walks down the hill to the mall. He steps over the ornamental shrubs onto the tarmac and he's in the car park. It's busy, bustling, as if all the townsfolk have moved here. He stares as they push their trolleys, unload bags into their trunks. There should be razor wire and rust, signs saying *Danger Keep Out*. If this is the place then his bunker is buried beneath a foot of tarmac. No one turns as he walks through them, scanning their faces. The walls of this place need no sadness, the cars do not blame or forgive. This must be what it feels like to be invisible.

The sign ahead of him says *Recycling Zone*. He watches a mother lift her daughter up to the bottle bank; the child raises a bottle, aiming for the hole; the laughter on the muted smash. Again, Mummy! Again! An advert for a mobile phone on the trolley stand says *The Future is Now*.

A sign looms behind him. He senses what it is before he faces it. He turns and surrenders to it. Yes. It is his store. Two thousand four hundred and eighty seven of them in the world. And the funniest thing of all, was that for just a microsecond there, a millisecond, he caught himself thinking: Thank God it's us. Not Tesco or Aldi.

Ted would laugh, Ted would hold him, Ted would say what I love about you is that you are absolutely incapable of profundity.

Joe can't stop staring. There's a display of beach balls and outdoor furniture by the door, beneath a sign that says Prices Slashed. And the faces: Asian, English, Scottish, young and old, all smiling with their boxed and bagged purchases. Electrical appliances, shoes, furniture, games consoles, paperbacks, school uniforms, digital cameras, rings, watches and perennial plants. Our company, Stefan used to say, has opened its doors to all races and classes. When we are in every country in the world, and everyone gets to share in our discounts, then everyone will be equal and there will be peace.

Joe feels a sudden thirst. He could go inside and get some Evian, they always stock them in a fridge within the first twenty feet. He could actually forget all of this and just do a bit of shopping. He could call Ted, tell him, Hey Teddy Bear, you've no idea where I am – you wouldn't believe it! And Ted would say. Oh hun, could you pick up some Chorizo and Zinfandel while you're at it?

God, you're pathetic, he tells himself.

He looks back across the roofs of the cars to the field. The two silhouette people are arriving. They step over the shrub border just as he did. Of course, they weren't pursuing him. They are teenagers. Their clothes are dated and dirty, the purples and greens betray fashions from years back. They've walked all the way from the town because this place has forced all local competition into closure. They walk on a homemade path because Joe's corporation did not lay down a sidewalk; it wanted to discourage customers without cars.

They head towards his store, grinning, holding hands. They have brought their own plastic bags. The girl could be

Laney's daughter. She has similar cheekbones, a prominent nose. The boy could be the son of Tommy, the blonde hair, the slight stoop in his walk.

But he's trying too hard. The truth is they look like no one he has known. Like everyone or anyone from any of the countries he's visited this year.

If he was to shout his name, no-one would notice or care. Everyone has forgotten everything, and they seem happy.

He could weep. For Christ's sake. A surge of anger then, not at Laney or Tommy, but at this place that has erased both them and his chance of forgiving.

He watches as the teenage couple stop before the entrance by a display of soccer balls and a cardboard cut-out of a soccer star. The girl pulls out her smart phone, she wraps one arm round the cardboard cut-out and the other round her beau. A flash and the image is saved forever.

If he was to call Ted, Ted wouldn't understand: Ted would joke and make puns and say Are you listening? Am I talking to myself here? Why did you turn me off? Are you even there?

There should be blood on the wall, nails and broken glass, he should be able to touch the ground, get down on his knees and kiss it.

A mother and child walk by with balloons that carry the logo of his company.

Joe turns back to the edge of the car park, and looks at the tiny little path worn over the hillside. He steps between the cars to the edge. He walks into the long grass. Once again he is running.

A Brief History of The Mall:
Parts 1 to 4 (500 BC – 1950s)

1. The Agora, 500 to 140 BC

Set in the city square at the foot of the Acropolis in Ancient Athens, the Agora is arguably the world's first urban marketplace. For historians and architects it represents an ideal balance of the two forces that vie for control in the history of the mall: on the one hand, uncontrolled trading; on the other, market regulation and social planning. The Agora is seen as a civic centre, grown from the roots of the village, where commerce is at one with community, where local issues are debated as goods are exchanged. This is the era of verbal selling, of exchange, of barter and haggling, of no fixed price, and negotiation as an integral part of the social fabric. Two thousand years later, the idea of the Agora would both inspire and haunt the architects of the 'modern mall'.

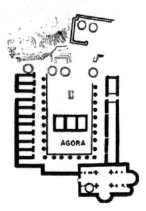

2. From Bazaar to Piazza, Middle Ages to Renaissance.

During the dark ages, while Europe falls into chaos and is visited by plagues and purges, trading and the concept of the central market place is kept alive by Islamic culture. Isfahan's Grand Bazaar, Persia (now Iraq) dates from the 10th century; while The Grand Bazaar of Istanbul – built in the 15th century – still stands as one of the world's largest covered markets, comprising 58 streets with over 4,000 covered street stalls. The word derives from the Persian word *bāzār*, meaning 'the place of prices' and as with the Agora, Bazaars are lively, colourful places in which haggling over the price of locally-produced food, clothing and spices is an integral part of the negotiation of everyday life. Bazaars still exist in over seventeen different countries, from Afghanistan to Kazakhstan.

Horse racing at the Piazza del Campo, from an engraving. 1682.

With the Renaissance in Western Europe, the ramshackle medieval bazaar is transformed into an organised civic market area, inspired by the Greek model, with the construction of ambitious, rationally-planned, civic areas like the Piazza del Campo in Sienna, created for use by weekly market stalls. The piazza adds elements of music, performance and even sport. This fusion of retail and entertainment foreshadows the phenomenon that will one day become the mega-mall.

3. From the Arcade to Department Store, 18th to 19th century.

By the 18th century, competing European empires require showcases to display their economic prowess and colonial power. Cathedral-like in scale and grandeur, arcades are city centre indoor markets, generally neo-classical in architecture (glass ceilings with mirrored walls, detailed ornamentation, gold leaf and frescoes) displaying the most exclusive retail for the newly-rich classes of the industrial revolution. Gostiny Dvor in St. Petersburg (opens 1785), covers one square kilometre with 100 shops and competes with Burlington Arcade in London in terms of opulence; while the Galleria Vittorio Emanuele II in Milan, Italy (1860) is the most iconic example of the grand style. In 1828, 'The Arcade' in Providence, Rhode Island, introduces the concept of pedestrianised shopping to the United States.

In the 1870s, in Europe and the US, the first women's guides to home-making, shopping and fashion appear. The newly emerging bourgeoisie likes to show off its wealth and its wives, and with it develops the idea of the women's 'separate sphere'. This lays down the model of women as principal shoppers and 'conspicuous consumers'. The feminisation of shopping favours the comfort and shelter provided by covered markets, and 'strolling' becomes the new model of retail (being on display as one looks at the displays). Industrial production then widens the differences between the classes and the sexes – 'men produce, women consume'. The arcade then gives rise to the department store – 'all under one roof' – without which the modern mall would never have been conceived.

With the department store, the era of verbal selling is superseded by the visual: mannequins and 'Do Not Touch' displays. For the first time in history, price tags appear, making cost non-negotiable and placing a distance between retailer and shopper.

Galleria Vittorio Emanuele II in Milan. Opened 1877.

4. The Car & the Strip Mall, 1920s – 40s.

While the European Empires struggle to survive war, industrialisation rapidly expands the US economy and city centres become crowded and polluted. Along with the invention of the affordable family car (Ford), this leads to the birth of the suburb (the dream of a new life beyond the city) and with the suburb comes the strip mall – linear roads many kilometres long, lined with single retail outlets. Strip malls spring up in Illinois, Missouri and California throughout the 1920s.

A typical innovator from this time is salesman Don M Casto. In 1928, Casto opens Grandview Avenue Shopping Center in Columbus, Ohio, with 4 supermarkets (Piggly-Wiggly, A&P, Kroger, Palumbo's), twenty other stores and parking for four hundred cars. Casto preaches his car-centred strip malls as the future for America and uses exotic publicity stunts – such as an 'old lady' diving 100ft into a six foot pool in a parking lot – to promote his properties. However, the Depression and World War II delay the proliferation of Strip Malls and there are, by the end of the war, as few as three hundred in the US. Traders like Casto, however, by handling construction, ownership, management, promotion, and through leasing units to individual retailers under one single entity, become models for an aggressive new type of entrepreneur who comes to dominate the landscape of postwar suburbia and the economic boom: the real estate developer. Strip malls embody the ethos of the *free market*; without state regulation they spring up along every newly-constructed state freeway and come to dominate the American landscape.

Meanwhile, in revolutionary communist Russia, the entire economy comes under the rule of centralised command and the former arcades and department stores of the Russian Empire are turned into state-run stores. In 1928, Stalin closes GUM (on Red Square), formerly the largest shopping arcade in Europe, and converts it into government offices (later, he puts the body of his wife Nadezhda, who commits suicide, on public display there). Although fighting the advance of Communism, much of Europe shares the Russian distrust of 'vulgar' US-style commerce, and so the global expansion of the mall is kept in check for over sixty years.

Soviet tanks in 1944 passing GUM – the former shopping arcade.

Incident in a Mall # 15

Vasyl and the Empty Space

Between 1987 and 1990, through a long and complex journey that involved shifting borders, detention centres, and changing laws on immigration within the EU, Vasyl Machenko emigrated from the Ukraine to the UK. He is now fifty and lives in a council housing scheme on the edge of Glasgow with his forty-one year old wife, Zhanna, and three children, one of whom, Tanya, he worries about constantly, as she has left home, after many arguments – and without his consent – to live with a young British man. Things have not turned out quite the way Vasyl expected, but he is a man with an indomitable spirit, and a hearty, self-deprecating sense of humour. One of his tales is of his first experience in the West, after scaling the wall; he recounts it to demonstrate his then naïveté. Bahh, he says, I am idiot, what can we do?

On his entry to West Germany, Vasyl was taken in by friends of friends, and as an outing, they took him to see his first mall – *The Europa-Center*. They led him inside and asked, So what do you think? They had expected him to be dazzled by the cornucopia of goods, the cheap prices, the infinity of brand choices.

But where is the centre? Vasyl asked.

His friends were confused.

There is no place to stand, he said, You are joking with me, take me to centre.

The West Germans exchanged a look of embarrassment.

This is it, they repeated.

Bahhh! Vasyl said, I want to go to centre!

Vasyl always laughs outrageously when he repeats this, and many listeners put their inability to grasp Vasyl's meaning down to his thick accent and poor English grammar; nonetheless, he was making an important point. As Vasyl looked out at the tiled central walkway, he was correct: there were no emblems of the state, no pictures of the leader, no central cenotaph, no clock or sculpture to meet under, only hundreds of people in constant movement, almost bumping into each other, apparently oblivious to the place itself.

He stood there on the spot for only a matter of seconds, frozen, as many people passed him by, unaware of his quandary. Vasyl always calls himself Idiot! when he recounts this, but what he articulated was something many people from former communist countries have experienced and something westerners feel periodically in times of estrangement: that there is something empty at the heart of consumerism.

In simple architectural terms a mall does have an empty centre: it is hollow, and the epicentre is only the point of greatest transit. The centre is a space, not a place. A space between outlets (shops, food courts, entertainments) but also between people. As malls are designed to keep consumer traffic flowing, any features of interest which might slow down traffic – fountains and display areas – are placed in the wings. Even store maps are kept to the side, so as not to block transit.

What made Vasyl shudder was the idea that there was no plan to all this, no overseeing eye. He was asking, How can a place be held together by little more than the passing desires of its populace? It was as if for a moment he was experiencing a nostalgia for the securities of the totalitarian state he had escaped from; for the monument, the memorial, the government building, the civic centre, the locus and panopticon. A mall in this light must seem to lack a core; it has no centre but its shoppers, for better or worse, are all free from each other. This may be why Vasyl found himself feeling very alone on the fake marble tiles.

It is perhaps worth noting that the only job Vasyl could get was as a CCTV operator in one of the six malls in Glasgow. He makes jokes now about how he is Big Brother, but you can sense that he gets some comfort from the job. They call him Stalin at work, because of his accent, and he laughs, but thinks them idiots. They do not know of the fear of picking up a phone or of one's own neighbours reporting your movements and intimacies. But still, these dots on his screen, these people, they seem to be content in a way he cannot quite access.

His daughter Tanya was happy to be part of them and to call herself British. She left home complaining that he tried to control everything. He wanted only to protect her from a place which had no heart, to save her from the mindless wandering he watched every day on his screens, but she thought him dated; she too called him Stalin.

Sometimes, in the times between looking for shoplifters, he searches for her on his twelve cameras. He has heard that she still lives in the city, although she has not called him in two years. He thinks she must shop in his shopping centre, as everyone seems to, as there are few other places for people to go, but after hundreds of hours of searching, has not yet found her on his screens.

Incident in a Mall # 22

A Solitary Car on the Top Floor

Once a week, in one of Glasgow's five major shopping malls, a BMW drives to the top floor of the car park, irrespective of whether there are spaces available on the other floors. The driver, a well-dressed man in his forties, parks the car at a spot with no other cars in sight and then takes the escalator to shopping mall, to shop.

Twenty minutes later, he returns with a shopping bag, goes into the trunk of his car and lifts out a sports bag; he then takes both bags inside with him and locks the doors. The windows of the BMW are slightly mirrored, making it difficult to see clearly what is going on inside.

Half an hour later, the same car drives slowly around all the seven floors, stopping finally at the attendant's booth. The electronic window goes down and reveals what appears to be a stunning woman, with a platinum blonde wig.

Hi Dave, she says.

And the attendant replies, Hello again Greta, how are you today? She has told him before that that is her preferred name.

Would you like to see my new dress? Greta asks.

The attendant concurs, as there is no one around and there is no harm in it.

Greta then opens her door and reveals herself in stockings, heels and an expensive mini-dress. She asks the attendant what he thinks, and he tells her, Terrific, you look terrific Greta. Over the last year, he has noted, she has taught herself to shop for clothes that flatter and learned how to apply make-up convincingly. She crosses her legs, plays with her hair and pouts for him. Not once does she step out of the car.

When her performance is over, Greta waves goodbye and drives back to the top floor, to remain there for up to forty minutes. Perhaps it takes all that time to effect the transformation in reverse and erase all signs of the change, or perhaps Greta just wants some time alone, to sit and look out over the city.

At the end of this time, the driver emerges from the car, in smart but casual gents clothing, puts the sports bag back in the boot and goes to the automatic payment machine, pays for the ticket and drives back down the seven floors to the exit.

This happens every week, and no one apart from the parking attendant has ever seen Greta in person. He has noted that the BMW has a baby-on-board sticker on the rear windscreen, but this does not bother him, as no crime has been committed and Greta brings some colour to his day.

N.B.

An almost identical tale has been reported in a second mall, fourteen miles away from the first. In this second report, however, the individual wears a red wig, drives a Nissan and has never spoken to anyone, although he/she goes for walks in high heels in the car park. These walks are brief, of about twenty feet, and the person appears to be recording him/herself performing to a camera in the car.

This new phenomenon is named Public Cross-dressing or 'daring' by cross- dressers themselves and has become a cult phenomenon. It has been facilitated, by among other things, affordable video technology (camera phones) and the internet. On

YouTube there are over 80,000 videos of cross-dressers, venturing out for their first test steps 'au femme'. The challenge is 'to pass' in a public space. These videos are self-filmed and have titles such as: 'Going out for the first time in my complete femme set', 'Cross-dressing at Next in Deep Stealth Mode', 'Some recent outings in Stilettos', 'Driving to the shops', 'CD cissy shopping' and 'Sabrina – a great TV day out in the mall'. The YouTube pages contain notes, tips, encouragement and appraisal from other cross-dressers, worldwide. In almost every case the locations picked for the first steps are retail outlets, malls and car parks.

For the uninitiated it may also be worth noting that CD and TV here, do not refer to mechanisms for distributing media, but stand for cross-dresser and transvestite, respectively. Whether there is some subconscious impulse on the behalf of TVs to model themselves on televisual images, and then record themselves for TV (or at least YouTube), is worth further investigation.

Incident in a Mall # 7

Rena the Cleana

You might find the nickname, the play on words, a little humorous. Rena does not. There is very little that Rena finds funny; in fact, local legend has it that she has not smiled for over a decade. Rena is a grandmother, forty-two years of age, from the east end of Glasgow. One of her daughters is a junkie; her youngest has just had a child and has also recently become a cleaner, like her mother. Rena's daily tasks include: picking up over two hundred pieces of dropped chewing gum, mopping up spills in the food court and car park and scrubbing the toilets every three hours. Rena hates customers and their children. Rena has had to clean up things she would rather not speak of: blood, sanitary towels, used condoms and human excrement, in places in the mall that could barely be imagined, one of which was the pot of a large plastic yucca plant on the main concourse.

Rena hates her fellow workers. They are younger, and foreign mostly; Russians, Poles, Slavs, Kurds. They make her feel like an immigrant in her own country. *Away and fuck yersel ya Paki bastards* is her most frequent expression. She calls everyone a Paki irrespective of their racial origin. Her other well-known phrase is: *Ya fuckin' animals – dinna come tae Rena to clean up your shite!* Given her racism and her language, it is highly unusual, and perhaps unfortunate, that Rena was called upon to be the prime negotiator in this incident involving an Asian man.

85

At the time of the event, Rena was cleaning up some soft-drink spillage in the car park, on level five, when she saw something unusual. The man in question had climbed the concrete wall and was standing looking down at the hundred-foot drop. She knew there were procedures for such incidents, there having been three such ones in the last year, three or four in fact, every year, but she did not like calling the security people, because they always 'took the piss'. Even though she had never attended any courses in crisis management, she decided to take matters into her own hands.

At this point, the people in the CCTV room had noted the problem and despatched security, called the police, fire brigade and ambulance services.

Rena pushed her trolley towards to the young man.

As the CCTV footage is the only record of events and no audio was recorded, the actual words that passed between Rena and the young man can only be speculated upon. The footage shows Rena gesturing over the edge as if encouraging the man to jump. Then shouting at him, spitting on the ground and walking away.

Perhaps, give her repertoire, she made some explicit reference to his ethnic origin; perhaps she said she was not going to be held personally responsible for clearing up the mess, after he jumped. Whatever she said, it nonetheless proved effective.

The emergency services had not arrived at this point, but many staff had crammed into the CCTV room to watch. What they saw was the young man staggering on the ledge, then getting down and running at Rena. He spun her around and shouted – Rena then grabbed his arm and forced him to the ground. By the time the police, ambulance and fire brigade finally arrived, Rena was sitting on the man with his arm up his back in something like a half-Nelson.

Rena had never studied manuals on dealing with potential suicides but she had correctly, if subconsciously, enacted all of the correct strategies.

1. *Tell the person your name.*

2. *Make them aware that there will be an aftermath to their act.*

3. *Try to provoke them into an argument on some subject other than their current situation.*

4. *When possible, restrain them till professional assistance arrives.*

A year later, Rena got a postcard from the young man. He had become engaged and was going back to college. He thanked her for saving his life and invited her to meet his family. Rena kept the postcard at her workstation, and it was noted by her colleagues – who had, since the event, started to treat her with something like respect, if not reverence – that one day she did almost smile while looking at it.

Then her walkie-talkie sounded and she was informed of an incident involving excrement in the ladies toilets. She got to her feet, muttered *Fucking animals*, and got back to work.

TOP MAN

This time it's for real. No more excuses, lads. This time it's a life-challenge. Are we going to do it in a pub, in a nightclub? Nah, that's the loser's way. You're going out there to the mall in broad daylight, and I'm giving you one hour to get an N-close. Not a K-close, which means kiss by the way, or an F-close, which I'll leave to your imagination gents, but a number. You gotta close the deal with a real girl's phone number, over the road in SilverDale. I picked up most of my top three hundred chicks in malls, dunno why, but it's a fact. So, I want you to form pairs again, cos picking-up is sixty-five per cent easier in twos. Right then, no time for losers cos we are the champions, right lads? It's just across the car park, under the flyover. Remember the Ten Rules: get out of your comfort zone; a ninety-nine per cent failure rate with a hundred girls-a-week is still one brand new lay every seven days. Warm up with some ugly birds to get the confidence up before going for that ten-girl. It's all about numbers gents. OK, see you on the ground floor between Gap and La Senza, one o'clock. The guy that scores highest wins a pass to the Platinum Plus Workshop in Los Angeles, December. May the best man win!

Dave stays seated as the others surge out of the conference suite. My God, this place, these people. This is so not Dave.

A hand on his shoulder. It's Raj, the six-footed acne-faced business start-up guy from Milton Keynes who, at the Who-We-Were-session, before the coffee break, talked at great speed about how this Neuro-linguistic Programming life coach saved his life by curing his stutter. Dave thinks Raj has probably never had a girlfriend or maybe even sex and it's a bit weird that he should go from being a virgin to a pickup artist, bypassing what normal people do, but Dave kind of likes Raj, because although he hasn't got a stutter anymore, something even stranger has replaced it. Raj takes a deep breath before he starts, and his face is usually blue by the time he's finished.

You-alright-mate-you-look-knackered-gotta-get-pumped-up-man-face-the-day-man-you-ready-gotta-get-over-approach-anxiety-man-you-know-what-I-mean-we-gonna-win-ready? Dave looks up at Raj's gasping face; it's maybe that, and Raj's extended hand, and the foresight that Raj may turn suicidal if Dave doesn't help him, which makes Dave rise from his seat to the challenge.

You're probably wondering what the hell a nice quiet guy like Dave is doing on a Pickup Artists weekend boot camp with twenty sharply-dressed single men, run by a man who has renamed himself after a type of weapon, looks like Brad Pitt's bodyguard and is 'bestselling author' of 'PPP' (Pussy Pulling Power) and 'FFF' (Find Fuck Forget) – well so is Dave. Dave is not what you'd call an ambitious or sexually-active person. In fact I don't think he's had a girl since Sally in 1993. He prefers to sit at home and collect old blues records from the 1930s and to walk dogs for house-bound geriatrics. Personally, I think he's got this kind of hidden genius, but most folk think that in the soccer-game-of-life he's the kid that always gets put in goal.

How it started? Well, it was Dave's thirty-third birthday and all us Facebook buddies got together and asked some fundamental questions like: is Dave seriously going to be alone forever? I feel kind of bad about it but about thirty of us chipped in and paid the six hundred quid – his mum even gave us fifty. She's nuts, her name's Tricia, but she calls herself Tree; she was a wild child in the 60s and fried her brains. She wants Dave out of the house, because that's where he's still living. A guy your age, she says; you should be out there, up to your neck in pussy.

I dunno, said Dave. Saying I dunno is just so Dave. Cos when he doesn't know he admits it – he's got a thing about truth. I think it's admirable, but it's probably why he used to get called *Rain Man* at school.

Anyway, it started as a kind of joke but Dave didn't want to let his mates down, plus it cost a lot and Dave worries about money, probably cos he's the only person who's been a barista for over twelve years, and we're talking by choice. I mean, you got to look at the irony of the words, like baristas and barristers – and more than a few of us are in law now, and Dave – well, personally, I put his stunning lack of ambition on all fronts down to Starbucks. They have this weird flexi-working rota thing that means you have to be on-call practically all week even if you're part time; we're talking like eighty hours on call to get thirty-two. Go do the math. So you can't really plan anything social or hold down another job or study, and dating is kind of tricky too. Dave doesn't complain, it's not like he even wants a promotion or a date; he's just happy serving coffee, drinking coffee. He even hangs out there when he's not working. In fact, coffee is probably his chief passion in life; he drinks about twenty cups a day. Maybe that's another reason, actually, why he accepts the challenge, cos he's thinking there must be a Starbucks in the mall and he could get a Frappe or a Grande Cappuccino, cos the craving has started.

Raj and Dave are standing outside Gap and it's been fifteen nervous minutes since Stealth left them alone with their POA, or Plan Of Attack. They have to stop random females in their tracks, 'force an opening' and 'split-up the set'. They are to 'isolate' one girl and 'accelerate' using the chat techniques, and Kino, which, as I might have said before, is nothing to do with cinema, and means touch. I know the lingo is kind of hard to get. Lingo is so not Dave.

Don't worry if you can't think of anything to say to the chicks, Stealth smiled, Use one of the 'canned-openers' I taught you, if you can't remember them, they're in the info-pack. Then he turned away swiftly leaving Dave with this unusual visual image of trying to undo a woman's head with a mechanism designed for tins of beans.

There were three canned-openers from the second morning session and Dave remembered them almost word for word, due to their high absurdity quota. The first went something like this:

'Hi girls, I'm looking for my friend, have you seen him?' As Stealth explained, this makes women ask, 'What does your friend look like?' At which point you get the 'hook' in and make 'the joke'. You lean down to your ankle and say, 'he's about this size and has red hair.' This technique is called 'the squirrel' – for some reason Dave cannot fathom, there are supposed to be squirrels in shopping malls.

Then there was this one that baffled Dave.

'Hey girls, my mate gave me two hundred pounds to buy a birthday present for his girlfriend cos he's stuck at work. Any ideas on what she might like?' According to Stealth this was ideal because it showed that you have both money and friends, and there's nothing chicks distrust more than guys with no friends and no money. Stealth's lack of irony in saying such things made Dave's left shoulder twitch involuntarily (which is another thing he does that is 'just so Dave').

At least a hundred girls have walked past with their shopping bags and extremely intimidating push-up bras since they started, and Raj is getting quite frothy around the mouth. You-gotta-believe-

in-yerself-gotta-think-out-of-the-box-man-you-gonna-go-first?
Eh?-eh? You-go-first eh?

Well, I dunno, shrugs Dave.

Got-to-fight-it-man-approach-anxiety-man-its-a-killer-
gotta-just-jump-in-I'm-just-warming-up-here-man-I'm-gonna-do-
it-I'm-gonna-do-it-it's-only-chicks-man-don't-fear-rejection-man.

Dave stares out over the forecourt: The Hugh Grant
lookalike guy and the cop-looking guy from the workshop are
chatting with a group of four girls, each one with a different hair
colour, like the Spice Girls or Girls Aloud. Hugh Grant is pointing
to one of the girl's shoes, he's touching her arm. There was this
thing Stealth had shown some of the other guys, before, some dance
move. Hugh Grant is twirling a girl in his arms now. Jesus.

Further down the court, Dave can see the short bald man
and the skinny guy stopping three young Latina-looking girls. One
of them shrugs away from the outreaching hand of baldy, then all
three move swiftly away, laughing. Over by the pillars, outside Gap,
Stealth is standing, judging all, arms crossed over his steroid chest.
He makes these big arm movements as if to usher Dave forward;
mouthing big slo-mo words like GO-FOR-IT. BREAK-UP-THE-
SET. Raj taps his shoulder, nods to an approaching set.

Quick-the-canned-openers-man-we-need-the-canned-
opener-give-em-the-lines-stop-em-isolate-ask-em-about-
themselves-keep-em-there-accelerate.

It's pointless Dave thinks, it's the same Latinas that ran
laughing from baldy man. Didn't Raj even notice?

Now! Raj shouts, make-a-move-make-a-date-no-no-no-I-
mean-get-an-N-close-yeah-an-N-close-wow-she's-a-seven-an-eight.

They do this, they rate women – it's like that self-monitoring performance form Dave has to fill in every month at work. He only ever gives himself a six.

I dunno, Dave says. But it's too late, Raj has leapt forward.

Hi-girls-I've-got-this-girlfrend-nah-nah-I-mean-my-mate's-got-this-girlfriend-and-shes-got-this-phone-ah-I-mean-shes-got-this-birthday-and-I've-got-two-hundred-pounds-and…

Their faces – as if accosted by a leper. Raj accelerating, getting louder, all the words in a glue. We-need-yer-help-yeah-yeah-that's-right-cos-I've-got-this-text-she's-gave-him-this-text-for-his-birthday-and-

Dave has to do something, Hi, we're looking for our friend, have you…

The girls laughing, the tallest, in the purple top, speaks in this Latina-way that Dave finds rather lovely.

We have already… your friends, over there, they ees looking for friend also. Ees thees market research? She points over to baldy man.

From the corner of Dave's eye he can see Stealth gesticulating vigorously to keep on, intercept, chat, Kino, Kino! Raj is starting to stutter and the girls are wanting to move on.

Sorry, Dave says, actually we don't have a friend. In fact we're just doing this because we need to get one, like a girl, I mean two, one each, maybe … or something.

This is so Dave.

You want me to be girlfriend? And this sends the girl's friends into hysterics. She is speaking to them now in Spanish.

Dave shrugs. He went to Madrid once with Sally Carter; Sally had a couple of secret addiction issues and that's maybe why Dave turned out so square, but that's a story he'd rather I didn't repeat.

Raj is giving him frantic facial indicators, much like Stealth's.

Sorry, Dave blurts out, My friends made me do this cos I haven't had a girlfriend in thirteen years. I dunno.

Thirteen years? The tall girl laughs, No sex?

He shrugs, nods. I dunno. She strokes his cheek.

You are joker with me, you are funny man!

Raj is nodding for him to move to Kino, she's touched his arm, it's fair game. But Dave can't think of anything to say. Jeeso, he could really do with that coffee, straight Americano, three sugars.

Bye-see-bye, the tall girl says, we have to go for shoppings now, see you, bye, you are very cute, these ees wonderful country, I hope you have sexy times soon, ees very best, Adios.

And they run off in hysterics.

Hey, that was nice, Dave says to Raj.

Nah-man-we-got-to-get-their-number-the-N-close-man-you-was-close!-I-was-shit-I-froze-man-fuckin-approach-anxiety-man-I-was-shit-you-got-style-you-was-good-you-believe-in-yourself-man-you-got-what-it-takes-man-you-were-that-close-to-an-N-close-whats-yer-secret man?

I dunno, Dave says. How about we break for a coffee to celebrate, and maybe a choco muffin? My treat.

JESUS! It's Stealth shouting, he's run over, hands on both their shoulders – That was fantastic, gents! You held them, you accelerated, you almost had Kino dude. Stealth is slapping him on the back. Dave isn't into back-slapping.

Look lads, I don't know what you've got going here, the geek thing, yeah some girls are into that, good cop / bad cop, the sensitive types, I dunno, but you've got to escalate to Kino, no point telling you, look…He leads Dave to one side, by the doorway of Gap.

What's that on your shoe? Stealth says to him.

Dave is perplexed, chewing gum, dog-shit? He stands on one leg to look at the sole, just then, off balance, Stealth offer his hand to support him and Dave takes it. In a flash, Stealth has locked Dave's hand, twisted it over his head. Dave flashes back to many humiliations in high school, but this is not that, Stealth is not going to force him to kiss feet, to eat dirt. No, Stealth spins him round, once twice in his arms, as if in a tango. Stealth takes his waist, and sets him back on his feet.

Didn't expect that did ya? And Dave cannot reply.

Kino, Stealth says, Adrenalin, did you feel that? I'm talking about setting off subliminal trust triggers in a woman in seconds. I'm talking about accelerated intimacy that it'd take a bloke in a pub three hours and three rounds of drinks for her to even get close to. This is primordial, this is cave man stuff, you get a woman's adrenalin going, she'll feel it in her dark wet cave.

Raj stands, dumfounded, almost applauding, his enthusiasm growing inversely to Dave's embarrassment as shoppers pass.

Once you've hooked them, pull the shoe trick, or one of the hand tricks from earlier. You think you could pull off that move, Dave?

I dunno, says Dave.

Stealth backs off. Hey, Dude, you want out, go join the masses, be a loser for the rest of your life. You want to go?

Dave is about to say – Sounds fine to me. He's thinking that an Americano with three sugars would be the answer to just about everything. Then he sees Raj's face, and Raj's future. Once he's abandoned him, back in the conference suite with nineteen strangers, an odd number and no partner, Raj will be paired up with Stealth, jabbering his way through the rest of the day's exercises and the final nightmare test (as outlined in the info-pack): the exclusive, high end nightclub where 'real models' hang out, where, rumour has it, Beyoncé was once seen. He has this image of Raj, drunk on the dance floor, trousers round his ankles, doing the only move he knows.

I'm cool, says Dave, I'm going nowhere.

Excellent, so what's your strategy? says Stealth. You got twenty mins, max, before we head back to compare scores. What you gonna do?

Get-an-N-close! Raj shouts.

We're gonna... Dave forces himself to say it... get an N-close.

But do you believe it, do you believe in yourself?

Raj's face says he'd like to have a self, one day, whatever that is.

Sure, Dave says.

Stealth puts his hand in the air. Hi-five! Raj hi-fives him. Dave puts his hand up and it stings when Stealth hits, hard, deliberately.

Great-man-fab-man-tastic Raj shouts to Dave, all fired up on Neuro Linguistic Programming. We're-gonna-do-it-man-gonna-throw-away-the-script-man-no-canned-openers-man-just-gonna-do-it-yeah!

OK, just for Raj, Dave tells himself. He scans the mall for girls and his eyes come to rest on two with baby buggies – they're all wrong, in many ways: the shellsuits, the babies most of all. He gets wondering if girls that young, that poor, ever had any romance, then he gets thinking that romance is probably outdated by now, and maybe it's just best to skip all the hoo-hah and make babies when you're fifteen and not have to be picked up by pickup artists.

LA SENZA! Raj shouts. She's-an-eight-man-maybe-a-nine-man-nine-at-nine-o'clock-man. Dave looks up and locates the pair of busty high-heeled mid-thirties types coming out with bulging shopping bags. Raj nudges him and heads over.

I dunno, Dave calls after him. I really dunno. What the hell is Raj going to do? Stop them and rant about their choices of intimate lingerie.

No way Raj, just let it go.

It's too late anyway, Baldy has intercepted first and in the seconds that follow Dave catches sight of Stealth, head in hands, as Baldy gets it all in the wrong order and goes straight for Kino before chat and the girls must think they're being accosted by a store detective. One of them whips her hand round and almost slaps the guy.

Jeeso, Dave is craving that Starbucks, a mochachino, an espresso with three shots. But Raj is heading towards the shellsuits. A quick flick of the head tells Dave that they've left their baby buggies with another teenage mum outside Mothercare. Raj is already running before Dave can stop him. When Dave gets there, this is what he hears:

Oy!-Hi-by-the-way-I'm-not-making-you-feel-nervous-am-I?-This-isn't-market-research-if-that's-what-you're-thinking-sorry-I-can-talk-a-bit-fast-my-name's-Rajesh-by-the-way-and-I-used-to-get-approach-anxiety-you-know-but-

The girls move from fear to scorn bypassing pity as

Raj accelerates into verbal oblivion. It's-cool-I'm-cool-I'm-just-wondering-what-two-babes-sorry-girls-sorry-ladies-are-doing-like-you-in-a-place-like-

Raj! C'mon.

Raj's eyes flash years of frustration. He unleashes it and strikes Dave, sending him flying across the tiles. It's fine, Dave tells himself as he tries to right himself, it's maybe from the stutter, understandable. Girls push past Raj, eyes spitting disgust, while others stop and stare. It's cool, he says to Raj, extending his hand to shake and to ask for a help-up but Raj is already raging away, towards Stealth.

Dave checks for broken bones. He's taking his time to stand because he's actually a little portly. Something strikes his chin and voice yelps – Fuck!

He scans around and there's this girl lying on the ground, with this heavy rucksack on her back.

Jesus fuckin' Christ! She's shouting, rubbing her forehead. It's only then that Dave feels the pain. Jees, he says, I'm really sorry.

Her eyes are anger, her hair is cut like a boy, but dyed purple, she's got these big army boots on, and they're sort of in the air, as she tries to kick herself back upright.

Ten minutes in this fucking country and... She sounds Canadian or Aussie.

He knows his apologies sound lame but he stands there offering a hand.

No fuckin' ta, she says as she tries to lug the back-pack back in place. Fuckin', fuckin'... He stands there as her hands struggle with the straps.

Can I?

Take your fucking hands...? But after tying herself in knots, she agrees and so he helps her up, gets her bag strap over her shoulder. Already there's a cluster around Stealth, laughing and pointing. Jeeso, as soon as he's said sorry he's gone, forever. Before that he has to make it all OK.

As you know, when Dave feels stressed Dave tends to crave coffee, which is not good for stress but it's very Dave. In such situations, he has also found it's a good idea to try to get the offended party to join you in the thing you need. So, it just slips out. Jees, sorry can I buy you a coffee or... he says, D'you know if there's a Starbucks in here?

What, she says, fuckin' what?

Now he feels selfish, You fancy a coffee?

What are you a fucking spaz?

I dunno, he says and thinks he should probably walk away, but she's laughing.

Fuck, what a fucked-up country, they kept me for an hour in immigration, pulled all the shit out of my sack like I was a fuckin' dealer, thought they were gonna strip me and get their rubber gloves on. Fascist fucks.

He was kind of shocked by her language.

So where's this fuckin' Starbucks, anyway?

He didn't know and that was what he said.

Fuckin' fascists, she said again as she shifted the weight of her rucksack. In the doorway of Gap, Stealth was amassing the troops, motioning to Dave, pointing at his wrist where a watch might once have been.

Dave didn't fancy the conference suite now that Raj was pissed at him, and he really did need that coffee. Must be around here somewhere, he said, You can usually smell it before you see it – it's usually near the entrance, or close to Magic Muffins.

You're weird, she said, then smiled.

So they were walking, not quite together, as his eyes scanned the shops and she was ranting behind him about the UK, how it looked just the same as Oz, and why did she even fuckin' bother.

He didn't really have anything to say about the subject that people hadn't said before so he kept walking, past the phoney fountain thing and there it was.

Cheers, she said, as he set her grande skinny cappuccino with soya milk on the table in front of her. She had her rucksack on the next seat like it was a person. She was putting her hair back in a headband. She was pretty, not pretty-pretty, but pretty much the OK-est looking girl Dave had seen in a hell of a long time, in a kind of fucked-up grungy way, what with her nose piercing and purple hair. He caught himself staring and sipped his Americano. It was hot and good like it should be. She was staring at him.

Sorry, I'm a junkie, he said.

You take smack?

No, no, he held up the coffee, nodded at it. Twenty a day – keeps the doctor away. She nodded, a slight smile.

I had a boyfriend that did crystal meth, she said. Toby Spencer, back in Melbourne, he's in rehab now, that's kind of why I'm here.

Wow, thought Dave, maybe it was an Aussie thing, not the drug thing, but that she was one of those folk who always told you the full names of people they knew, like you were supposed to know who they were, which was something he did too.

So you just going to stand there or what? She said.

Oh, was I? Dave said. Of course he was standing. She patted the other seat beside her.

Weird fuckin' country, she said again. And he sat.

Well Dave, she said, I'm Daisy by the way; she put out her hand to shake.

He wondered how the hell she knew his name. She smiled and pointed to his sticky badge that he must have forgotten to take off. Jeeso.

Oh that. He fumbled with his cup and took her hand. Her shake was vigorous. Yeah, it's a long story, he said. Stupid fucking name, she said then laughed, mine not yours, my mum was a hippy.

He could have told her about his mum and asked about crystal meth but he didn't want to pry. He was just savouring the good hot black coffee and her face and the way she'd go sort of nuts when an idea shot through her, a bit like this dog he knew — you could tell when it was going to bark because this kind of power started in it's belly and few seconds later a bark came out, and it was always really funny, like the dog wasn't even in control of its own bark. Sal it was called, she was old Jim Thompson's dog. It would have been nice to tell her these things but he kept quiet and just kind of smiled at her.

So what you doing here in hell? You got a job here? She had a frothy bit of chocolatey milk on her top lip.

Yeah, Starbucks, but not here, another one.

Fuckers, she said, every cup goes to a kid in Africa or shit, I dunno, I dunno, she said, and that made him smile. So, are you just... she paused to add some sarcasm, which seemed to be her thing — shopping?

Well, he could have said 'yes', but that would have been a lie. He could have even come out with that old canned-opener about shopping for a present for his best mate's girlfriend, but no. Out through the glass he saw Stealth and the guys looking for him. They were heading in this direction. He bent down behind her rucksack.

What the fuck?

Are they there? He tried to cover his head.

You *are* a fuckin' junkie, she said, did you steal something? I don't want to get fuckin' deported!

Nah, nothing like that, the guy with the tan and the stripe shirt is he...

Shh, she said, yeah, he's snooping round, slimy lookin' motherfucker. She put a hand on his shoulder, Stay there a min. He did as she said, crouched. Beyond, he could see the staff staring.

OK, it's cool, she said finally, Coast is clear.

He got back up; he'd spilled some coffee on his trousers.

Why do I always end up with junkies, she said exhaling loudly, I must have a fuckin' sticker that says co-dependent. Jesus.

I'm not, he said, brushing the coffee from his crotch. Honest to God.

Through the glass he saw Stealth and the team heading back in the direction of Gap, away from the main doors, Stealth checking his mobile. He sat down next to her again, looking cautiously over his shoulder.

So, why don't you stop fuckin' me around and tell me why the cops are after you?

He apologised, trying to hold in the laugh but it farted out the sides of his mouth.

I'm, I'm... he said.

What? What the fuck are you?

OK, she was freaked and she'd been so honest with him, so he had to level with her. I'm on this dumb course, he said, and, after her initial shock, it was funny when he told her the details, she was all eyes and they were incredible eyes, like a locked door that suddenly opens and she laughed like hell when he told her about the N-close and Kino and NLP and 'the squirrel'.

No fuckin' shit! He really liked her accent; the swearing seemed part of it, not something put on for show. So he went on.

Yeah and you do this thing where you get this girl to show her your foot then you spin her round and you touch her but she doesn't notice, I don't get it but she's supposed to feel it in her 'primordial cave'.

She roared like old Thompson's dog when it got barking. God, she said finally when she stopped, my friend got me a book just like that, *The Rules*, you've heard of it, right? Jesus, it's totally fucked up. I mean, what if all guys have to read *The Game* and all women read *The Rules*, there's like books to tell you how to have sex and how to have babies and how to split up. Anyway, what a mate eh? Giving me that shit, what was she thinking?

Who's your friend? Dave asked.

Debbie, Debbie Carter, she's like this uptight career chick now but she's sweet, she has these weird teeth she's going to get fixed but I think she's probably nicer with them the way they are.

Wow, said Dave, I can totally see Debbie Carter. I used to know this girl just like her called, with braces, Sharon Mackay.

Really? Daisy asked, and there was this moment when they both could have been trying to imagine Debbie Carter and Sharon Mackay but not quite making it.

Anyway, Daisy said, She thinks I need to get some self-esteem and believe in myself.

Self-esteem, I dunno, Dave said.

She says self-belief makes you a winner.

Weird, Dave said, I mean, how can everyone be a winner, when there's like gazillions of people in the world?

Here's to losers, Daisy said, toasting him with her cup.

She drained her coffee, then stood, Yup, I think it's time…

Sure, he said, though he wanted it to go on and he could have done with a second double shot. He set his cup down and stared at the floor, Well, it was nice…

Nah hah, she said and stretched her arms, I want to try out this fuckin' Kino shit. Seriously, so what you say – nice shoes and…

Dave couldn't help but laugh.

Yeah, well, I say, nice heels or something, or I could neg you, women are supposed to like being put down, like I could say – you've still got the price sticker on your sole.

For real! She roared then put on a funny face, he thought maybe she was pretending to be Debbie Carter, she did a funny voice and stood on one leg, reached out and balanced on his arm.

My God, you're right, she said, with the funny voice, I'm never shopping in Shoe Shed again, I'll get my stilettos from Dolce in future. And it was funny, what with her army boots.

So, she said, Aren't you supposed to take my hand? So he did, and then she nodded, and he raised it above her head and with a bit of pressure from her, leading the way, he spun her round, like in those old fifties dances, like in *Grease*. People were staring.

Again, she shouted, laughing like mad, so he spun her again and she looked like she was going to fall, so he took her waist and balanced her.

Just then there was a knocking behind them, Dave didn't care. Her laughter took on whole new devilish quality like she was laughing at someone, not at him, but not with him either, and now she was pointing to the window. Dave turned and there were Stealth and Raj and all the gang staring back. Stealth holding up his mobile to take a photo and Raj giving a hi-five to the bald guy.

OK, OK, OK, kiss me, Daisy said, and Dave sort of really did want to, but not in front of those guys. C'mon, just to fuck them off.

She took her hand from his and held his face and planted her lips on his. It went on for a long time and all the folks in Starbucks and the pickup artists were forgotten in the smell of her patchouli and sweat. She took his waist and held him tight and it was arousing in an uncomfortable way but she didn't seem to mind. She whispered to his neck, Shhh, they're still staring, looks like you've got your K-close, after all eh?

Dave didn't want to open his eyes, but when he did he saw her waving away Stealth and the gang. Then she gave the gang the finger. Dave tried not to look as she went up to the window and mouthed FUCK OFF and finally they sloped away. Fuckin' retards! She shouted.

When they were gone from sight she said Hey-ho and got her rucksack on her back and had the same trouble as before with the last arm, so he helped her, hundreds of question in him, but none for the asking. And this sick feeling. He probably shouldn't have had the coffee on an empty stomach, should have had a blueberry muffin to soak it up.

Cheers matey, she said, turning to face him. What the fuck

is there to do in your country anyway? I just got the stupid flight cos it was cheap.

Well, he said, I dunno. There was a whole bunch of tourist stuff she could do, but it was all pretty much the same stuff you'd get anywhere. He was thinking he could show her around the city but she'd not asked and it'd probably be too hard for him to get time off work anyway. He was thinking of the solitary walk back across the car park, under the flyover, the entrance to the conference suite, and the round of applause he'd get, and the slaps on the back, and Stealth handing him the gift voucher for the Platinum Plus Executive Workshop in Los Angeles.

She paused, as if waiting for him to say or do something, and when he didn't she said, Have a good one. An Australian expression maybe, and probably meant life, and she probably did have major problems with addicts in her own life and she may even have been a junkie herself – these were the things Dave told himself. She took the weight of her bag, I hope you find your friend, she said.

My friend?

The little guy, and she bent down, and made a sign, at about ankle level, tricky with the weight of her rucksack – You know, with the red hair and the fluffy tail.

Oh, right, he said, feeling himself smile.

She didn't stroke his cheek or kiss it goodbye. He had to step out of her way as she passed so as not to get knocked over by her rucksack.

See ya, she said, and she walked out into the mall.

So, he calls me, and I'm telling him, this is so great, good for you Dave, and he's asking me, So what should I do? And I'm like, Wait, did this just happen, like right now? And I'm telling him run after her Dude, but he's saying well I've been on the phone to you for half an hour, so she'll be long gone by now. And I'm like Jesus, Dave, why the hell didn't you run after her, why d'you waste all this time telling me? And why the hell didn't you ask for her number, she kissed you for chrissakes! And he's like, I dunno, I dunno. And I could weep with laughter or just plain weep cos this is all just so Dave.

Etymology

The evolution of the word 'mall' involves several international migrations and the unlikely transformation of a 'mallet' into a 'street-shaped retail area'.

Contrary to the propaganda of French anti-mall activists the word has nothing to do with 'mal' (bad, foul). It does however have French origins.

The earliest usage of mall in English is derived from the word 'pallemaille', a now obsolete French game dating from the 13th century which took its name from the Italian 'Pallagmaglio' (*palla* – 'ball,' and *maglio* – 'mallet'). The game – which was popular with the aristocracy and was later to form the basis of what would become croquet – was described by one Joseph Strutt in a book on European Sports (1611) as follows: 'a game wherein a round bowle is with a mallet struck through a high arch of iron (standing at either end of an alley) which he that can do at the fewest blows, or at the number agreed on, wins.'

Thereafter, once the game had spread to England, the name was anglicised to 'Pall-mall', and former Pall-Mall alleys were named after the game (Pall Mall and The Mall in London – 1656 & 1673 respectively).

The word, as words do, quickly proliferated and was transformed through popular usage into many things vaguely associated with the game and the places it had once been played. It then came to represent (a) a walkway bordered with trees (1702); (b) a grassy or paved pedestrian area between two roads or adjacent to a road; (c) an open area between buildings reserved for pedestrian usage. From there, in the 19th century, inspired by the grand malls of London, other cities designed their own long pedestrian walkways and in turn named them malls. Mall then came to mean any walkway between two rows of shops, or in an outdoor shopping area (often including trees, flowers, fountains, benches, and other such features). It then was a simple linguistic twist for mall to become the name of the shopping area itself, and this occurred in the transmigration of the word from Europe to America in the 20th century. The US was ever-keen to invest its commercial enterprise with something that would signify European sophistication, thus 'mall' proliferated throughout the US as a signifier of quality.[1]

Ironically, although the UK had 'shopping centres' which could have been designated as malls in terms of size and content (according to the conditions of the US based International Council for Shopping Centres), up until the 1980s, the word did not fit culturally, as it was associated with American private enterprise, while the land on which most British 'shopping centres' stood was council-owned. It was only with the selling off of such public land to private developers in the Thatcher-Reagan era, and through the adoption of American culture, fashion and slang within the UK at that time, that the word mall came into common usage.

Proposition:

Picture a 13th century French gentleman, frock coat and britches, striking a ball with a mallet. Then imagine that ball speeding through time and space till it gathers size and weight to the point where as a

---

1 The leading cigarette in the US of the 1940s was 'Pall Mall'. The branding slogan was 'The finest quality money can buy'.

'wrecking ball' it tears through the wall of a mall in the 21st century. Consider the date 14th July 2004, and the first recorded destruction of an abandoned US mall, Detroit, Michigan, and you might find the linguistic line from ball and mallet to mall wrecking ball closing in a way that might seem fated. *(See section entitled Dead Malls, Ghost Malls)*

A game of Pallemaille, 16th century France. Note the suspended hoop and the scoop-like mallet.

Naming a Mall

Mall names follow a simple but rigid linguistic system; the samples below are from the UK, post 1981:

Bargate	Bluewater	Braehead	Bull Ring
Cockhedge	County Square	Crossgates	Crowngate
Eastleigh	Fishergate	Golden Square	Grace Church
Kingsgate	Meadow Gate	Meadowhall	Princes Mead
Princess Square	Queensgate	Queensmeer	Silverburn
Swans Walk	Tweedmill	Vicarage Field	Victoria Square
Wellgate	Westfield	West Gate	West Quay

Points to note:

1. The recurrence of rural motifs: field, church, brae, burn, walk, mead. In naming a mall, it is common to invoke a feudal, pre-consumerist era and 'local' identity that existed in idyllic form before the invention of the very things – cars, motorways, malls – that destroyed such an idyll.

2. Nearly all names consist of two words, the second designating a space i.e. gate, square, park, etc., and the first adding a quality to the place, either adjectively: blue, silver, etc – or geographically: east, west. Or by using signifiers of status, heritage and 'authenticity' (see 4. below). In China, Golden is a popular mall name (as it is for Chinese restaurants in the UK).

3. In cases when geographical signifiers are used, these, generally, have no direct correlation to bearings on a map relative to a specific city. Which typically begs the question: to what is West Gate west of? And for that matter, what or where, is, or was, the gate?

4. In the UK, the recurrence of motifs from the British Empire: King, Princes, Victoria. This is anachronistic, since in every sense the values of feudal monarchy are contrary to the values of modern mass consumerism (the mercantile bourgeoisie destroyed the rule of royalty in almost all developed countries – the American constitution designates kings as tyrants). These royal signifiers then simply stand for 'class-i-ness'.

In much the same way that King and Queen are used in British mall naming, malls in America often use the word 'America' as a signifier of tradition and higher values. Thus, the 'America' in 'Mall of America' does not designate a locality but, in an act of circular reasoning, acts as a guarantor of qualities that are 'American'. In this sense, every mall, everywhere is a 'Mall of America'.

5. As most large regional malls are owned by international conglomerates (for example Braehead Shopping centre – on the outskirts of Glasgow – which is owned by a UK-based corporation that also has properties in the USA) the use of signifiers of belonging and history is at best tokenistic, or, perhaps, accidentally ironic.

6. The notion that malls are 'local' and pay homage to their environment is confounded by one notable example in the UK. Since 2000, there is one corporation that buys up failing shopping centres and re-brands them with a common name. This company

owns seventy-six properties, and each, irrespective of locality, is called 'The Mall'.

An image of the Brock Burn (a burn being the Scottish name for stream) which runs alongside Silverburn Mall on the Outskirts of Glasgow – after which Silverburn took its name.

Incident in a Mall # 4

The Key to Happiness

Happiness: the word does not seem immediately synonymous with market research, but since the late 50s, corporations have been keen to tap into and exploit this illusive phenomenon in the search for what they call 'the key to happiness'. This was, in fact, the name of an extensive market survey, conducted in 2002, by a shoe manufacturer, with over 500 focus groups and 2,000 head-to-head interviews, know as 'depths'.

The results, however, proved both disappointing and disturbing. None more so perhaps, than the interview conducted with Susan Thompson of Shawlands, Glasgow, thirty-four years old, childless and recently divorced.

Susan openly admitted that the only reason she was doing the interview was because she had too much time on her hands after having lost her job at Debenhams. The interviewer guided her back to the first question: What was the product in your happiest retail experience, ever?

Susan said they were a pair of shoes, very special, maybe called Mary-Janes, with these delicate double straps, which were quite daring, and this three-inch heel, in this off-white colour by the designer known as *Chloe*.

The interviewer asked where the point of purchase had been, and was told a long story about how Susan had seen these in a window the year before, and they reminded her of her student days when she was quite 'alternative', but they were too expensive and then of course there was the heel. This was when she was married and her hubby, James, had been quite short, so out of sympathy she'd worn only flat soled shoes. And they couldn't conceive, because of his tubes, but that was a long story. Anyway, so she decided to do a bit of self-esteem shopping.

Was that when you found your perfect Chloe shoes? The interviewer asked.

No, no, no Susan said. They were a whole year out of date by then and everyone was wearing pumps or those wedgy stiletto thingies. Me in pumps or stilettos? So I was pretty depressed, not just about that, but other things. Totally slash-my-wrists actually, if you must know.

The interviewer tried to lead her back.

So when did you come across your happy purchase?

And here Susan digressed – a friend of hers, Debby, knew about her fancying these Chloe shoes and bought herself a pair, online. That pissed her off, because Debby was always copying her and getting there first, and there was no chance of borrowing them from Debby because she was a size three. Anyway, this was a year ago and they'd stopped making them since then.

The interviewer, pen and fact-form in hand, pressed the question as to where and when again.

Susan went off on another tangent and talked about how hard it was being single again, doing online dating, and going to Cumbernauld for this job interview, and then being on this date with this guy from PC World, or was it Staples? And waking up in his bed, and he was too square and wore too much aftershave, and she felt a bit sordid and sick to her stomach; but then before getting her bus back she went to the shopping centre, just because it was next to the bus station, and she had time to kill, and she didn't want to sit in the bus station for too long because it was... well, not exactly hygienic.

And then?

Well, she was just killing a bit of time, like she said, and watching all the lassies, thinking about how much slimmer and trendier they were than her, and feeling a bit old and sad and fat – the usual – but then, by the doors of John Lewis, on this discount rack – she couldn't believe it, there they were, in the right colour, which might actually be called eggshell and not off-white, and they were her size, a nine – she had large feet and James had never liked that – and they were only a fifth of the original price and the sign said End of Line Clearance. So this was the last pair of Chloe shoes in the world, and like, only thirty quid.

OK, said the interviewer, So, price is a factor for you, and exclusivity?

Naw, naw, naw, Susan said, the fact was, right... I was just about to get them, when this old dear in this fancy coat saw me, and she marches up and grabs them and walks right to the tills.

Sorry, the interviewer said, inquiring as to whether Susan had made her happy purchase at all.

Naw, naw, wait, So I went up to her, and what d'you think I said?

Here the interviewer was further perplexed as it was highly unusual for an interviewee to ask questions over and above the standard ones about how much they would be getting paid, and when the interview would be over, and if they would be getting their promised free gift pack.

Right, Susan said, saving the interviewer from risking a

response. So, I'm running after her and I don't normally use language like this…

Go on.

So I said, Excuse me, those are MINE, by the way. I mean this is totally not me, but I'd wanted these shoes for over a year, right?

OK…aha, so you acquired the shoes, and completed your purchase, yes?.

Yeah, well, no exactly, you see the old bitch wouldn't let go, so were both tugging at them and I say – If you don't stop that you're going to break them! Because they have these lovely wee straps, right? And, so I yell at her… I can't believe I actually said this…

Go on. What did you say?

I said… If you don't give me them right now, I'll smash your fat fucking face and stick it right up you arse!

… OK.

I'm sorry, I can't believe… it was dreadful.

So, did you…?

Aye, I mean no, she let go and ran off, and I paid for them and that was that.

And… this was your happiest retail experience… ever?

Aye, absolutely. Yes.

(Here she paused.) Mind you, afterwards (laughter) I felt just a wee bit silly, because really, they were just a pair of shoes, right, and to be honest the wee straps were a bit daft-looking.

Susan received her complimentary gift pack of perfumes and lotions and a cheque for fifty pounds from a subsidiary co-sponsor. It was observed that was not wearing her favourite shoes during the course of the discussion, (she commented in fact that she had never gone out in them and probably never would). It was also noted that she did not agree to sign up for further interviews on similar products in the future.

The findings of this session, and many others like it from the same study, pointed to some alarming facts about happiness and consumer choice.

Rather surprisingly, factors such as affordable prices, a pleasant retail environment and easy access to a wide range of fashionable up-to-date products scored low on the happiness scale.

In the one-to-ten rating, every time, what hit the top – and concurrent experiments by the Psychology department of Yale University on the phenomenon known as 'Peak Experience' backed this up – was the same story of struggle: of an individual overcoming terrible odds to finally gain a victory over their competitors to possess their desired product. The greater the obstacle, the greater the happiness. All the factors, it must be said, that are common to the earliest stages of agrarian markets, with seasonal goods and scarcities, to haggling and fighting; and in our modern era, to food queues, looting and revolution.

Ironically, following this logic to its conclusion, corporations would have to suppress the mass-market availability which they have spent a hundred years trying to streamline and revert to – or at least simulate a regression to – a pre-consumerist era in which scarcity and violent struggle are part of the retail experience. Of course it was neither advisable nor desirable to try to recreate any of these conditions within a modern retail environment, so the study was, it was claimed, shelved.

It must be noted, however, that a number of retailers seem to have taken on board the results, albeit in test scenarios. Most notably Microsoft, who 'manufactured a scarcity' by imposing a finite number on a much-hyped mass-manufactured product on the first day of release, resulting in stampeding and violent conflicts in over fifty noted locations.

The same phenomenon has been noted at the opening of Ikea stores, in over ten countries, with injuries in three locations and one closure because of the same, due to opening-day-only special offers.

Consider, also the phenomenon of mass discount stores such as TK Maxx and Walmart, in which designer labelled goods retail at discounted prices 'hidden' among cheap produce, inducing similar experiences of 'the accidental find' and 'combatitive covetousness'.

Notable also is the queue – some with sleeping bags, all wearing nothing but lingerie – awaiting the opening sale of La Senza, Charing Cross, London (Free prizes given to the first hundred entrants). This effect is also used during the annual Black Friday (the first day of the winter sales in America) which in 2010 went 'out of control' with over two hundred reported injuries. Footage reveals shoppers racing each other, tripping each other up, fighting, hoarding goods and leaving stores with faces expressing something close to religious ecstasy.

Note also that the riots of 2011 in most major cities in England, may have started out 'political', but were soon transformed into violent looting for designer products – shoes being highly prized among the trophies.

CHANGING

1.

One day Victoria entered a lingerie store to buy a brassiere.

Very little of this is entirely true – so let's start again.

First of all, Victoria had not set out to buy the brassiere. Her real goal was entirely different: She was in the store because she had an hour to kill while waiting for a blind date with a man called Max. The meeting was secret, because she was engaged to someone else – Michael.

Secondly, her name was not even Victoria, but Sarah, and it was no mere coincidence that she was shopping in the store known as Victoria's Secret.

Thirdly, she had told herself, and almost everyone she knew, on many occasions that she would 'rather be dead' than be seen in Victoria's Secret and so the entire event was itself a secret.

Lastly, Sarah had a long and troubled history with secrets and with secret lists.

Let's start again.

2.

There were *People-I-Want-to-Meet-Before-I-Die* lists; *Ways-to-Lose-Thirty-Pounds* lists; *How-to-Save-the-Rainforest* lists and *Reasons-to-Go-On* lists. Whenever she sensed the seams-of-it-all about to burst, she always started a numbered list of practical problems and things-to-do, and hid it somewhere safe. The lists, however, were far from safe in themselves, and always triggered some imminent burn-all-bridges transformation.

There had been the one year studying law, and the fumbling lesbian experiment, and the transcendental meditation classes, and the surgery. Worst, though, was scoring things off before she'd even given them a chance and drawing up new lists, starting again from 'Day One', with the passion of an amnesiac or an addict-turned-fundamentalist. There were other possible diagnoses in her *Problems-With-Me* list, but list-making was number one on her list of failings. So it was, as she turned thirty-two and found herself for the first time holding down something like a relationship and a job – albeit, both being somewhat random, and accidental – that she decided, once and for all, to write:

> *1. Stick with the job at Debenhams, for God's sake (even though I don't believe in God, or Debenhams for that matter). Sorry. OK!*
> *2. Please, please, no more of your bloody lists again ever – finito!*
> *P.S. This is not a list.*

3.

Sarah had been losing sleep over the situation at work, and every morning after the hours-long drip-torture of Michael's snoring, she was left brittle and bitching and hating herself for it. So she'd moved to the sofabed in the front room. But still she found herself ceiling-staring beyond reasonable hours, angered at the clock's slow mockery. Four twenty-one – five sixteen – six thirty-nine a.m., and then it would be staring at the floor and things – her things – Diazepam and mineral water, her copy of *Who Moved My Cheese? An Amazing Way to Deal with Change in Your Work and Your Life*. And his things: *No Logo*; *The Essential Dylan Chord Book*; his sweaty socks that actually seemed to stick to the sofa like velcro.

When she was counting sheep she never made it past thirty-four or five without having to start again. Sheep had it easy probably cos they had small brains and were all the same. The only thing that bored her to sleep was her self-hate list. She'd lost count but estimated it around the mid two-thousands.

> *2579. I can't stick to anything. Even my post-it notes come unstuck.*
>
> *2580. I have the sexual charisma of a slug. It's been over a month since you've even brushed against me by accident!*
>
> *2581. Try a new career/ life – loser.*

The couch had bumps and trying to read anything just proved how stupid and ugly and cowardly she was. It was not really her, but some insomniac-self, that leafed through the copy of Cosmo sitting next to his copy of *9/11 – The Truth* at four a.m. one morning. Inside, beside a photo of some perfect person was *Top Ten Tips for Self Empowerment*. I know, I know, she told herself, yeah, yeah, yeah, but still. Whenever she brought these rag-mags home Michael threw them out. An irrational degree of violence in the gesture. 'Book a facial spa, because you're worth it' – his sarcastic tone in mimicry of an American bimbo – 'Survive and thrive with a diet of dates' – 'Write a hit-list/ hate-list of your problem body parts'.

> Worst of all was when he found her self-assessment form.
>
> *24. I have to be more positive. Remind myself that I love teaching staff how to sell, and hearing them interact with customers.*
>
> *25. Could do better at setting weekly task targets. There's no excuse for failing to make our sales plan!*
>
> *26. Formulate a sentence that describes all my best qualities. Say 'hopeful' and 'ambitious' ten times a day.*

He'd laughed, not at it but at her. He'd said they only ever made people write this shit when they were about to lay them off. So after that she kept her lists secret, even though she knew that was bad.

She flicked past more of the smiling girls and another list blossomed in full colour.

5. Try a pedicure. Your feet need the limelight too.

6. Cheer yourself up with a new laptop! Next to it was an advert for Dell Computers. Maybe Michael was right after all, she hated that he was right. She was struggling to resist writing the unwritten list: Things I hate about Michael.

In the front room, at two a.m., she checked online to see if any of the CVs she'd sent out had gained replies. Nothing. Michael's snores sounded almost triumphantly from next door as if to say 'told you so.' Above the nothingness was a flashing banner for Victoria's Secret. She clicked, just to defy him.

The no-frills purple push-up bras were tacky but cute. Maybe she'd buy one just to test his reactions. She noticed that there was a list on another page – *10 Ways to Win Your Man Back Into Bed.* It was all crap, crap, and she was crap for reading it. There was another banner flashing. Michael said concentration spans were diminishing because of internet addiction. Sea-of-love.com. *Date your perfect mate now.*

She laughed – What bollocks! But why not have a peek? *You're worth it.*

There were 12.9 million people worldwide, 351 men from her city alone, right at that moment, looking for a date. She clicked on face boxes: One was a Sean Penn lookalike, another looked like the Incredible Hulk without the green. One was a trader who listed Mozart and Dvorak under his favourite pop bands, had a room in the Hilton 'for one night only', and boasted of 'expertise in cunnilinguistics'. One had a surfer-look, bare-chested, worked out and said he was 'fun fun fun'. Another had an arty goatee and was looking for a 'terrible slut' to 'dominate' his 'every dream'. Those were the least shit ones.

An IM window popped up with a *Hi*.

She checked to see if Michael would wake. She wanted to read the message but the screen said she had to register first – for free, no hidden extras. She knew the routine from a few years back, before she'd met Michael.

She filled in the profile swiftly: age, weight, height, job, location, likes, dislikes. Exactly like the online job-searches. There were top tips on how to be attractive to the opposite sex.

3. Send each other a virtual bunch of flowers or glass of champagne, greeting cards, gifts, pictures, songs or fun attachments. You can buy credits for these at…

8. Discuss seriously the traits you desire in a partner. Display concern for their feelings and well-being. Download our Top Tips package.

The shite of the world, the Shere Hite shite of it.

It asked her for her chosen ID name, and she worried they might send her an email, saying 'you have messages' or 'hello and welcome' and Michael might stumble upon it. She tried to think of another name and the flashing Victoria's Secret banner gave her a clue. She typed in Victoria and it said 'name already taken'. It offered her the option of Victoria435 or 32Victoria. Thirty-two was her age and her chest size, and if it had not been for these serendipitous technical accidents on the automated server that made her feel chosen and welcomed, she would have shut the laptop and none of what followed would have occurred. Perhaps. Or perhaps it was a particularly loud roar of Michael's snoring, which in some body-memory evoked being woken by her parents fighting. Whatever it was, she hit join and she was in. She was on sea-of-love as a single, feisty, 32-year-old woman called 32Victoria.

4.

Figures, numbers. Debenhams lingerie floor was losing millions to Victoria's Secret. It had been a gradual bleed for the last five years, but recently, the floor which Sarah managed had been almost entirely abandoned by the target market, the under-thirties. She knew that when dust gathered on shelves it was time to start looking elsewhere.

Sarah had walked past Victoria's Secret many times, and every time experienced a quivering, withering feeling in her gut.

Through the window she watched all the tarty young things with their pink clothes and fake tan faces, the vulgar displays, the sheer intimidating vitality of juvenile sex appeal. She could not rise to the level of enthusiasm demanded by the in-store music with breathy voices and pounding rhythms. A dusty old bra left on a department store shelf, that was what she would be if she didn't start drawing up a new to-do list.

5.

Sarah checked for email replies to job applications, and when they failed to arrive she checked for messages on sea-of-love. In over a month she had received nine hundred messages from total strangers, and this surprised her as she hadn't even posted an image of herself (as the site had recommended). Instead there was a black silhouette with a question mark inside it, and underneath were the words 'awaiting image'. Sarah thought this was pretty bloody funny because it looked like the interviews they had on Crimewatch UK, with psychos and crime witnesses. And she laughed because it proved that guys would try to shag anything, even a very ugly anonymous psycho.

Most of the messages were almost identical. The guys must

have taken the tips template rather too literally. *1. Talk about your hobbies. 2. Talk about your goals and aspirations. 3. Talk about yourself and what makes you unique. 4. Talk about your taste in music.*

So Jeff239 said: *Hi, I'm Jeff. I have lots of great hobbies and I love sport. My goal in life is to own a yacht and have a beautiful wife. I am a warm and unique person with a great collection of classic 80s pop.*

All said they 'drank socially', and all claimed to be 'single', although half of them must have been divorced. Over a hundred said: *Hey babe, You look so hot!!! Wot U up 2 2nite?* She worked out, after reading so many profiles, that there were a lot of Maxes and a lot of Jacks and their replies were always brief. It was pretty clear that all the Maxes and Jacks were married and typing with one hand.

Since her advert was secret, she tried not to give too much of herself away, but little tell-tale bits kept creeping in. She wrote:

Hi, I am blonde but not a bimbo. I'm blue-eyed, have a curvy hourglass figure and always dress to impress. I love a good debate but not first thing in the morning, and hate bigots and people who think they know better than anyone else. I'm adventurous and I'm not scared of spiders or snakes. My friends would call me funny, friendly, caring, dependable, sensible, feisty, sexy! I love nights out and cosy nights in. Victoria xxx

Since most men were blatantly dishonest, she was taken by this one message from Max1410, which said:

Hi Victoria, my name is not really Max. xxx

He didn't have a photo either; he had a black silhouette.

6.

Sarah stepped inside. An advert showed a teenage model in a purple push-up bra with front-fastenings — *Smooth lightweight ultimate cleavage maximum impact.* Another sign on the back wall said *Sizes now up to JJ.*

She walked the aisles fingering the Silky Sheen and Sporty Smooth. One was so frilly it seemed to have no structure at all, like some gothic spider-web. There were bras with gel inside to increase the cup by two sizes, bras with words on them like HOT and another with the Playboy logo. Bras covered in diamante and with see-through plastic shoulder straps. The lighting was much better than her store and she told herself that she was, in fact, doing a bit of market research on the competitor's staff practices and store layout. Like a secret shopper she would do a survey and send it to head office with her recommendations. Maybe they would promote her.

- *How many customers were served within 30 minutes?*

- *Were the staff attentive/polite or intrusive? Did staff use the branding greeting phrases for hello and goodbye?*

- *Were there any odours in the store?*

- *Did staff seem to be well informed and enthusiastic about the product?*

Yes, that was what she was doing as she touched the textures and measured herself against the pictures. It was not true at all that she was fantasising about wearing the *Miraculous Subtle Lift*, or the *Glamour Demi-Balconette*, or the *Pink Push-Up Strapless Nakeds* for her blind date who she would meet in forty minutes, and for whose benefit, she had, this morning, put on an almost sheer silk chemise through which such a bra would be visible.

7.

In the year in which she studied feminism (for a BA that she later abandoned) at a local Women's Group, in which they discussed Dworkin, pornography and rape, and their interconnection with women's magazines, she had her list-making critiqued by the others.

So she started an anti-list-list.

1. I see myself as an alienated victim.

2. I need to judge myself for what I do, not how I look.

3. This list is not a self-improvement list, it is all about awareness.

Sarah did not last long in the women's group. She fell in love with the older woman Sylvia (who was not a leader, as they were not a competitive patriarchal unit).

This was another thing and another time and another Sarah, that she had never told Michael about.

8.

1. Teeth.

Aged ten, Sarah had found one of her mother's copies of *Cosmopolitan* and discovered that the way to be beautiful was to list your failings. There had been a large space between Sarah's two front teeth; she tried once to fit a fifty-pence piece between them and it got stuck. No one else in school had a gap. One day Sarah took the mirrored sliding doors of the wardrobe and put her teeth between them; she squeezed the doors on her teeth to push them together.

'You filthy sneak.' Joan shouted as she ran in and yanked her arm. 'Tell me right now madam, what were you doing in my wardrobe?'

Sarah cried and confessed about how kids called her Bugs Bunny. Joan held her tight and called her poor baby, as they stared at the plastic casing of the wardrobe where the teeth marks had bitten. Joan said all she needed was braces – she'd had them too when she was young and look at her lovely teeth now. So they got the braces fitted. Then the kids called her Metal Mickey and R2-D2. But that was nothing.

Number 2 was the ears. Sarah had straight hair – not curly hair like Joan – and her ears stuck out. No matter how many times Joan showed her how big her own ears were, Sarah could see that hers were much bigger. The kids called her Dumbo, making elephant noises, and when she blushed they pointed and said her ears were bright red. Then they would pull and twist them and she worried that all the pulling would make them even bigger. No matter how much Joan consulted doctors and put scotch tape on them at night in bed, it only made Sarah more anxious. So Joan booked a consultancy with a plastic surgeon, but when she found out the cost she said no. There were months when Sarah stuck her fingers down her throat so she didn't have to go to school and this went on until Joan got Doctor Jameson round. He said she didn't have a temperature so she had to go back to school. But then she started passing out when the kids teased her, so Joan took her to see a psychologist and he said they could get the operation done on the NHS, for free, if they could prove 'trauma'. Joan said it was best to say the worst answers in the psychology test, but to keep that a secret. There were a hundred questions and some were weird, like: *Have you ever thought of hurting an animal? Do you sometimes feel like vomiting before you meet people?* The doctors said yes, she had to go to hospital. And so they cut bits of ear and skull-skin away and then made her wear this big headband that became smelly, like cheese, and used to itch like midgie bites. She got a month off school but that was the worst because that was when she realised that her mum spent most of her days in bed and took pills. And she worried that when she got back everyone would notice the change and tease her again, so Joan agreed to pay for a hairdo: all big 80s curls to hide the ears now pinned to her skull. They were bruised and purple like cabbage leaves, with white veins and black charred scars but the hair hid it all. You look beautiful Joan said, fluffing her new curls, then one night she said something that confused Sarah. Joan sat her down and told her that all that stuff she'd said before about how bad it was to keep secrets, well that was fine for kids. But she should know the truth, because she was going to be a woman, maybe quite soon, and the thing about being a woman was that you were actually allowed to have a few secrets, and this was called feminine allure. So, it was probably best if Sarah never told anyone else about the ears. It would just be their little secret. OK?

Sarah thought everything would be fine, but in that month at home, all bandaged-up, a pain started growing in her chest. Joan was very buxom and like Sarah, she said, she'd started developing at the age of ten too; Joan called them her 'breasts of burden' and then explained the joke but Sarah didn't get it. 'Poor baby', Joan said then climbed up on the stool and from above the wardrobe brought down an old dog-eared copy of *The Joy of Sex* and some of the copies of *Cosmopolitan*. Sarah thanked her and had to pretend to that she had never read the magazine before. Joan winked at Sarah and put her finger to her lips in a *Shhh* shape. So more secrets were born.

9.

'Can I help you?'

The assistant was in her early twenties, her tiny breasts hoisted up in some Wonderbra or balconette. 'Just looking,' Sarah said, and couldn't work out why this young woman was making her fret to such a degree. To try to calm herself she spied on other women, as if trying to learn how to do this thing called shopping.

Three rows away, a suited woman in her early twenties was

flicking through one frilly bra after the next. So Sarah copied her. One after the next.

She went through her calm-yourself list.

1. Don't be silly, no one's staring or whispering, and they can't read your bloody mind.

2. They're not going to call Michael and tell him what you're up to and … stop this bloody list immediately!

First it was a black bra, no frills, no underwiring. The size was her usual, which she liked to think was on the slightly generous side of average, although Michael had read somewhere, in one of his radical eco-papers, that because of growth hormones, pollution from chickens and cows and oestrogen in the water system, women's breasts were growing a cup size every five years. Bloody idiot. She couldn't focus on the bras now that his list of failings was in the way.

1. I hate the way you make it seem like I'm the sell-out.

2. All that coo-chee-cooeing that masks our total lack of communication. I'm not a bloody pet. And why do I call you Babe? It makes me sick.

3. The way you always do the cooking and think you're a feminist but who cleans up the mess after you've been Masterchef?

4. You are balding and you do actually have a big beer belly and you have no right to get offended when I imply these things. Join a gym and shave your head or get an Elton John.

5. The way you always pre-empt me, so that I can't initiate anything. Not even a fight.

6. Worst — when you're not laughing at my post-it fridge lists you ignore them, and me, and I know you've been judging us both.

7. The way you distract me from my final list and so all of this will go on and on and on. And you turn me into a sniping little bitch, because I lack the guts to end it and pretend I'm not the guilty party, but I am this time, Sonny Jim.

She grabbed another two bras then another on the way to the changing room. Inside, there was a woman in her twenties parading around between the cubicles in a bright blue lace number, showing off in the floor-length mirror. Sarah shut herself in and hung the four bras on the hook. As she started to undress, her BlackBerry beeped.

'Hey Vic, I'm on my way, stuck in traffic tho. Might be late. Probs 25. Wot U wearing? How will I recognise u? Max. XXX'

It wasn't panic, there was a whole new level of agitation. The tasks were getting confused. They had agreed to meet at Pizza Express, but how they would identify each other had somehow slipped her mind. Was his hair blonde or brown or grey? Was he tall? She had absolutely no idea. A whole month of late-night instant messaging and the thrill of secrecy had somehow prevented her from asking these basic things. Was he even fat? Or fifty?

She went back to the bras. The black one was pretty tarty and when she tried it on it was too small and she was getting twitchy. What would happen if she didn't reply to Max? Would he lose interest? How would she describe herself? What does your bra choice say about you?

The pink one wasn't really her; it would give the wrong impression and attract the worst kind of guy. And it was made of some kind of vinyl; it would cause sweating and she'd get a rash. The white one was too like the old ones from the department store, when she tried it on, it said same 'same old'.

She peeked over the top of the door. A woman in her thirties, long red hair, was stuffing a huge amount of flesh into a vast structure. White silver stretch marks over her belly, the flabby skin of post-pregnancy. The woman reached under her armpit and unzipped something, her breast fell out and came to rest near the belly button.

'Hey, how you getting on in there?'

It was the assistant standing by her cubicle. She slipped her BlackBerry into her bag.

'Have you been measured recently?' the girl asked 'Our sizes are a bit smaller than Debenhams.' The girl had known where she worked just by looking at her. Maybe she'd seen the old bra. The embarrassment; the once white, now washed grey, the writing on the label long since faded, the edges frayed.

'I can measure you if you'd like, you've no idea how many women wear the wrong size. It's a free service, by the way,' the girl said.

She let the girl in with her tape-measure, feeling like a fool as she raised her arms as per instruction. The two of them in this tiny cubicle; the sight of dimples on her arms, cellulite tummy. Porker, she thought.

'You're a 34 double D,' the girl said, and that was a surprise. Maybe her back or shoulders had become fat.

'You want me to pick out a selection for you, save you getting dressed again. I'll take these back if you want.' The insult of it, that you weren't even allowed to buy a bra that was the wrong size. She waited, folding her arms over her chest. They were playing some song about girlfriends and boyfriends.

She'd not replied to Max, he had wanted her to describe herself and so now she tried, for herself. Mousy was a word, busty another, fat – a possibility. She took first one then the other breast in her hand, weighed it, turned to the side and looked for sagging.

'Breasts of burden', for sure. She tensed her muscles and her breasts sat more upright; she looked at her profile and that little bit of extra weight she'd put on was not all gravity-borne. For the eyes of Max or Michael? Or even me?

'Hiya.' The girl was back with three new bras. They all looked rigid. Underwired.

'Do you think I need … support?'

The girl smiled silently, as if for a photo.

'OK, well, I'll try.' She looked at the bras on their plastic hangers in the girl's hands. One was green, a kind of modern filigree; the other black and grey striped – eslasticy sporty and supporty; the third was black traced with red, with an abstract design, not floral, sewn into the cups. It said not 'slutty' but 'not dowdy'. It had a kind of power-dressing sophistication about it.

'I thought you'd like that one.' The girl said.

Even before she put it on and saw the elegant line and flattering uplift in the mirror, and how invisibly the straps touched the skin without nipping or digging in to cause bulges, she knew this was her special bra. It felt like a new her. It felt very Victoria.

She asked the girl if she could put it on properly, and keep it on, and if they'd wrap her old bra for her. She didn't even notice or care what the price was as she swiped her card. She texted Max. 'I will be carrying a Victoria's Secret bag! And wearing a new bra!!!'

10.

Over the five weeks in bandages before school, Sarah memorised all the hand-drawn illustrations of the beardy *Joy of Sex* man putting his thing into the long-haired skinny woman, and worked out that the woman didn't have any feminine allure. But the ones in *Cosmo* did.

She also worked out that the women in *Cosmo* were always alone.

At school, the girls stopped taunting about her ears and teeth, because the boys had taken an interest and protected her. But the protection came at a price. Now it was squeezes and gropes in the bike-sheds. She accepted the deal because it felt like a better kind of attention. Sometimes they kissed her and put her hand on their hardness and told her she was pretty as they jerked and writhed.

Sarah was caught and reported to the school counsellor. She expected a row, but the night her mother found out, Joan did not scream or shout. Joan stroked her face, her ears, saying sorry, sorry, saying beautiful, beautiful, over and over. Sarah couldn't work out what she was sorry about and what or who was beautiful. Her mother whispered: 'I have to tell you something, promise, you won't tell, not your father, nobody.' Sarah nodded. 'Promise you'll never do what I did. Promise me.' The weight of her mothers crying body pushed down on her. 'I'm sorry, I'm sorry. I'm shit, useless shit, useless, useless.' Sarah stroked Joan's back. 'It's OK. S'gonna be alright, Mum. I won't tell. Promise, promise. Shhh, shh…. what is it?'

'I cheated on your father,' her mother whispered. Sarah didn't know what cheated meant, not then. It sounded to her like something you'd do in a game.

11.

She was wearing her new bra and her old one was in the Victoria Secret's bag. Only five minutes to go and she was sweating with nerves. She moved quickly, forgetting what floor she was on. Pizza Express was down and she was up, so she would have to take the escalator. Why was she even doing this?

She tried to resummon the list of things that were supposed to happen with Max: They would talk about food and music and films – He would ask her where she bought her clothes – He would maybe offer to buy something and she would refuse, then accept – They'd walk very close and he might point out how funny this passing person looked, or this advert – They would go to Body Shop and smell perfumes and touch display gels and those things like jelly for the shower – They would hold hands over a bottle of Pinot Grigio in Pizza Express – They would kiss in his car in the car park – They would drive to the Holiday Inn across the motorway – And she would go back to Michael and never tell him and know what it felt like to be worse than the whore that ruined her life – Then she would be free.

Funny how the mind worked, she was just shopping in the mall and saying hello to someone new. That was all.

As she took the escalator, she sensed that the hundreds around her were staring. Pizza Express seemed a disappointment in advance, and there was no one who looked like a Max standing outside. What if he spotted her and didn't fancy her? She was early. She should have been late, and less eager, less visibly eager. She was worried about the Victoria's Secret bag.

She decided to walk past, do a detour, ditch the bag and do a second pass. What if he was that fat man drinking red wine alone in there? Her BlackBerry beeped, but if she looked at it, she would be exposed. He could have been that ugly guy by the door on his mobile. He might have texted, waiting to see who in the vicinity picked up their phone. She tried to look like she wasn't looking. She was still carrying the stupid bag.

1. Find a bin for the bag.

2. Stay and chat and see if he is anything like what he says.

3. If you don't like him then just pretend he's made a funny mistake and you're not Victoria.

4. Give him the run-around to another shop.

5. Text him to say 'another day'.

6. Run away. He doesn't even know what you look like.

Round the corner, she folded the plastic bag and the old bra into her handbag, opened her phone and checked his message.

'Is that you sitting by window? U look cute. Text yes and I'll come over.'

He was looking at some other woman and thinking it was her. As she stood there, staring at the window, a man got up inside and moved towards a blonde. He looked not mysterious or handsome at all, balding, bellied. He looked very much like Michael.

She moved swiftly, imagining glimpses of their point of contact, of him asking 'Victoria?' Then the girl's face. She ran towards the exit and that was where and when she saw it: a Victoria's Secret window display by the turning doors where three mannequins stood, all wearing her bra – the same colour and fabric. A big bold red sign said *70% off. Final reductions.*

She felt the eyes of all in the car park measure and assess and laugh. And how many millions of women had bought that same discounted bra and wrote dating ads that said *I'm fun, feisty, dependable, and like a night in with a Chinese and a DVD*. She stopped by the car and waited for a second, waited for footsteps, as if Max might have pursued her, but there was nothing.

12.

There were hundreds of photos of Joan, partying in the 60s, posing by pools in bikinis, in sunglasses by the Eiffel tower, a wet T-shirt at the Trevi Fountain; always laughing, hands in the air, hair in the wind. Then from the 70s – clippings from Selfridges and Littlewoods catalogues, posing in swimsuits, slacks, pyjamas or lounging on sofas with price stickers. Other women Sarah's age had photos of themselves crawling or on a swing or on a pantomime stage dressed as a witch or a fairy, or wearing flared jeans or copying Abba dance routines. But there were less than ten images of Sarah from that time.

Joan said there'd been Polaroids and they'd faded and looked greenish so she'd thrown them out. Her dad had been the photographer, Joan said, that was why he wasn't in the pictures, and he never had a steady hand anyway. Joan always insulted her father, and sometimes, back then, their fighting woke Sarah in the night. Then he would be away for days on end. Sarah was sure all the arguing was because of her, because they were trying to protect her from the truth – she was their ugly disappointing child. So she wrote '1.' on the top of a page in her secret diary.

13.

1. The way you defuse every argument I try to have with you.

2. The way you turn every 'me' into a 'we'.

All the way on the drive home she had been through the negatives and had this gnawing sense that they were the very same reasons why she started with Michael in the first place.

3. Because you have stupid ideals.

4. Because you always say what's on your mind and are so fucking retarded that you are incapable of a lie.

5. Because you make me forget my lists.

As she opened the front-door, she could smell dinner. Thai maybe.

'Hey-ho Lady-O,' he said in that American accent as he handed her a glass of wine. 'So whassup? Hunky-dory?'

'Yeah… but tired,' she said, hiding her face, pulling her coat tight to hide her chest. 'Look sweets, I have to check my messages – be a min, OK.'

She grabbed her laptop from its place by the sofabed and ran to the bedroom, climbed over his mass of unwashed clothes, and pulled off her bra and blouse. She folded the bra, doubled it up, scrunching it in her hands, searching for somewhere to hide it.

'So how was the daily grind?' He called through.

'Usual, usual,' she shouted back. It was stupid to have brought the bra back home. If he found it he'd ask questions. Under the bed? No, his trainers were there. There was space on top of the wardrobe but that was where he kept his DVDs. She could have thrown it out of the window if the frame didn't jam. The dirty laundry bag – he never went near it. She dug through his rancid socks and buried the thing at the bottom. 'Just checking my work mail,' she called through.

She logged onto Sea-of-love.com. She typed Victoria32 and accessed her profile. She had forty-five new messages, four from Max. She deleted them all. 'Be another few minutes,' she called out, 'I've got a reply to my CV'.

She tried Help on the menu. Edit/change/delete your profile. Before the site let her delete her profile she had to fill in a quick questionnaire on why she was leaving. *Did you (a) find love, (b) experience a disappointing number of replies, (c) experience harassment?* She clicked 'b', re-entered her password and heard him at the door.

'Hey babe, dinner's ready, c'mon.'

She hit return. The egg-timer symbol came up. The door was opening. She leapt at it, putting her weight against it. 'Wait, I'm getting changed! For fuck's sake!'

The door closed with his apologies. The dating site was still on-screen. Finally the delete button appeared and she hit it. It was done. Every trace erased.

There was just a moment where the absurdity of it hit her. Over a month of late night intrigue, hundreds of IM messages and texts and nights without sleep as she typed and typed, and nothing had actually taken place in the real world, other than the purchase of a sale item in shop. Silly cow.

She pulled on a T-shirt, threw back the wine and walked into the kitchen. The mess of his cooking was everywhere, his CDs were mixed up with the food and the music was too loud. He opened his arms to hug her and she let him. He held her tight, muttering intimacies, his rough beard against her neck, his wooden spoon dripping sauce onto the floor. Over his shoulder her eyes roamed. On the fridge there was a new list. The writing tiny, spidery, his not hers. It was his first list ever and she had to read it. It was hard to make out at first.

1. Tidy up more.

2. Join a gym.

3. Remind S – her mum's 65th Bday, Sunday.

4. Buy something sexy for S.

She couldn't contain it, the spasm in her, craving release. He stroked her hair, fingers brushing her ear. 'Shh, babe. What's wrong?' The soft strength of his arms. How could she hide anything any longer?

She would have to tell him.

But even just thinking about it drained the energy from her: where would she start? There was so much to explain, it could take years more than they'd even been together and it would all come out a mess. She buried her face in his chest, hiding her eyes. That was it – she'd have to make a list of all of her failings and give it to him. Everything in it; the teeth and the breasts and the ears and the secrets and the sea of love, nothing spared. All of it, off her chest, once and for all.

As he held her tight, she tried to work out a way to untangle herself from his arms, without seeming to pull away, or raising suspicion, so she could go next door alone, and get started.

Countdown to Zero

673 stylish and pretty ideas
478 genius budget buys
387 ways to make your life easier
365 star style secrets
321 ways to look ten years younger
278 killer ideas
200 glossy new looks
150 ways to spend less and live lots better
dying to be thin – I took **120** slimming pills
and **40** laxatives in one go
63 small changes with big results
54 foods that fight fat
20 lbs in **30** days and still losing
19 dresses that show who's boss
12 poses for self empowerment – how to create positive change
10 hair myths busted
9 secrets of women who enjoy best sex
8 steps to a calmer happier life
7 day dressing: your work to weekend wardrobe covered
6 instant confidence boosters
flat tum in just **4** days
3 ways to lose weight in **21** days
how I dropped **2** dress sizes in **4** weeks
his # **1** sexual fantasy

*Compiled from the cover titles on women's magazines in Tesco, Silverburn Mall,
Glasgow, on the first of January 2011.*

A Brief History of the Mall.
Parts 5 to 7 (1950 – 1980s)

5. From Suburban Centre to Supermall, 50s – early 60s.

While Europe and her colonies struggle to rebuild after WW2 and the fall of the iron curtain, cutting off 18 countries from the west, the US is in economic boom, and exploits the defeated countries of (West) Germany and Japan as experimental bases for both military sites and manufacture. At this time, the US extensively uses the image of the shopping mall in cold war propaganda and the threat of Soviet invasion as a ruse to develop an active philosophy of consumerism as 'freedom'. News of soviet citizens queuing in lines all the way across Red Square for rations of scarce, bland products is paraded in the US press, so as to demonstrate the failings of the Soviet Planned Economy.

In 1954, a US congress ruling changes tax rules, allowing developers to set the depreciation of their buildings in the future as losses set against profits, making it easy for developers to make their accounts show losses instead of profits. This makes malls effectively tax-dodges and opens the floodgates for investment. By the late 60s, facilitated and encouraged by lax zoning restrictions and incredibly cheap suburban property rates, the promise of huge profits draws venture capitalists, who begin constructing even larger supermalls, which serve entire states. These massive structures take advantage of the new Federal Interstate Highways and are built in advance of new suburban housing developments – implying that government and local government are in the pockets of mall developers. Mall construction on a vast scale follows the US model in the UK, Germany, Japan, Canada and most 'developed' countries throughout the 60s, with the help of American aid and investment. To promote expansion, the International Council of Shopping Centres (ICSC) is founded in New York in 1957. Supermalls exponentially increase city sprawl and urban decline – a set of problems that the US begins to export to the rest of the non-communist world.

In the UK, entire 'new towns' are planned and constructed with shopping malls at their centres: Cumbernauld, Glenrothes, East Kilbride, Milton Keynes, Tyne and Wear, Newton, Aycliffe, and Telford. These malls include many community facilities such as libraries, pubs and community centres, attempting to blend commerce and local civic life, to strike a compromise between social planning and capitalist growth; an enterprise that would end up with the undoing of the former.

6. US expansion and malls as targets, the 1970s.

CIA coups, black ops and other US interference in Middle Eastern, third world and South American nations, expand US influence, while the World Bank and the IMF guarantee that development in foreign countries happens on US terms. These systems operate through vast high-interest loans that place a country in perpetual debt, forcing them to adopt 'austerity measures' – these involve currency devaluation, privatisation of all public assets and an open-door policy to US investment. Malls start to be constructed in former third world countries and become symbols of acceptance into the 'global market' – the 'golden arches' gateway of Macdonalds being a metaphoric case in point. US-dominated corporations began extending their trade through global ad campaigns such as 'I'd like to teach the world to sing (in perfect harmony)'.

Shopping malls in Europe become targets for anti-American political protest during the May '68 riots in Paris and Berlin. During the Vietnam War, German communist radicals pen the manifesto 'Consumer why do you burn?' and firebomb department stores. On the other side of the wall, in Czechoslovakia and Hungary, the Soviet Union aggressively puts down protests for 'freedom'. The terms 'freedom' and 'free market' have not yet been fully merged.

By 1972, after 20 years of steadily expanding construction, the United States has a total of 13,174 shopping malls. The ICSC does not have reliable statistics on the rest of the world, but Japan and Germany are both growing centres of consumption and cheap manufacture. Many products carry the label: Made in Japan or Made in Germany. The first food court is introduced in 1974 at Paramus Park in New Jersey, while the first Regional Super Malls (over 800,000 sq ft), serving several cities at once, are constructed in the US and become tourist attractions.

In 1976, after over a decade of population and commercial flight from city centres, Faneuil Hall Marketplace in Boston and Chicago's Water Tower Palace (the worlds first 'vertical mall', with 7 retail levels and 40 stories of hotel and condo apartments) spark the beginning of the return of retail to the city centre and the use of the mall as an urban revitalisation project. The mall has returned to take over the city centres it has gutted.

7. Entertainment centre. Mega Mall. Post Wall Mall. The 80s.

With a booming US economy, the 1980s sees the construction of more than 16,000 shopping centres, taking the total to over 47,000 in North America. With so much competition, developers introduce exotic amenities to attract shoppers, such as the ocean-wave water park at West Edmonton Mall in Alberta, Canada. (Completed in 1985 at a cost of $750-million, it remains the largest enclosed shopping mall in North America, with 800 stores including 8 anchors, a 360-room hotel, 110 restaurants, a full-scale amusement park with 47 different rides, and a miniature golf course.) Megaplex cinemas are launched in malls, and the phrase 'shopping playground' is introduced. Malls not only have cinemas, they also appear in Hollywood movies: *Mall Rats* and *Valley Girls* become a staple of US culture. Gallup claims that Americans average four trips to a regional mall per month.

Urban regeneration malls, such as Baltimore's Harborplace (1980), and New York City's South Street Seaport (1983) and in the UK, Glasgow's St. Enoch Centre (1985), receive acclaim despite criticism of the apparent gentrification (displacing the urban poor) that they create. Meanwhile the New Towns in the UK (built around central malls) are, after only twenty years, voted the most hated buildings in the country, an architectural and town planning disaster – 'concrete carbuncles'.

After two decades of struggling against a growing black market in US consumer goods, financial stagnation and the failure of the 'planned economy', the Soviet Union starts its western style reforms (known as *Perestroika*, or 'restructuring'). In 1989, the Berlin wall falls, with all 18 former soviet countries, scrambling to modernise and westernise. With a collapsed economic and political structure, a wilful rejection of any social planning and a desperate need for foreign investment, these countries are hungry to catch up and are wide open for the next wave of the mall explosion.

Meanwhile in the US, the first signs of retail saturation are beginning to show, with the appearance of the very first 'dead malls'.

Incident in a Mall # 24

Bill and the Pregnant Infrastructure

This is not an incident and it does not take place in a mall. Actually, it takes place in a mall-to-be. This is a series of small, nondescript events that are the foundations of a mall; that will spawn many thousands of other incidents, some favourable, some adverse; that you might question the source of, although, on reflection, it seems no one asked you, and you cannot recall consenting to any of what then follows. Who even started it in the first place?

It was a man called Bill.

When you first come across Bill, he will, most likely, be wearing chinos and loafers and a denim shirt; he'll look so Joe-Public that you think him just that. He is good at what he does. You'll probably first meet him at an obscure thing called the Monthly Town-Planning Meeting of your local council.

You may, or most likely may not, take an interest in such things. They can be a rather tedious bureaucratic procedure, dealing with applications for sunroof extensions and loft conversions, or the use of previously residential spaces for retail or the selling of foodstuffs or alcohol; there are also proposals for and against slow zones in residential areas and recycling bins, and so on.

You won't notice Bill at the back of your local planning meeting, until he stands up and says 'Hi, I'm Attorney Bill Broughton and I represent the Pyrell Pyramid Development Corporation. We're hoping to build a mall on the 400 acres that we've just optioned on the South Side.'

You would be taken aback, as hundreds of civilians and council members have been on encountering their first Bill. Not to worry though, you will soon be bumping into him at the local rotary club, coffee mornings in the church, and community fundraisers.

Or it may not be rotary clubs and coffee mornings, it may be fiestas or bar mitzvas (actually, the chances that you would meet Bill or anyone like Bill in the UK or the US are much diminished in the last decade, as rules and limits have had to be placed on the activities he is involved with, which some have described as 'vampiric'). Let us say, then, that you are in one of the forty or so countries that has accepted a loan from the IMF and is opening its arms to the many Bills. In which case Bill will have turned up with a well turned-out and carefully auditioned translator and through him he'll speak eloquently in the language of your country, even as he represents the interests of a company from another.

But at this first meeting, Bill doesn't want to bother you with details, he's just, if you have time, presenting some of the positive benefits the proposed mall will bring to your community. He wouldn't be here if your area didn't offer something unique and special, he says, and he means it. From extensive research he knows that your area is either (a) an area of growing affluence, (b) recently connected to a new motorway infrastructure, or (c) under-represented in terms of providing goods that adequately represent the aspiration of its dominant demographic.

So, he tells you that the mall will bring prestige and glamour to an under-performing area. It'll create employment for hundreds of local people, at first in the construction business, then in retail. The mall will be a safe place for teenagers to hang out and for old folks to meet, well away from the overcrowded city centre. (In a tiny aside he may hint at some of your local social problems and you might wonder how he knows such things.) In conclusion (and sorry for taking up your time) the mall will provide a post-office, a community meeting space and also sports and leisure facilities, such as a swimming pool, and even, potentially, an indoor adventure park.

Bill comes across as serious, sober, and highly intelligent, and his argument is persuasive, as it should be. The corporation he represents have paid a lot for his skills and this is not the first time he has done this. Bill knows the laws of local, national and global planning inside-out. What's more, he says, after the lease of this land (which will guarantee occupancy for fifty years) at a value of x million in your currency, the mall will create ongoing revenue for the town or city, attracting visitors from other counties and even countries. And, of course, he's expecting the city council will want to extract a premium from the developers as a price of entry, perhaps 10% of the project cost, plus the occupancy rates and taxes, which, given the size of the development will be substantial. The city can dedicate these funds to schools, housing, old folks homes, disability projects, urban regeneration and children's play-parks. This would be something in the region of several million, negotiable of course, as per contract. Think it over, he says, we'll be in touch, and he shakes your hand.

Your fellow board members may be in shock; they may also be divided, some may oppose such a development on principle, but will be argued down by those that bring up the pressing issue of the deficit, the cutbacks and the need for that swimming pool that the council has been saving for a decade. None of this bothers Bill. Bill is in no rush. Bill is not even there.

You might make enquiries about Bill, and if you do, the

chances are you would probably not discover that Bill's consortium is backed by a lobby group, who include land owners, real estate agents, developers, construction companies, banking, insurance, energy and utility corporations, car and truck manufacturers, technical firms and subcontractors in engineering. And political figures (depending on your country and its laws on such things) who may or may not receive campaign contributions to facilitate such projects.

The next time you see Bill may be when he has filled your little council board room with well-dressed lawyers, planners, architects, and engineers, with beautifully-crafted miniature models, charts and PowerPoint presentations. You might be intimidated, sceptical or impressed. During his 'questions and answers' session, after confronting him, you may discover that he knows more about your local area than you or any of the other board members do – on the subjects of local demographics, road usage, consumer spending power, ethnic profiles, even local history, local family names, clans, tribes and traditions. He may at this point mention that Pyrell Pyramid are looking at another location, in your neighbouring city, as the possible 'alternative site' for the mall (which he now calls 'mega-mall') should you choose to reject the proposal. He may mention that your city currently has an adverse market leakage of 250 million to its neighbouring competitor, which could be reversed by the mall (which he talks of in the present tense). He may also say that some of the world's leading architects are now 'competing' for this contract; and all have drawn up plans to pay homage to the area – let's say a once proud shipbuilding centre – with a building that will represent the long history of ground-breaking world-class shipbuilding. This new mall will – and he might pause here to joke that he's no architect, but that he loves the idea and thinks it'll really touch people – take the shape of a boat.

It may also happen at this time that local elections for the council are taking place and that Bill appears at a fund-raiser for a particular candidate, or perhaps he hired the opulent room, or paid for the flowers or the drinks. The pockets of the people Bill represents are deep and they can sit and wait for a time when your town or city is in more urgent need of his offer.

If you are opposed to Bill and form a community group or campaign, Bill will meet with you and hear what you have to say. The Bills of the world have learned a lot from the 80s in which they were seen as brash and aggressive and acquired a reputation for bulldozing public sentiment. But still, in countries indebted to the IMF, local opposition will be seen as threat to a government's 'co-operative' image and will be crushed by top-down pressure. And he knows this. A rejection of planning permission for a mall, and the hundred or so multinationals it will house, will be seen as a refusal to allow free trade and foreign investment which any government will find necessary if they are to ever pay back their IMF loan.

But Bill will not say any of these things; they amass behind him in the many unspokens. I hear what you're saying, he'll say, Yup, I take it all on board.

So there are those in your council that talk about the mall, like it exists already. The tendency is always to talk of the mall as just 'the building'. You or they would be wrong in this, but Bill would not correct you on your error. It is important in these final stages of planning that you put some things into place, on paper, if you want to have some say in what the mall does to your community. These include: making sure that the development is covered by a well-defined site plan with specific borders; that there is a body regulating the plan; that the plan is passed by the community; that the permit you allow is a special permit, which includes re-negotiable criteria concerning 'feedback factors' such as environmental, traffic, and community character issues; and also that the developer will cover all legal costs incurred in its negotiations with the community.

If you do not put these processes in place then you can expect some of the following processes to occur. (These will be things that Bill did not tell you about before you granted the corporation he represents permission to reshape your city, and its social fabric.)

Firstly, all malls lay eggs. It sounds absurd, but they give birth to strip developments along their road arteries – McDonald's, Shell, Toys R Us, TK Maxx. This greatly increases traffic and takes it to a point higher than that projected by the mall developers. Legally, mall developers are not to blame. They are not financially liable for road improvements or construction of connecting pavements, pedestrian crossings and walkways needed to cope with the massive increase in human and vehicular traffic, unless provisions have been made in their initial contract with the local body.

Secondly, all out-of-town malls have historically impacted negatively upon retail in local city and town centres. Retailers relocating to malls send a strong message to the consumer that a better shopping area has been found and that they should follow suit. At first, local family-run stores close, then larger national chain stores start relocating to the mall. This is part of a herd instinct, but also a genuine response to threat. This effect grows exponentially, and enters a vicious circle as it leaves a great number of premises vacant in the city centre, making it a less attractive place to shop. It also places a burden on owners to meet mortgage payments, on councils in gathering taxes on vacant stores, and on policing crime around abandoned buildings. In some town centres this has led to almost total retail wipeout. (See the Scottish towns of Paisley and Renfrew with respect to Braehead Mall.)

Thirdly, massive increases in traffic will impact on quality of life in adjoining neighbourhoods, on property values in those areas, and on pollution levels. Malls can also alter sewage and waste requirements for an area, drastically and overnight. New, bigger sewage pipes will have to be laid for the mall and all of its offspring, as existing domestic sewage structures will not be able to cope, and so it is important that the financial burden for rapid infrastructural redevelopment is placed upon the mall developers, not the tax payer.

Fourthly, malls feed off other malls: developers figure into their calculation the amount of 'leakage' they can get from other malls and retail zones. Basically, a new mall will damage its competitors, deliberately, and no one will be held responsible for the consequences. If you have one mall in your city centre already, it makes little sense to have a second bigger one, as you will destroy the first. Councils must be aware that mall developers care only for the success of their mall and have no social plan for a city and its inhabitants.

Lastly, in terms of 'employment' for your community, mall jobs pay little more than minimum wage, short-term or part-time, and do not build communities. Vacancies are filled by passing workers who may not contribute in any way to the local area, and all of the profits go to multi-nationals, and not to local or national businesses. Taxes due also vanish out of the country to 'safe havens'.

Of course, years later, when you've struggled against and maybe survived some of these blows and you come looking for

155

someone to blame, Bill will not be there. He'll be in another country on another job. Anyway, he is not the corporation, but only its social face, and he's not to blame. If he hadn't done the job then someone else would have. He's a survivor, like you, like all of us (and he doesn't like this situation anymore than anyone else), and he has a family to support. In his shoes, what would you do? This is what Bill would say, if you ever get near enough to speak to him again.

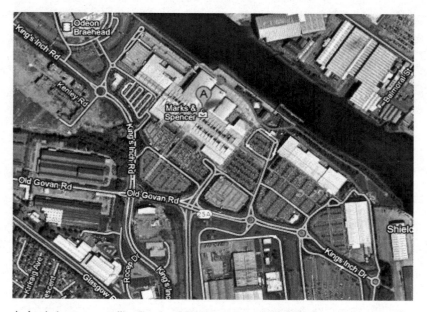

A classic 'pregnant mall' – Braehead Shopping Centre, Glasgow. Note the vast retail area that has been birthed surrounding the mall, with the Odeon to the north west and Ikea to the south east.. Imagery © Digital Globe, GeoEye, Getmapping plc, Infoterra Ltd & Bluesky. The GeoInformation Group, Map date © 2012 Google.

RECYCLING

157

She's in the cosmetics aisle and that's the tricky one, cos Jungle Jim – that's what she calls him even tho he's no black but cos he bought a Jungle Gym for his bairns – well, he's Security, and he says they have more cameras there than anywhere, even in the shelves, among the medicines, cos o the junkies and the gangs o organised criminals. The stories he has, like this one time it's a granny, a ma and these two wee lassies out o school, an one's got wire cutters for the security tabs, no, no wire cutters, *what ye call them?* She's ay forgettin the words these days. For trimmin roses. *The brain's mince,* she ay says. They got caught anyway, but ye wouldn'y believe the stuff – Xboxes and Chanel and DVDs. Secateurs, is mibee the word. Real professionals like – no like her.

There she is tellin herself, *be quick bout it for Christ's sake, pardon the French, and stop lookin around like a dafty cos it's a dead give away and how she's got the wrong kind of jacket on, cos of the bloody elastic in the wrists and she'll fart about tryin to stuff the stuff up afore she gets to the queue and the have-you-got-a-loyalty-card and it'll fall out or they'll see the bump and how she's a silly arse for bein back at this malarkey. This time it'll be the last, this time it'll be the slammer.* She thinks that every time and that too is part o' the buzz and the why she does it.

Ye probably think ye've seen her type afore, but she's no like that. She's probably only pinched twenty, thirty quids worth o stuff, and the stuff's no the for-why o it. No, it's the feelin, nothin like it, no like the shaggin or the drink – naw, they just give her the dejas now. To get rid o the dejas is why. That's how it started. She knows fine well, it's no excuse, havin a fancy French word for it, it's no excuse, but still. The dejas – that's what she calls them. She's been havin the dejas a month now and it's no the HRT and no the panic attacks cos she's had all them afore. No, the only thing she's found to stop the ole dejas is the thievin. It's like a drug – no that she's done that many in her time, in fact she's dead against it now, seein what it does to the young lassies, and Manda. She could blubber so she could, thinkin bout Manda.

But honest to God, a whole month o the dejas and ye ken exactly what's gonnae happen next. Folk are talkin and it's like the repeats on the telly and she hears all the jokes afore they say them. And it's no funny. Serious, she's wakin up and right away she kens what song's gonnae be on the radio. She's thinkin, *Aye, it'll be that Beyoncé,* and right enough, like a million times afore, it's her or some lassie sounds right like her. She gets a call and kens it's Manda afore she picks up and she's hearin what Manda says afore she says it – *Hey Ma, can ye loan me a twenty… my giros' got lost,* and no kiddin, word for word. Honest to God, it's like she's in that film with whatsisface an that rat-thing comes out the hole and him stuck in the same day forever, aye Bill …the Merican, he cracks her up, Murray, aye that's him, *Groundhog Day.* That's her, right enough, stuck in fuckin Groundhog Day.

And Shaz-the-Raz in the back at change-over, she's tellin Shaz bout the dejas – sayin *I've been in this weirdy way for days,* and Shaz says *Aye, you should get a…* and she just knows Shaz's gonnae say *Crystal Ball,* and Bob's yer uncle, there she is, crude-as-oil, the Shaz sayin how she spends most her nights starin at guys' balls, anyway, and that's her future right enough. And Jungle Jim says mibee she should see a doctor cos it's mibee a brain tumour or whatsit, early onset – and she just knew he was gonnae say that too cos o his ma, just like her own, bless her – dementia, aye, early onset. Aye, same ole story.

And dinnae get her wrong. She's no meanin she's heard it all afore and folk are stupid. She's no a snob like that, she cannae stand snobs and she'd be the first to tell ye she's no some fuckin Einstein herself.

She's got it bad though, the dejas. Ye've mibee no had them since ye were wee, but ye might mind. It feels like fallin, but ghosted, like everythin's slow motion, like faintin, but yer still standin. Like that but every minute and no escape from it. Maybe it's the music at work, like how it's always the same CD on repeat, God knows how many times a day and in yer head when yer tryin to sleep, some song about girlfriends and boyfriends and ye never asked for it to be there in the first place. But, it's no that and maybe worse. Mibee she should see a doctor was what she's been thinkin, well, till she started the thievin.

And it wisnae like she was bored. No, no. She's been at the tills God knows how long and there's wee games she's picked up, ye know, like folk in prison and the loony bin. *The ones that put up a fight are the ones go daft*, she says, *Like fuckin Johnny Rotten* – that's what she calls him – *wae his sticky up hair, always takin the piss, rantin about the price o this and that and the capitalist bastards. There's always one fuckin Socialist right enough at the tills thinkin he's better than every other poor cunt. Bloody students.* Don't get her started.

Or there's the zombies. A million times she's seen the new lassies here, and they start out all full o lip and ambitions for this and that, then the days go by and the months then it's drainin out them like blood. Then they're all starry-eyed and sad- mouthed at the magazines and Posh and Becks and queuin up for their Lottos. Same ole, same ole. If ye dinna expect nothin ye canna be disappointed, is what she tells herself. *Did I say that afore?* She's aye thinkin she's repeatin herself, worries it's the dementia, the early onset, like her ma.

And old Frank, always wae his big smile and his old wee lassies voice, camp as fuckin Butlins and *How are you today madam – would you like a plastic bag – do you have a loyalty card*, like he's retarded. Always the same lines, wae a smile. Shaz- the-Raz said he was queer but she can tell that's pish by the things he buys – six packs o shoe laces, Radox bath salts and Pedigree Chum.

Aye, some folk just live alone.

And that cunt Kenny, the supervisor, seen his type afore, right enough, always leerin at her tits, finds any excuse to come and peer over her shoulder, like when they're checkin some kid's age for the booze. Always givin it the flirty shite, *How you today Debbie, out on the town last night Debs?* Fuck knows where he gets this Debs shite from, and it pisses her off. Her names no fuckin Debbie or Debs.

Aye, the games. The start o it, she thinks, was mibee the wee games. She jokes about it with Shaz-the-Raz. Ye might mind *The Generation Game*, she says, *Bruce Forsyth, I must've only been wee when it was on.*

And on the conveyor belt tonight! Soda siphon and an ice bucket, a carriage clock, a fan heater and… aye, always the cuddly toy. So yer at the till and ye look at the stuff goin past and ye try to work out what kind o person would buy it. It's like this skill she's picked up, makes the day fair fly by. *Didn't he do well!* This is what she says to Shaz. This is her game.

Mibee it's a six pack o Carlsberg Super and a four pack o meat pies and some paracetamol and no veg, and she works out the guy's an alchie, and she should mibee tell him, *Mind yer greens, an apple a day keeps the doctor away* and in a wee whisper to *Lay off mixin the booze wae the pills or you'll fuck yer liver,* like her old man. So, she looks up and right enough Carlsberg-Super-man has a yellow face and a boil on his neck and reeks o it. *Thank you for shoppin at Tesco's,* she says, *Every little helps.* But they never get the joke.

Next on the guessin game: there's a three pack o' tights and yuppie salad in a bag and a smoothie and a low-fat pre-cooked chicken ala somethin and some o that Dior Ultra Anti-Wrinkle shite and she can just tell it's some poor single lass in a suit, mibee forty. And sure enough she looks up and there she is, like a million times afore, a mobile phone stuck to the face. *Poor souls, they work that hard and they'll never have bairns, sold a pack o lies, doon the river, eh? No that bairns are everythin mind you. Mine's a thankless wee bitch and ahm glad to be shot o her.* It was just after Manda moved out that the dejas started. *Silly wee hoor,* she says to herself, *getting herself up the stick for a council flat. The thanks I get.*

But the wee games, they've even stopped workin and started givin her the more of the dejas, it's the always being right about folk. What, two, three hundred folk a day, ten years. There's folk buyin Redbull and reduced packs o mashed tatties, and sure enough they're students, there's Birds trifle and Ibuprofen Plus and it's some old dear with arthritic knuckles like golf balls. She could bawl. The folk. Mibee it'd be better no to look and just say next, but that'd be rude.

One day, she starts prayin she'd get it wrong, just the once, really wrong, like some lass'd come up and lay down some sirloin steaks and a g-string and a fishin rod, just to put a wee sparkle in the day. Not that they sell fishin rods, but most things, more than most places, cos o the size o the place.

See, she's at that new Tesco's. *Tesco Extra,* they call it. The one that takes up half the Silvergate. Her flat's on MaCarthur Street but nobody minds the name o it now. The flat's behind the Tesco's car park. They knocked down all the rest and ye canna see her house from the road anymore. She jokes sometimes with the taxi drivers after a night on the Raz.

Take me to Tesco's! She shouts, which usually gets a laugh out of them, like this one time.

Is it no a bit late luv, or do ye live in the supermarket, eh?

Aye, in the drinks aisle, she says. *In the two for ones, Honey.*

Sometimes she says, *Just let me off in the car park, fuck knows why they didnae knock my block down too, but who am I to question the divine order.* And she does mibee believe, in some thing, a voice, mibee watchin over her, mibee she just wants it there, mibee it's just started since she wanted it. Mibee cos o her ma.

This one day she's doing the game and guessin five folk in a row and it's gettin to her. So she just scans the stuff and doesny look them in the eye or say *Do you have a loyalty card – have a nice day*, the usuals. Then this lassie with a card and she's seein it's Mother's Day so she's thinkin that bitch Manda never minds to send her one, but she's just as bad cos she's forgotten her own ma too. So carnations at the end o her shift and then the bus to the home, that's what they call it, a home, like for the one where they put dugs to sleep.

The place though, it gives her the shudders. The muffled tellies behind closed doors, squeakin wheelchairs and rubber soles on lino, and the stinks, how they can stand it, the lasses that work there, like bleach and lavender spray, hiding things she'd rather no name.

She's in Rose now, that's her mum, she's called Betty but they've named all the wings after flowers. Wings, like there were angels there, mibee there are. Mibee she should go to church for once. Room 28. She feels bad for puttin her there but what can ye do. Every time she goes it's the same, they never mind who you are and ye have to say, *I'm here to see Betty. I was here afore... her daughter,* they never mind a face. Then it's the corridors and the things through the wee windows, old folk like, she doesny like to think o the word, but it's Belsen.

Hi Mum, she calls as she opens the door, there's no point knockin, no now she's so deaf. She could blubber. Early onset. Only fifty-nine.

She's in and thinkin it's the wrong room, this body there, near naked, spine stickin out like fists and this big saggin nappy, this hand like a skeleton hand waving in the air, and bluey knuckles reachin for the bars, the face buried against the wall. But she sees this mole on the arm like her own and she's callin out *Mum, for Christ sake,* and tryin to haul her up. Her ma's heavy as hell and then she's slidin on the floor cos it's wet with maybe piss or things she'd rather no think of and pullin the emergency cord. For Godsake. The red light goes on but she cannae hear no alarm cos the TV's so loud – *The Weakest Link,* aye, it's always *The Weakest Link.*

This hand on her shoulder. This carer, is what they call them, a fine name. She's shoutin, this carer, to her ma, over the telly.

At it again Betty, I told ye not to put the side down. This lass hoists her ma up and now she sees the face, all pale and blood drained outy it. And for Christ sake, she's thinkin *How long's she been lyin like that? Jesus. Hours and no one would know. Days.* But she's no sayin it, and her ma's no lookin at her, so she takes her hand.

And this carer, this lass says to her, *It's like the Great Escape in here. She thinks she's going to the dancin, that right Betty?* She winks at her. Winks at her. And the way she talks, the mouth on her, she could fuckin slap her.

And her ma, smilin like a dafty at the telly and still hasny said hello. She could blubber, and she's feelin the old guilties again, like how long since she was here last, cos her ma's so... what's the word? The carer lassie puts her hand out to her and she's sayin, *Get some water for those, shall I?* And it takes her a minute to click – The flowers, aye, right, right. The lass touches the remote and the telly goes quieter, but no much.

She's a real telly-tubby, aren't ya Betty? Loves the telly. Ye've got a visitor, Luv. The way they talk, the cheek o it. All this, she's sure the carer said last time. It's maybe where the dejas started.

But then she's tellin herself, *Right enough, everyone's got their wee games, and ye have to pity them an all, I mean they get to know the old folk, then they pass away, then it's more o the same, it's a wonder they even mind the names. It's the ones have stopped jokin ye should worry about, the zombies.* She's read about them in the papers, overdoses they give them, smothers with pillows.

So how you feelin, Ma? And the voice saying it's a stupid question and said a hundred time afore.

But her ma's still at the telly, stickin her tongue out, lickin the sides o her mouth. Her teeth. She looks round to find them, so her ma can talk. *Why the fuck they do that, eh? Hide the teeth? Jesus fuck, these folk, pardon the French.*

On the telly the folk are turnin over the name o the poor soul that's the weakest link. Four o them vote for this guy called Jerry. She tries the shoutin.

You feelin any better Ma? Where r' yer bloody teeth?

Is that you, George?

It's always that. That George, and who the fuck is George?

No my da, for sure, for what little she's telt me. She tells her, *It's me Ma,* but her ma's no interested. This George thing, ghostin for months.

Is it tea time? Her ma says. And she checks the mobile. *It's eight thirty Ma, soon be time for bed,* she says. Then her ma's twitchin in her hand.

Oh, I'm burstin, and she knew this was comin cos it's the same oles, but she gives her the benefit o the doubts. But then she sees it and she minds, under the bed. The bag and the tube and tells her *It's fine, ye can do it here Ma, no-one's lookin, just have a pish in the tube.*

Oh, I'm bloody burstin, she's sayin. She never used to curse, but these last months, always the cursin.

Is it tea time yet? Starvin, she says and starts to blubber. And she gives her the benefits. Cos how would she know, they starve them, that's what they do, get them in and take their council houses off them, and the bank accounts, don't get her started, kill them off and get the new ones in. What can ye do?

Is it tea time, is that you George, oh, I'm burstin, she's hearin it all goin round and round, waitin for the next, goldfish like, as the next round starts on the telly.

What is the chemical name for…

Carbon Dioxide, she thinks, *CO_2.*

… Carbon Dioxide? The lass asks.

Nurse, she's callin out, pullin the chord again and in a minute the lass is back and she's sayin *Sorry, she's hungry, is there any chance she could have a…* and she's heard this answer that's comin afore.

You at it again Betty? Eh? I don't know where you put it love. Hollow legs. Hollow legs.

CO_2 is the correct answer, the telly says.

The lass winks at her again, hands her the chart.

Lancashire hotpot with brussel sprouts, mashed potatoes and peas and then ice cream and jelly, that was an hour ago, see.

And right enough, it's all there, next to what she had the day afore and afore that and the times for nappy changin, room cleanin and the piss bag change and it's always Lancashire hotpot or maybe it's just the dejas at it again. So, she's sayin, *Sorry to bother you, sorry, sorry.*

S'awright. She loves her grub, the lass says. *That right, Betty?* And the lass gives her ma a hug. *Sweetie, isn't she? We changed her bag an hour ago and gave her a bed bath. She doesn't like the tube, but we can't lift her anymore, they're like big babies, you gotta love 'em though, eh?*

The lass is near shoutin in her ma's ear. *Got to pish in the tube Betty, no need to burst, let yourself go, love.*

Is George here? Her ma asks again.

Naw Betty it's your daughter come to see you for Mother's Day, with flowers, then she leans to her and says *Was he yer da? George?*

And she's like, *Naw, I've no idea, serious.*

It happens, the lass says. Then raises her voice. *Who's George then Betty? Ya old rascal – yer toy boy, eh? George Clooney, eh?*

And the lass nudges her. *If I were you, I'd tell her you're George, might get some conversation out her then. Closing time's in ten minutes by the way.* And walks out, closes the door.

Is that you George? Round and round. Just three things. And worse is the changes, getting faster now, like how she greets when she says she's burstin then she's forgotten about that and is all hopeful when she thinks it's George.

She turns the telly back up, and they're askin, *Who invented the light bulb?*

And she's thinkin, Thomas Edison.

Thomas Edison is the right answer.

What is the capital of Afghanistan? And she's saying *Kabul.*

And she doesny know these things, she's sure she never did afore, maybe it's a repeat and she's seen it last time.

Is it tea time? Her ma asks.

Kabul is the right answer, they're sayin.

I'm burstin, burstin.

The flat, though, now that Manda's no there screamin at her. It's the marks in the carpet where her bed was and the balls o fluff by the skirtin. It's no the smell o her tarty perfumes, but the no-smells, the smells that have gone, the fags and the air fresheners. But worst it's the quiet as she steps in, and the voice. *Yer gonnae need that voddie* it says, *I ken you well enough, I seen yer kind, I gie ye ten seconds, a wee voddie and diet coke,* and so she stops herself afore she starts.

It's like a ghost, mibee, the voice o the dejas. Or God. Say a Hail Mary. But no, he never answers.

So it's the SKY on the telly. Three hundred channels and she can guess the next as she's flickin. Home makeovers, lassies in bikinis, fast cars, click, *Big Brother*, cop shows, some folk confessin about shaggin, home makeovers, lassies in bikinis. And adverts, always the adverts, she flicks as soon as she get one cos they're givin her the dejas.

And the movies. She pays extra. She doesny know the why o it, but it's all remakes now: *Karate Kid*, and *Planet of the Apes* and *Willy Wonka.* She's swearin at the telly now, *Jesus, ye'll be remakin Gone With The fuckin Wind next. Is nothin sacred, I mean can ye no think o somethin new, what's the point if ye know the endin afore ye see it!*

And her head's fair spinnin with dejas and she canna drink

cos it's the same ole story so all there is is callin Manda, even though the voice is sayin, *Yer gonnae call Manda now, look at ye,* and she tries her on her mobey, but its dead like always so she tries her new flat and the first thing Manda says is:

Hey Mum, I wus gonnae call ye, thing is, can ye loan me a bit for a new mobey?

Why, did you lose your giro again? Did we no have this conversation last week?

And she's hearin some guy in the background, like afore, and she's askin, *Is that Tommy,* and Manda's sayin *Naw, it's Ben, Ma, Ben, for fuck sake, are ye goin daft? Ye been to the doctor's yet?*

And she's like *Whit ye need a new one for?* And Manda's, *Are you fuckin startin on ma love life again, ma, dinna fuckin start.* And she's like, *For Christ sake, I was meanin yer fuckin phone, no yer man, ya dafty…* and the name callin and every fuckin hoor under the sun, she could tell it was comin. Word for word.

So she's in the local, and the voice all the way across the Tesco's car park tellin her it's the same ole, *Look at ye ya sad soul,* and she knows she shouldnae, but what can ye do? At the bar and this guy's gettin closer and she cannae mind if she's shagged him afore, a real joint it is for the pickin up. But he's from down south, tacky business suit and stinks o beer, but nice big shoulders. And most likely he'll say, *So what do you do for a livin?* Then there'll be the ole brushin o his hand against her arse and nudgin in closer. Then he'll say *You mind me o that lass fae off the telly, yer her double,* and they never say which one, and so she'll say, *Away te fuck, that's a fuckin line if I ever heard one,* and all o this happenin with the voice tellin her what's comin next, word for word, afore the fact. So she's downin the voddies to kill it off and tryin to think o somethin new to say.

You ever get the deja-vus?

Days o what?

I'm havin one right now, she says, *A big one.*

A double is it? Vodka Diet Coke. And he's pointin to her glass which is always empty and always a double vodka Diet Coke, tho she cannae mind tellin him that. Then he's askin *So where ye live?*

The mornin, and the wakin, and it's Beyoncé again, and she's hungover and chucked him out and cannae mind his name or what happened, but she's sure it wisnae much cos he was probably drunker than her, and sometimes it's just like that after all the flirtin. It's the flaccids and the sorries, and the guys are no so bad like that, all they're after is a bit o a cuddle, an some nice words, like you were their ma.

She's at the tills and there's this bag o organic apples goin by and this organic broccoli and this organic wine, and she's thinkin this dame'll be really uptight and thirty and she's guessin the next thing'll be the snobby vitamins or nuts – and sure enough it's the poshest lookin walnuts on God's green earth. But then she looks up and it's this guy. And fifty. So, she's thinking, *Thank fuck, wrong, for once.* Then he's baggin it all, fast and puttin it inside his trolley, and this is a bit weird cos usually they stack the bags up the end then put them in. That's when she get his game, when she peers over. There's a litre o red wine still in the trolley and he's puttin the bags on top to hide it, and it must be worth a tenner.

There's procedures and she knows them well enough. Like you're supposed to get on the intercom and say *Customer Services twelve to checkout…* whatever, and twelve is this code word for shoplifter.

But this is new and she's no had the dejas through the whole game. So she lets him go. And he wheels it out through the doors and the bleepers don't bleep and he's away and she thinks, *Good on you son, good on fuckin you.*

The next twenty folk she's still thinkin about the guy and the in-house trainin and how they lose twenty-six million a year and how we have to be vigilant. And no once is she havin the dejas.

Then she's on her break, and she cannae face the back room and Shaz-the Raz on about who she shagged last night and Johnny Rotten and wage slavery, and the supervisor leerin at her tits, so she's just walkin the aisles, thinkin mibee most folk are shoplifters, given the chance. She's in the cheeses and sees there's this empty wrapper for a packet o Oreos, pack o twelve, and there's only one reason she can see – mibee this is some wife with screamin bairns and she's been feedin them Oreos to get them to shut the fuck up, but she's near the end o the aisle and her patience and she's gonnae join the queue but thinks, what the fuck and dumps the empty wrapper. And put yourself in her shoes.

She gets this feelin in her gut, mibee cos she skipped lunch, but mibee no.

She's back at the tills, business as usual, then there's this item won't scan, and this uptight bloke wearin all the latest and she's on the intercom to customer services to get another, what is it even, aye, hummus, and she's never tried it herself, it's a vegetarian thing, and maybe he even sees her hesitate cos he says, *Just leave it, forget it.* So she puts it to the side, and then it's the next and the next. But all the time she's thinkin *No one knows it's here.* She's thinkin, *I've got my own bag o shoppin here and I'm gonnae take this hummus home*, and it gets her though the day. Halfway through she slips it down off the counter into her bag, and when she's done and out the front door she gets the cold sweats and the guilties thinkin o the bleepers. But there's no bleep, so that's her. That's how it starts.

And thrill or fear, mibee. She's walkin the car park back home and its cameras, mibee they let her go deliberate like, and the next morning there'll be the supervisor, calling her in, or mibee big Jungle Jim'll run after her, haul her in the back and there'll be the polis and a photo with numbers underneath. Mibee it takes weeks and then you get a letter from the government with a photo o the moment. In flagrante. All this buzzin in her head and no once the dejas.

She's home and hyperventilatin is mibee the word. And tellin herself she's been a right arse, and take it back the morra. Set it back where it belongs, discreet.

That night there's no telly, there's no her tryin to call Manda and fussin about the drinkin or the no drinkin. There's just her and this tub o hummus.

It's no her thing, it's a yuppie thing. But no care even what it tastes like. She's stuffin it down and lettin the chips fall where they may and that makes her laugh.

She pukes it back up, it was mibee the nerves. She's just thinkin *If I lose this job now, I mean c'mon. No exactly like I can go to the dole office and say have you got work as a CEO. It's no like the song says, like The Only Way Is Up, baby.*

She heads out to the local to drown the ole sorrows but then the ole dejas is back, or mibee it's Manda in her head tellin her she's an old hoor and an alchie, *Have a drink, go on,* same ole fuckin story. This guy at the bar is doin the usuals and she just knows he's gonnae say *Like, so where do you live?* He's like, *Is it a Double Vodka*

Diet Coke? So for the first time in a fuckin long time she's givin it the arrivadercis and back across the car park at Tesco's, alone.

It's dark and the mall's all locked up and Burger King across the way and PC World, and all the baskets stacked up inside by the main doors and the lights on. There's a few folk movin around inside Tesco's, the nightshifters stackin shelves, their music thumpin, and she never knew they did that, one o them dancin like an arse in the aisles – never seen that afore. And a thousand empty spaces and no a car in sight. And the light from the Tesco's signs doin this green glow over the ground and the sky, and she looks at her hands and they're green too. All quiet and no a wind, and no lights or voices passin, fuck all, just the motorway far off like a sea sound. She's over the tarmac and starin at the arrows and stick men on the ground to tell you where to walk. And it's daft that, like followin instructions wae no one watching. So she steps off and walks where the cars should go. And she does a wee skip and a hop to herself, thinkin *Look at me and no a drop to drink.*

But she knows what's gonnae happen next, she's gonnae get mugged or worse. Someone's gonnae come up, a psycho or zombie, just askin for trouble, and where would she run if they chased her, cos all the doors are locked, a junkie wae a knife mibee. But nothin, no dejas. Just the breath and the sound o her heels, the echoin. Nothin happenin and nothin keeps happenin. And no dejas at all.

So she takes her shoes off and carries them and the tarmac's cold and nice and it's like she never walked in her stockin soles afore, though she must've. The chilly ole bones, eh? And there's seagulls, walkin on the pavement outside the Burger King, just like folk, and it looks like they're havin a chat and she's laughin like a dafty. Never seen that afore. *Mibee the birds take over the world when we're sleepin eh?*

Like whatsisname, aye Hitchcock, eh.

And this shiverin feelin, like when she thieved the hummus but even more. And the clouds movin, and her breath too, like wee clouds, green.

There's a noise as she passes the end o the mall, just by the recyclin bins, and she's feared then, thinkin it's some guy. But no, just an advert, turnin. She's seen them afore. They're on some kind o roll machine thing, one slides down and clicks then it's there for a bit, then the next one and the next.

She's standin watchin them change. The first one's for Disney, with Mickey Mouse and Goofy and Minnie Mouse, the whole gang in a green field, and it says *Believe in Yourself.* Aye that'll be right. The next one's got a lassie's face on it and says *Killer Volume Mascara.* She closes her eyes and tries to guess the next. Mibee it's God's wee test. To see if she can tell, see if the dejas have gone for good. She's thinkin it's gonnae be Xbox or Wii or what have ye. She waits for the sound o the thing windin on and opens her eyes and there's this advert for Next. That cracks her up, the next one wis Next!

She could blubber wae the ole happiness. She's gonna be alright, the fuckin dejas are done. God's sendin her messages. So she's standin there watchin the sign go round and round but the good feelin doesny last long. Cos there's only three o them ads, so after the Next it's back to the Disney and then she knows it's gonna be the Killer Mascara again, then the Next, then the Disney again. And it's always next next next and always the fuckin same and her standin in an empty car park starin at adverts as if they wos the meanin o life. What an arse! She wants to smash somethin and no the bottles in the fuckin bottle bank. That's it. So tomorrow, she's goin back to the thievin.

She slept fuck all but she's mad for it with this plan. It's spot on. The bees knees. Like the hummus. All through the day it's singin in her head, all through the sex talk from Shaz-the-Raz and camp old Frank with his pedigree chum and have a nice days.

At tea break she's scopin the aisles, doin a bit o' personal surveillance: there's Hob Nobs and big chunks of Edam, and tights, packs of three and deodorant and dishes, and she's no thinkin about the price or if she needs them, but about her belly and where she'd hide a pack o Durex or a pack o Duracells. And the cold sweatin buzz o it, like pure magic, and a hundred folk she's served and no once the dejas. The weakest link, is what she's thinkin, what's the weakest link, it's the bleepers, how d'ye get stuff past the bleepers?

She waits till near the end o her shift and she's up to Jungle Jim, just tae check, tae do the job right. Givin it the small talk and he's askin her about her ma, and how she's doin, cos his has just taken this turn and she's sayin *Sorry. Sorry to hear it, poor soul,* and thinkin tho maybe it's for the best, cos it's no life, no life at all, but she's no sayin that. So she's askin him about his job and the shopliftin, and how interestin it must be and like did he catch any folk this week, and how d'they even get away wae it? And he says *Between you a' me the scanners at the bogs dinnae really work proper. Aye, ye wouldn'y believe it, they take the stuff in the bogs and out the boxes and stuff the boxes down the bogs, the things he's found in there. Wan time, it was all the wrappin off a turkey, maybe the cunt ate it in there, and flushed the bones, mibee stuck it up the jumper.* So she's laughin like hell, but thinkin aye, get the box off of somethin in the bogs.

So, she's huntin, that's what it feels like. Bread's too big, fruit

– no worth it, meat – too cold against the skin. There's CDs and DVDs but they're all shite. She comes to a stop at cosmetics and this Oil o Olay is just askin her to take it, eleven pounds forty nine, the promise o eternal youth, and thinkin about it, with the shite she gets paid it's worth about two hours o her life. So then it's in, up the sleeve and she's headin tae the bogs, and Jungle Jim was right enough, the bleeper didny go off, but there's still the front door bleepers to get through. So then she's gettin it out its box, double checkin for barcodes and tags and sure enough there's nothing. She lifts the lid o the cistern and sticks the box inside then she's got this thing in her hand and she's thinkin, if she had some sellotape she could fasten it round the ole waist then thinkin *Wonder if suicide bombers worry this much?* And she's no for a second thinkin *Why the fuck am I actually doin this,* no a second o the dejas. She's wild and sweatin with the fear, like it must like be for the animals, and maybe they're the lucky ones.

Down my pants with it maybe – but then there'll be a bulge. So a weirdy way o thinkin then, like put it inside herself, like cocaine smugglers, but it'd be too big and sore and... and then just laughin over what an arse she is and she could just leave it here, the Oil o Olay, put it in the cistern too, but then mibbe the cistern would clog and they'd open it and maybe think it wis a bomb. For Godsake! And she could still get fired, cos they'd check the cameras and see who's the last in the bogs afore the one that reported the suspect package. *Why did I even pick this bloody thing in the first place?* It's an old ladies' cream. It must be her ma. Aye! She used to let her have it when she was wee, the secret o youth, squeezed some out on her hand, *Only a wee bit but,* she said, *cos it's dead expensive, mind.*

She's sayin to herself, *What a state o affairs.* It's only a matter o time, if she keeps on at this. *Give it up, afore it lands ye in the clink or worse. Cos there's always worse. Ye know fine well where this is goin. The dejas. Aye. Pathetic.*

She's seein herself tho, like if this goes wrong, how she'll be back there just workin, no theivin, just watchin the conveyor belt and it'll be frozen chips and Diet Cokes and camp Frank givin it *Have you got a loyalty card?* And can he no recognise her just for the fuckin once? And if she doesny thieve this thing now, that'll be her, like the ole ma, on the loop forever and ever amen.

Down the knickers it is then and she's headin out fast, but no too fast, towards Jungle Jim at the doors and a wee nod to him so it's like business-as-usual and the pulse up now, and mibee say somethin so it's no a dead give away.

Night Jim, she's sayin, even tho it's no night yet, and feelin like an arse, then steppin into the bleepers.

But for Christ they're goin off, alarm bells, like all God and creation and Jungle Jim's face like a skelped arse. And the voice in the head says, *Aye, tell him yer a numpty, say sorry, how could ye have just walked around and forget to pay, the dementia, aye the early onset.*

Keep on walkin. Jungle Jim's reachin out now, cos she's no stopped. Keep goin. She's out there, five feet and he's no grabbed her. There's folk with trolleys and she's dodgin faster, keepin on goin. A car comin and she runs in front o it. Across the car park, but no to home. Where but? Anywhere, onwards, but no lookin back. There's maybe folk in hot pursuit – if she's stopped she'll no let them put a hand on her, no unless it's the polis, they canna hold ye, they havna the right. She kens this from somewhere, mibee Manda. And no lookin back, aye, no lookin back. And she'll have to move away now, leave it all behind, even her ma. And footsteps behind her, so she's runnin, runnin. The dejas have gone now, but so's everythin else. No going back, no to work, no ever. No even the house, cos the door'll ring and the polis'll be there and the game'll be up. Where'll she go, eh? Manda's? Aye right! She keeps on over the lines and through the cars, no lookin back, and she's muscles and sweat and breath and she cannae see what she's gonnae do next, or where she's goin, she cannae see it, the body'll tell her, like an animal runnin and she keeps on goin, keeps on goin, no lookin back, no lookin back.

She doesny say her ma's name or hello as she comes in, just goes to her side. Her face against the wall again, like always, her wee skelly arm in the air.

Is it tea time? she asks, no to her, no to anyfolk.

Aye Ma, she says, *It's tea time.*

The Weakest Link is on loud, the only time they let you in is when it's on. *What is the chemical name of Carbon Dioxide*, the lass is askin.

She sits down aside her ma and takes the hand. *Got ye a wee present,* she says.

Is that you George, her ma says. And mibee George was her real da, how would she know, it's no the time to ask.

In what country is Puttanesca a local peasant dish?

Italy, Naples, and she doesny know why she knows this.

Oh, I'm burstin.

She takes the Oil o Olay out the box and pushes the pump and it's wet and nice in her hand and sniffs it and puts it on her ma's hand and rubs it in. A bit more.

Italy is the correct answer, the telly lass is sayin. *Fingers on buzzers. Who invented the light bulb?*

Edison, she says to her ma, and it's no a deja, this time it's no going to be the dejas it's just that they do it twice a week and four times on cable, or mibee they only have so many questions.

She smoothes it into her ma's skin. *I'm burstin,* she says. *I know Ma, I know.* She keeps on with the smoothin and the cream, puttin more on, and strokin the hard veins to make them soft, the promise of eternal youth. She's waitin, just waitin for the line *Is that you George* – but no.

Thomas Edison is the correct answer, her on the telly says. It's gettin less now, the tension in the hand. The man called Tom is the weakest link and the crowd applauds as he leaves and the theme tune starts again.

Where's George gone? Her ma asks.

And she's no heard that afore, and she doesny know where it's come from, but if she doesny keep pushin and tryin, it'll be back tae the dejas.

George has gone for a while, she says, *it's me, Ma, Lizzy, Elizabeth,* and her ma's hand tightens round hers and her face turns from the telly, looks at her, strugglin with somethin, chewin.

Lizzy, Ma, mind, yer lassie, Elizabeth May, wee Lizzy.

And she waits then for her ma's next words, and they might be *Oh, I'm burstin,* or *Is it tea time?* But in that waitin there's a bit o hope, just a wee bit, that it'll be somethin new, somethin she's no heard a million times afore, maybe just a wee bit o recognition.

Twenty Top Tips for
Brightening Your Day in the Mall

Edited from a collection of over two hundred tips found in a chain mail on a networking site popular with teenagers, 2010.

1. Locate a soap emporium, buy some bubble bath and a selection of bath bombs (failing this, regular washing-up detergent will suffice). Deposit these items in the mall fountain, waterfall or wishing well, and make a swift exit.

2. In a supermarket, sample the apples by taking a bite. Then place the apples back in the display, bite-side down.

3. Walk up to a security guard and in an official tone tell him: 'We've got a Code 6 in Mothercare'. Wait and see what happens.

4. Buy a picnic then eat it inside a display tent in a camping store. The staff will be far too overworked to notice you're there. Be clean and discreet. Bring a rucksack of food, and you can stay there, undetected, for several days and nights.

5. Find a store with stick-on metallic security strips on items and tear them off. You can then either (a) restick them on people's backs (b) lay them on the floor, sticky side up, so that they will attach to the feet of a passer by, or (c) stick them on a shopping trolley. In every case, innocent people will set off the security alarms on leaving the store. Step back and watch as they get searched.

6. Throughout these activities be sure to wear a large hat – Stetson, sun-hat, basketball hat or fedora, so as to obscure your face and

protect your identity from the surveillance cameras, which are usually mounted above eye-level.

7. Drop a used condom in a high-end department store. Place it in the kitchen section by the Le Creuset pans. Dove shower gel is an ideal and realistic substitute for real semen. Don't leave your DNA behind!

8. Buy a bag of marbles and drop them in the automatic rotating doors of the main entrance, just before jumping free. The doors are programmed to stop whenever anyone or anything gets too close to the motion sensors. The marbles will roll back and forward every time the door rotates, triggering the stop/start mechanism. No one will be able to get inside the rotating doors to fix them, rendering them effectively 'Out of Order'.

9. In the pharmacy aisle, pick up a home pregnancy-test kit, and drop it into a man's jacket pocket or basket.

10. With a friend, take a walking stick and request a 'shop-mobility' electric buggy from security. Get two and have a race.

11. It is relatively cheap to buy standard security clothing, so why not pose as a mall security guard for a day and give shoppers false directions? The real security staff cannot arrest you, as there is no law against impersonating an employee of a private company (as there is with impersonating state police officers).

12. In the wedding gifts section of a department store, walk up to a couple in their thirties and flirtatiously say to the guy, 'Hi, Tiger. Where have you been hiding?' See if he plays along to avoid embarrassment or protests innocence. Wink at him as you walk away. This works even better if you are male.

13. Pick a random person and tail them, while whispering (audibly) into your lapel (as if you have a hidden mic) giving a running

description of their characteristics. E.g. Caucasian Male, 5'10", early twenties, green jacket, white trainers…

14. Wait for the toilets to empty then go into the first cubicle, locking it from the inside. Climb over the top into the next cubicle and repeat. Customers will think all cubicles are occupied and queues of desperate people will form.

15. Make up nonsense names for non-existent products and ask newly-hired employees if there are any in stock. For example. 'What do you mean you don't have any Bod-Bods!' After they have searched all the aisles looking for Bod-Bods, insist that they fetch the manager. Then make a discreet exit.

16. Find a bathroom display in Homebase or Ikea and really relieve yourself in one of their display units.

17. Collect all your small change in a big bag, go to buy something really expensive and make the staff count out all the coppers for you. An angry queue will grow behind you. Then change your mind, say you don't want it and walk away.

18. Bring an umbrella and buy a candle from the Body Shop. Go to a clothing store, and in a changing cubicle light the candle. Walk out and put up your umbrella to protect yourself from the sprinklers which will activate throughout the store.

19. Leave small sacrifices or symbolic gifts in the upturned hands of store mannequins. These might include Ferrero Rocher, a crucifix or a small dead bird.

20. Read this list – add to it – pass it on. Remember: the only way to make things better is to make them worse, first.

Incident in a Mall # 57

Taking Care of Number One

Try to memorise the following three numbers: 35711 – 01988 – 21087.

Now match the first number to an item in a shelved stockroom and while doing that, hold the remaining two numbers in your head. Then, locate all three items and bring them to three separate customers within a time frame of four minutes. Repeat the process fifteen times an hour for seven hours and this is a typical day of your working life.

But this is not about you, by a long shot. This is about Joe.

Joe McCormack is a 'runner' at one of the country's leading sports shoe retailers in a mall on the east coast. There is no intended pun in his job title. He does not run for miles in the latest sports footwear; his job is to 'run' back and forward between the storeroom and the front of shop for the 'servers.' He never runs, he walks quickly, at a pace he thinks his own, and there is some dignity in that.

The job of 'sales staff' is split into 'server' and 'runner' because, although there are 3,000 shoes on display, each shelf has only one size of shoe, and there are 24 other sizes in the stockroom, making the total number of pairs of shoes available between 40,000 to 50,000. One person cannot both serve and retrieve the shoes as this would leave customers stranded and waiting, so the runner fetches, while the server keeps the customer distracted from the pain of boredom and waiting.

Behind the scenes, the shoes are arranged linearly from 00001 (by the back-of-store door), to the final number on the last shelf at the far end, which is currently 45683 – where a pair of Nike Unleashed Mid iD running shoes in a size 13 is to be found. You would think there would be some computerised system, scanners, barcodes numbers, bleepers, with numbers on some portable screen that Joe can read. But in this and every other sports retailer, the products are space age and the staff conditions Dickensian. Joe has to memorise all the numbers and search by eye.

At weekends, when it's busiest, and he's running for two or three servers at the same time, he'll be in the back getting three boxes when his walkie-talkie calls in another number, say: 13993, Reebok Track, size 3. The more customers, the greater the chance Joe will get the numbers mixed up, but this is rare as he's worked here for three years.

However, this is also a problem.

Joe is running out of time. Head office rarely employ staff over the age of twenty, as they seek to mirror the demographic of their main customer base. Already at nineteen, he is getting 'too old'. And Joe is about to become a father. On the wall at home at his mother's, where he lives, he has a calendar, and every day he scores off another number till the due date. Forty-one days to go. His girlfriend, Sally (18) has done the maths on his wages and thinks they'd be better off on the dole with her getting child support. Joe's against this though, 'cos they'd have to pretend Sally was a single mum and social security could do them for fraud.

Fuck that and fuck them all.

He never knew his dad, and his mum's never had a job. He wants to have a real family for once. Sally says if they're gonna live together he'll have to make more money and get promoted out of the stockroom, but this scares him, as he's fine with numbers, but it's folk he has the problem with.

Promotion means moving from runner to server.

Today is his trial run as a server and a new kid of sixteen will be his runner. He's sure the kid'll get lost in the stockroom and screw everything up, and he's kind of hoping for it. The kid's called Nick; he wears Vans, has a lip stud and an eyebrow piercing, both of which, Karen, the floor manager, has insisted he remove. When Joe explained the job to him, Nick said: Jeeso, can they no get a fuckin' robot to do that?

The first customer arrives; a young mum. She wants Nikes for this toddler in a padded suit that's crawling around Joe's feet and can't even stand. Joe thinks it's insane, that she'd waste sixty quid on these things the kid'll grow out of in a month, that might even damage the natural growth; but he calls it in on the walkie-talkie to Nick, reading back the shelf number from inside the left shoe: 15774. He adds: Kids, size 1, just to help Nick out. Minutes go by. The kid is trying to climb up his leg and there's no sign of Nick.

Due to the layout of the mall, with each retail outlet being a long thin rectangle with no basement or ceiling storage, the stockrooms are essentially narrow corridors wrapped around the shop like a sheath. Their stockroom has only one entry point, so you have to walk past the same numbers every time you enter – over two hundred times a day. Staff get bored, they do secret things to try to make it more engaging. Jemma – smoking, till she set off the alarms; Tim – popping tabs; Sally texting her mates (phones are banned from front of shop); Debs and Tony doing things for which they got fired.

Nick, is finally back, with the right box, smiling and lurking about; he wants to stay and watch Joe fitting the shoe. The kid will not sit still, it wrestles and screams and will not let its mum nor Joe put its feet in the doll's house versions of real trainers.

Joe used to be well into trainers. He thinks about the 486,000 they sell a year and how maybe only one person actually needed a shoe scientifically designed for a world-class athlete, and how most folk just wear them to the shops. And it's not like the kid's going to grow up to be Michael Jordan just cos he's got Air Jordans. And when his kid's born, they'll have to go through the same shit, or the kid'll get teased for having the wrong trainers. And that's more fucking money.

The mum hums and haws about the price and asks him again, again, if she can get them in the sale and why not? And it's clear she couldn't afford them even if they were, but he can't lose his rag cos floor manager Karen is hovering. So the mum is dragging the kid off muttering the price like it's a fuckin' liturgy, over and over 59.99, 59.99.

Next it's a group of lads in Reeboks and Lacoste and he knows they've no readies for the Adidas they say they want; knows fine well where they're from, cos he's not too many streets away from that shite himself. They'll no buy a thing; just here for the wind-up, a bit of mayhem. He tries to bottle it and get them out as fast as possible, but they're shouting instructions at him. Him. And he feels a bit of the power of it, cos it's not him that has to run, it's the runner. So, quite the thing, he sends Nick off for four pairs of this, four pairs of that. They're laughing as soon as the kid's turned to get the shoes. Karen loiters and stares. Joe has to make a sale and they're hogging his time and the old anger is coming back. He leans in and hisses in his own voice, not his sales voice, the one that scares Sally, the wee whisper.

Hey ya scum, get the fuck out of here!

They give him the finger as they go, knocking over a stack of football boots, which he then has to pick up.

Next it's this hefty bloke, forties, stinks of fags, and he wants a pair of Usain Bolt Yugo Run Pumas in a size 9. He hands Joe the shoe from the rack and it's a 6. Joe contacts Nick by walkie-talkie, reads out the number and asks for a nine. Try on the shelf above, he says. The man grows impatient in the time it takes Nick to return, empty-handed. Nick can't find a nine, he apologises; there's only 7s and 11s. The man looks them both over and asks Are you sure? Nick hesitates so Joe takes it on himself to go into the back to double-check. The kid was right. Joe hopes to hell the guy won't do what he thinks he's about to do, but that's what he does.

Let me try the 7 then, he says.

If you haven't got their shoe size, they take it like a slap. They probably work in a job just as shit as you, but when they come in here they want to be treated like David Beckham. They want you to call Puma or Nike personally and get a pair of handmade trainers flown in by jet. All you can do is try to interest them in something else, which is what Joe does, showing the guy a pair of almost identical New Balance.

No, no, no, The Pumas! the guy says, the 7!!

Joe nods at Nick, Best bring the 11 too, save yourself a trip, he says. The kid doesn't understand how the guy will try on the 7 and grunt and swear as his toes nearly break, then he'll insist on trying the 11, then he'll complain that it's too big, and all the time, you can't say Maybe you'll grow into them, or Maybe the leather'll stretch, because if you do, the next day, they'll be back, with damaged shoes, demanding a refund, and your name will be dragged through it and you'll have to pay for them.

It happens, just as predicted – the guy trying to stamp his foot into the 7, balancing against Joe, face bloating purple, saying, They're a wee bit tight. Then it's the 11s, and as the guy tries to walk in them he trips on that whole two inches of empty space at the toe, and curses the shop and Joe.

Three customers and no purchases and supervisor Karen watching.

What other sizes have you got? the guy asks.

You are a 9, Joe says, you need to buy something in a nine.

The guy shouts, Get me your supervisor, smart arse! Joe sees the time that he has left not in days or weeks, but in seconds. Look, he says to the guy in that voice, hissing through teeth, There's three thousand trainers in here and they're all the fuckin' same. So, take yer pick and be on your way.

As he passes the man's frozen face, Joe takes the shoe boxes from Nick's arms and says, I'm going back into the back. Karen heads swiftly over, asking the customer if he is happy with the service, calling after him – Joe, Joe! But he keeps on going. Joe is a runner, not a server, and he has just run out of time.

Incident in a Mall # 103

Beethoven and the Toxic Trolley Dolly Dance

You would not have seen Beethoven before, even if he had been standing right before you. Invisibility is one of the requirements of his profession, as he is a 'Trolley Dolly' – also known as a 'Yankee'. Beethoven is, however, neither American nor female, although he does push a trolley. Beethoven is one of thirty-seven men and women employed to clean the floors and toilets of Eastvale shopping mall; an area which covers two square miles of tiled floor space and one mile of behind-the-scenes, windowless, concrete service corridors. Among other things, Eastvale is known for one unfortunate fact: it spends more on air-freshener than any other mall in the UK, due to a lingering unpleasantness that some believe to be a product of the rather hasty construction of its complex fourth floor atrium food-court sewage system.

During the day, Trolley Dollies work silently; they are not permitted to chat to mall customers. Even if they witness one engaging in the process of littering, they cannot interfere, by shouting (for example): Hey, you! Set down that Ben and Jerry's! This would be a breach of protocol. They must use their headsets to contact security. Security will then, in turn, re-contact a Trolley Dolly (very often the same one) and instruct them to clean up the mess, which could have been avoided if the Trolley Dolly had been permitted to intervene. Having to cow-tow to security and being unable to prevent avoidable spillages before your very eyes are just some of the small humiliations that Trolley Dollies face daily. This may go some way to explaining the motivations behind the infamous 'Beethoven incident'.

But first, a little must be said about hierarchy, power and naming.

Typically, mall security workers have a history of working in prisons, the armed forces and police, so they enjoy using walkie-talkies and asserting their authority over the only people who are beneath them – Trolley Dollies. A certain alphabetical hierarchy exists in walkie-talkie speak, with A at the top – although no-one is actually called Alpha, or would admit to this. Security were once known as Sierra, but are now named Charlie, as in: Come in Charlie, this is Roger Foxtrot, over. This is because the spin-doctored phrase for security is now 'Customer Services' and this starts with a 'C'. Cleaners also start with a C, but because security had already claimed this letter, and because cleaners are at the bottom of the pecking order, they had to be renamed. Thus the designation 'Yard Operators' was coined. As Yard starts with 'Y' Trolley Dollies became known as 'Yankees' – as in 'Yankee nine, we've got a ketchup incident outside McDonald's'. Y is also closer to Z, and Charlie is only two letters from A, so this, again, enforces the Charlie's sense of superiority.

Note: there is some subtle irony in the fact that those at the bottom of the capitalist food chain are called Yankees, while Charlie was US army slang for the Vietcong.

The lives of the Yankee and the Charlie are not without their rewards in terms of running-gags, black humour, gossip, and of course derogatory nicknames. Beethoven's real name was known only to a few superiors. Some said it was Ted, others Tom. Several Charlies used to have their fun on the walkie-talkies saying things

Beethoven

like, Can Beethoven waltz his down way to the toilets, please. Or even just, Give us a tune, Ludwig. There was a rather convoluted gag about a child having been crushed by a falling bin, and could Beethoven please go to the recycling area and clean up 'a-flat minor'. But the jokes about music were slightly off-mark because, as you might have guessed, this Beethoven, like his predecessor, was deaf, or partially deaf, or maybe even selectively deaf. The latter became the popularly accepted version, since if there was a spill report over the headsets, Beethoven was somehow always the first Yankee to arrive at the scene.

Of course, the name was particularly funny, given Beethoven's appearance and probable class background. You see, Beethoven was the only Yankee in Eastvale that wasn't an immigrant. Poles, Portuguese, a few from the Ukraine and Serbia, were the only people willing to do such work for the minimum wage and they came and went in vast numbers. Beethoven, however, had been there since the mall opened, over eight years ago.

There were rumours that he was an ex-con, because of the amateur tattoo of a star on his neck, and the LOVE and HATE on his knuckles. But if you tried to ask him questions about such things, like Tatyana did, he'd just point to his ears, and shake his head. Some said he pretended to be deaf out of contempt for the others, that this meant he was possibly a racist or even a neo-fascist.

Others, like Drago, believed he'd been a soldier, probably in Northern Ireland, given his age — which was somewhere between fifty and sixty — and because his head was shaved. Plus he worked so diligently and humourlessly, standing as if on patrol at tea-breaks, without ever talking to another soul. He had undoubtedly been shell-shocked, deafened by an explosion, and this explained the hunched shoulders and defensive posture. Furthermore, he was always the last to leave; he never seemed to take toilet breaks and had never once called in sick – all signs of military training. There was only one occasion when he'd asked for some time off. He'd called a supervisor early one morning to ask if it was OK to come in an hour late. When asked why he'd replied slowly, in mumbled words, something that sounded like, Am getting evicted. But this was not known beyond the main office and only raised more questions than it answered.

There were those such as Istvan, another Serbian Yankee, who thought Beethoven had been a drug addict. He believed that the deafness was due to an overdose, or perhaps it was a perpetual LSD trip, which would explain the slow, almost pained moves and occasional twitching as he mopped. Since there was little mystery to their work, Beethoven provided it for them. Much of the speculation at tea-break happened well within what might have been Beethoven's earshot, but he never rose to the bait to say, No, I was a farmer, or, I was a shipbuilder.

There was one clue though, one night; the week that Ula and Tinto got engaged. There had been a little celebration after they'd finished mopping and re-fragrancing the floors at three in the morning. Tinto had pulled out a bottle of Rakija, and, with plastic cups from the food court, all ten Yankees shared a drink. Apart from Beethoven. Even though Ula took his arm, and kissed his cheek, and put a party hat on him, which said FUN with a big sparkly star, he would not touch a drop and shook his head over and over, mouthing, No, no, silently. He stood there with his mop, waiting for them to spill some of it, then as they tried to sing songs from their own countries and danced for five minutes more, he wheeled his trolley away. Ula drunkenly whispered that he had obviously had his heart broken, by a dancer or perhaps a daughter who died, as she was sure she had seen a tattoo on his upper arm with a heart and an arrow stuck in it, or possibly a crucifix. There was a big scar where a name had been, she said. He is so sad man, she wept, So broken in his heart, this is why he no play piano no more. Then Ula wept and they all concluded that she was either very drunk or very stupid, or perhaps that her English was very poor and she had misunderstood all she had been told.

The next day, when all the Yankees were slightly hungover, they decided that Beethoven had once been an alcoholic. Yes! His hands had twitched when he refused the wine. Or maybe every one of the stories were right: prison and army and drugs and drink; to this was added wife-beater and murderer. For sure, they'd seen a crazed look in his eye when Ula had taken his arm. No doubt he was a sex criminal too. They even made some reports, perhaps unfairly, to central office. They claimed that Beethoven was unclean and slovenly; and as Central office didn't care much for Beethoven either, it was decided that he be moved away from all other staff and the eyes of the general public, to the rear of the third floor atrium. Beethoven barely shrugged as the notice was delivered to him in printed form so as to make sure there was no possible aural misunderstanding.

To make matters worse, after months of working in solitude, Beethoven was the victim of a prank perpetrated by a superior: Tommy the Charlie (such incidents being very common among low-ranking mall staff.) The action that Beethoven then committed, perhaps in direct reaction to this humiliation, was described by Tommy as: The most fucking obscene thing to ever happen in this mall.

Earlier, on the day in question, Tommy had been chatting with Sam (another Charlie) on the third floor, when a woman with (perhaps uncomfortably) large breasts and a prominent cleavage – that in the words of Tommy – You'd need crampons to climb out of – passed beneath on the escalator. Seeing that Beethoven was directly above the woman, Tommy hid himself behind a display sign and threw his voice. Fuck me, check out the gazongas on that bird! The woman looked up and saw only Beethoven above her. He had been busy mopping and hadn't heard a thing, so when the woman clambered up the escalator and aimed a sharp-toed boot at his crotch, he, quite literally, had no idea what had hit him.

Later that day, there was one more event which was, no doubt, a trigger. On the ground floor, in the central arena, there was a promotion for CHILL: a vodka- based highly-sugared alcopop, that has since been illegalised. The promo involved teenage girls in frosty blue sparkly mini-skirts and stilettos handing out free samples and dancing to loud R&B, which blasted out from mounted speakers filling the entire mall. It had been noted that Beethoven, although supposedly deaf, looked angered by having to work on the ground floor, so close to the loud music, and/or the presence of girls in this kind of attire; perhaps also by the things the girls were shouting, such as, Hey guys, you wanna chill? It's cool to chill, etc. Fellow Yankees reported Beethoven's facial expressions as sad, sullen, grumpy, furious and pained, although this may have been to do with his physical assault of a few hours before. What is known is that he was certainly having to work very hard indeed, due to all of the drink spillages, and the great number of CHILL boxes that had been opened and discarded, and were littering the concourse. As has been said, the promotion happened on the ground floor, but the infamous incident occurred on the third floor, in Beethoven's area in the middle of the night, and was only discovered the next morning.

At nine a.m., when the doors opened, an acrid, vinegary smell was reported outside Mothercare. At nine-fifteen, a child vomited in the doorway – the mother complaining about a nauseating stench. At nine-twenty-two, Yankee Ula reported that the entire third floor was sticky, and that the smell was like 'many many cat pee pee'. Charlie Tommy was sent to the scene, slid on a still wet patch, went face-down on the sickly floor and vomited violently. By nine forty eight, the staff at Mothercare were complaining of headaches and nausea, and a dispute had broken out between their staff and those of Hamleys who both blamed each other's premises for the stench. By ten a.m. the third floor was closed, and Health and Safety specialists were brought in to assess the situation, which was assumed to be something to do with the plumbing. By ten-thirty-four several different departments, including head office, corporate level, PR and five retailers were involved in the dispute and in the shifting of responsibilities. It was suggested that this was an 'attack', perhaps by protestors, or maybe it was a gas leak. Ultimately, the executive decision had to be made to shut down the south side of the mall and bring in police sniffer dogs, to see if there was any more of 'the threat' lurking. Checks began on the sewage pipes to look for leakage, while sniffer dogs barked in a frenzy. The police then determined that CSI specialists be brought in to determine the exact nature of the noxious pollutant.

While the loss in revenue for the day was calculated as in excess of three hundred and eighty thousand pounds, the investigation began in earnest to see what could be reclaimed on insurance. Around this time, the paper recycler was reported as broken, as someone had jammed over thirty empty bottles of CHILL into the mechanism. Security were told to check the in-house CCTV footage to see if there had been a break-in that had somehow gone undetected. CCTV were then found to have been remiss in their duties, as only two of the cameras had recorded anything from the previous night. Calls were placed with Beethoven, to ask if he had seen anything suspicious, but his number came up as out-of-service.

Camera twenty-nine showed a wide-angle view of floors two and three. There were no vandals, no sign of pipes bursting. On the footage a small distant Beethoven was seen lifting his arm back to his mouth repeatedly; there was no sound, other than that of the other cleaners below. Beethoven then started dancing by himself; the moves seemed old fashioned. If one were not scrutinising his behaviour in the negative one could have said he was a fine dancer, 'fleet of foot'. He then returned to his trolley, appeared to open another bottle then proceeded to waltz with his mop. The mop seemed to become animated, like a woman throwing back her hair on the turns. It was a moment of endearing vulnerability caught accidentally on CCTV.

Beethoven then stood before his trolley, and unzipped and relieved himself into his bucket. He took his time. It was one of those pees that stop and then start again and give the pisser great pleasure. He was drinking Chill as he was pissing. Then he zipped himself back up, picked up his mop, dipped it into the piss and mopped the floors. Eight senior staff watched the footage in stunned silence, in fast forward, and slow-motion, as Beethoven consumed over twenty bottles and drew piss circles on the floor, while doing a dance with his trolley, the like of which Fred Astaire could have been proud of. This went on for over three hours and involved over eight litres of chill and urine.

It was then that the corporation insisted that the CCTV archive be examined, to see if this was an isolated event. The process took weeks, as thousands of hours were sifted. Wide shots of the mall were blown up to close-up, searching for footage of Beethoven, in some corner somewhere, leaning over his bucket, fastening his fly. Although the images were heavily pixelated and no explicit evidence of such acts were uncovered, there were a sufficient number of 'loiterings' over his bucket for the corporation to conclude that this had not been an isolated incident, that it may have even been going on for many years.

Tommy the Charlie and his immediate superiors, including the mall manager, were fired. The mall was closed for three weeks. The total cost to the mall owners and retailers is a closely guarded secret. In the press it was claimed that the mall was undergoing 'refurbishment'. When it re-opened the entire third floor had been re-tiled, but a stigma has haunted place, which is now in slow decline.

The police went to arrest Beethoven, but no one was at his address, nor had anyone lived there for many months. Some say he never existed at all, that the whole story was invented by Charlies to keep Yankees in their place, to prove how disgusting and base cleaners really are. Or perhaps the tale was manufactured by the property owners, to cover up their long-failing sewage system. Someone would have to find Beethoven to prove that any of it was true. But he, like his stain, vanished to become a tale, told and retold, added to and shared, sometimes in laughter, sometimes in secrecy, by Yankees all over the country.

EXITS

I'm in living rooms, no wait! I'm somewhere between beds and home office units. Sometimes when Eva calls she'll start without even a Hi, and say, I'm in potted plants or, I'm in toiletries, the way some people say, I'm in Banking, or, I'm in Life Insurance. Wait Evey, he'll ask, just tell me, is this IKEA? Is this Habitat? Where the hell are you? It was always the old mall, not the new one; she hated the new one. The old one she found 'comforting', she said, 'like an old family dog'. She'd taken to driving to the old mall, then calling him to ask what they needed.

Comfort Blueberry and Jasmine Twist eco-fabric conditioner, Durex Sensitive 12 pack, Cadburys Flake snack packs, Bird Songs From Around the World…

A large nose and big eyes. Like an outsized elf, is how she describes herself. She went grey prematurely at 21, with various subsequent uses of dyes that she at times called 'Cruella De Vil' and 'jet-brown'. Her breasts are too small and her feet too large, she complains. I'll never be able to breastfeed but I can run a mile in a minute. She often makes jokes about not having had children.

Her clothes are a mixture of designer labels and Save the Children. Polka dots beneath filigree. She likes to tell people she got her 50s style Marlboro T-shirt from Cancer Research. She quit smoking after the twin towers, but still has nostalgia for what she calls 'the salad days of nicotine'.

She has her own personal soundtrack. When she feels close to tears this orchestra starts in her head. It's like the score for *The Piano* or *Platoon*, she says, but it's for some film that doesn't exist – yet. She hums along, and because it's so corny, it makes her laugh and saves her from crying; other times it makes her cry even more.

This is what she means when she says, Shit, here comes my string section.

She mouths along to the words of the advert: '... it offers the thrills of a 100ft climbing wall, a "real snow" all-year winter sports slope and Virtualworld, the country's largest interactive games centre. RiversEdge is more than a mall, it's an experience – Live Life at the Edge.'

Jesus, he laughs, how did you memorise all that shit?

I wrote it, she said.

They are in an trendy authentic Russian restaurant in the Merchant City and he feels under-dressed and worries that with so many waif-like model-types all around, and Eva so stunning in her Prada, that he will fail to impress. And also – why the hell has she fixed this meeting outside work hours?

Jeez, how'd I end up like this? I spend every single day studying the consumption patterns of housewives, she says. Is that a life? At least housewives do things. I've never once touched a box of DREFT. Do you know what the world's leading women's body-hair remover is called? NAIR! It's one letter short of NADIR – I find that ominous. Does your wife use NAIR? Fuck, I think I'm actually just dying to just be a housewife. They're a threatened species by the way. Surrender is a dying art. Do you know how few housewives are actually left in the known...

She stops mid-rant, I'm sorry, she says, My seduction technique really blows. That means the same as sucks by the way. Blows, I mean. I once directed an advert for Hoover. I'll probably just keep on talking and talking and talking until...

And so he touches her.

We're in Heaven is a Place on Earth, she was shouting down the phone, On the second floor. Your child hates me. Save me before I jump. He'd been in B&Q buying a hammer, because Eva needed some shelves, but that was just an alibi. The real reason was to leave Eva and Stella alone together so they could 'female bond'.

Eva stood up as soon as he entered and rushed to him. In the booth, Stella's face was covered in ice cream of many flavours. Stella wasn't allowed to have ice cream; he'd maybe forgotten to tell Eva this. Now was not the time.

The minute you left us she started screaming, Daddy Daddy Daddy, then it was Momee Momee. She wouldn't let me take her hand, or go to Disney or Gap. Seriously, I had to pick her up and practically kidnap her. Everyone was staring. Eva impersonated the child: Put me down, you're not my Mommeee! Security in here is a bit lax. Frankly, if I'd seen me I'd have arrested myself. Your daughter hates me, but she seems to like knickerbocker glory.

Stella ran her finger round the bowl of multicoloured mess and grinned.

After Stella had been cleaned up, driven and handed back to her mother, Eva asked him to Stop, park the car – Anywhere, stop!

I'm sorry, I'm sorry. God, I'm so fat and useless right now – Look at that – she grabbed her chin – You ever see cellulite on a neck before? I just wanna vanish down a hole, then again I'd probably get stuck. Look, why don't you just dump me right now and go find some tight-skinned eighteen-year-old fuckbuddy.

Where the hell would I find an eighteen-year-old fuckbuddy?

Wrong answer, she said.

Sainsbury's organic gala apples, Echinacea tablets, 50mg Nicorette patches, Absolut Vodka. Agent Provacateur brassiere, Gordon's Gin, Anne Summers Rampant Rabbit, Sonic Youth, Nurofen 500mg, Recherche du Temps Perdu.

The rent on Eva's Merchant City 'warehouse conversion' is one thousand four hundred a month and she has eighteen thousand in credit card debt. He asks her to live with him. On the third day of her move-in Eva is exasperated: there's not enough space left to unpack, her boxes fill every room. He gently tries to suggest that she throw some of it out. Edit, at least. You are not just the things you own, he tells her, You're so much more than that. And she laughs.

You can read the future through furniture, she said. She should have seen the signs. First her company removed the permanent wall partitions, then the offices went open plan – this was 'sharing' and 'non-hierarchical' – then the desks and chairs vanished to be replaced by beanbags, bar stools and laptop ledges. Everything was fluid, they said, 'free-flowing', 'creative'. All the top new ad agencies had done the same: they had 'standing-meetings', then they went wireless, no cables, nothing to tie you down; then portable, BlackBerry. Meetings took place in corridors, elevators; then outside in Starbucks – the office itself was then seen as an unnecessary overhead.

In 2005, two nineteen-year-old flash animators, with 1,000 terabytes on a laptop somewhere in India, landed the contract for NIKE. Almost overnight the average age of an advertising creative went from thirty-five to twenty-two and the length of a contract went from three months to no contract at all. Still the cuts were not enough; within a year, the leading top ten 'top-down' advertising empires had gone bottom-up. Markets moved east, staff were as impermanent as stock values; even the outsourcing department had been outsourced to Singapore. The whole idea of the A&M Scottish Office had been part of an old colonial mindset; there was no reason to have a permanent office in an outpost or any post for that matter. You invested in one place and you withered. Eva had explained all of this to him many times, but when the company shut her office to relocate to a site 'yet to be confirmed', Eva decided enough was enough. She decided to stay behind and nurse her wounds, with no career, no plans, just him and his brat kid, who he only saw at the weekends, who he had yet to introduce her to.

Her laptop jiggles on her belly in bed as she laughs as she reads: A vast island of non-biodegradable plastic has been found floating in the North Pacific. It includes 100 million tons of soda bottles, shopping bags, mobile phones, flip-flops, kiddie swimming pools, condoms and sneakers – it is estimated to be six times the size of the United Kingdom. Fuck! she laughs, Hey, we should go live there!

She was walking through the old mall, she said, down the mobile, and told him what she saw. One shop had been stripped of everything, even its name, then body parts of abandoned mannequins – mirrored walls reflecting only herself – an escalator grinding, metal on metal, devoid of people – that she was scared to stand on – the window of the place Borders used to be, smashed. I'm so sorry, she said. Like it was her fault.

She's making a salad, chopping carrots aggressively. Two TVs, she says, two gas bills, a second sofa, two cars, right? She holds the knife in mid-air; now that you've moved out, that's two homes with two woks, two sets of pots and pans, two… a new wardrobe, stereo, wireless subscription…

Evey! Don't start.

I'm just saying – now that they've exhausted the family market, they're doubling their money with divorce. There's forty new adultery websites every week, twelve billion people who claim to be married-but-looking. We're actually doing a pitch for banner ads for a site called Affair.com, she shouts, Seriously we're chasing the Divorce Dollar. Did you know that people who've been fired are 43% more likely to have an affair?

All of her stats were made up. It had taken him a while to work that one out. What the hell are you actually saying Evey?

Your knives can't cut through shit, she says, We need to buy some new ones.

Media Sales; Virtual PA; Telesales – commission-based; Compliance Administrator; Customer Adviser; Online Marketing; Reliability Consultant; fun and flexible vacancies – part-time, which anyone can do instantly, make £25 to £250 a day.

There was a trace of London in her Yankee drawl. Perhaps from her days in the Saatchi sweat-pits. There were other traces, other twangs and cultures. I have a past, she said, a real one, don't ask. My parents are dead, she said one time, then another time it was 'dead to me'. She spent over four hundred pounds on calls to the US and when he asked who to she said her mother. There were gaps too in the chronology. He did not pursue them. Separation had taught him not to ask for what was not divulged; he was grateful to be permitted his own omissions.

Eva calls out something from the shower as he dresses. It sounds like – If they droop anymore I swear I'm gonna have to tuck them into my jeans! She calls out something else he can't make out. She walks through wearing only a towel round her hair. He reaches to hold her – What did you say?

I said, D'you think they'll take waspy pseudo-intellectuals with saggy tits?

Evey, your tits are great! What? Who?

Al-Qaeda.

Evey!

Well, when I kill myself I'm might as well take out as many of the fuckers with me as I can.

Should I be concerned?

C'mon, do suicides talk like this? No, they go silent, they get moribund, they do lots of washing and ironing and write everyone thank you letters and useful lists.

Don't worry, he says, stroking her arm, You'll find a job soon.

She jumps on top of him. What if I don't want to work, what if I'm pregnant?

Jesus Christ, Evey! Are you?

My God, she says, You should have seen your face.

In the last days she empties her office, shreds her files, throws out her yukka plant and tries to avoid the office in-jokes and camaraderie of the young advertising wannabes that she hired. This is the first time they have been 'let go'. They are so happy to work for next-to-nothing, with no promotion, no pension, no learning curve, not even a glass ceiling cos the building will soon be gone. They will leave here and find something and someone else. They have not worked freelance for twenty years for over forty companies; they have not been told it's too late to start a pension; they will not fail the boob-pencil test; they have not had so much casual sex that they lost track of names or had their third abortion, which may have damaged their chance of conceiving. They are not old enough to feel an ache in the joints at the prospect of a night club or a date, or to dread that new version of the same old song about boyfriends and girlfriends by that latest pop star who is a copy of a copy of a copy of something once believed to be genuine; they are not old enough to feel nauseous at the sight of celebrity-endorsed perfumes, bedding, watches, shoes and credit cards. They have never once thought – brands will outlive me. They have never had to spend three weeks clearing out an apartment they once shared with a lover, taking care with scheduling so as not to cross paths at the door with boxes of possessions they have reclaimed as their own; avoiding the fight over the toaster, the microwave, the collection of second edition Proust that they'd planned to read together over the next decades. These objects that will be packed into boxes and left in the street for the bin men and the hands of rummagers.

Ray-Ban, Versace, Schuh, Nike Air, Victorian pearl necklace, Orbit Sensasound three speed electric toothbrush, Clinique Youth Surge Night Age-Decelerating Anti-Wrinkle Cream, Brite 24-hour detox tabs, The Jesus and Mary Chain, Temazepam.

'Where RU?' You're like a text maniac! She says. Think about it, twenty years ago that message didn't even exist. Where RU? How could you call a landline and ask that? Where am I? I'm in the world, OK. I'm not having an affair, if that's what you think. Seriously, every time you can't get through and start texting like a schizo, I'm in the mall. Those new jockeys you're wearing, they're from TK Maxx. Seriously, this is what I do with my life now – I have all the Xmas presents for your daughter and moms and pops and all and sundry wrapped and stored under the bed already if you'd care to look. Truly, I've found the mall within, I think you should come with me sometime. Did I tell you about my formative mall experiences? Really, we're talking virginity, we're talking love on many levels, with an atrium, were talking the ups and downs, the escalators, the hopes and dreams of an entire…

Eva, just fucking STOP!

Did I take it too far? she said. I wouldn't be like this if you could actually force yourself to make love to me once in a while. Was this how it started with your wife?

His bachelor pad is an unfurnished one-bedroom third-floor walk-up in an area populated by students and the long-term unemployed. There is dampness on the walls, the stench of the bins that the junkies on the third floor never take out. The music blares till four a.m.; sometimes there is screaming. He sits and listens to the sounds of Bhangra mixing with rave and imagines he is twenty-one, hitchhiking in India, then he weeps at the walls, fighting the need to call Eva.

The ex didn't want Stella to meet 'the Yankee bitch', so Eva had to vacate the flat for the hours when Stella came to play. This they had agreed upon. He had pleaded that he needed more time to negotiate; he didn't want to confuse the child, seeing her father with another woman, the awkwardness of hidden intimacies. So Eva made herself scarce and walked the streets. But he worried, because the duration was three hours and sometimes it would rain and she would text – 'Is the coast clear? xxx'

One time, Stella's mum is late for the pick-up and Eva has returned. There at the door she sees the child on the steps with her father. The child has his hands, his slight stoop. He pretends not to know her, she smiles at the child as she passes and runs past, up the communal stairwell. She climbs to the next floor and hides in a doorway, hoping no one will see her, think her a mugger, a hooker. She crouches and spies on their feet, father and child, through the spaces in the banister, then she waits and waits and hears the voice of the mother. Only after all the goodbyes and footsteps are gone does she retrace her steps to his door. He knows all this because she recounts it later through tears, so he will not ever force her or any woman to do that again, as she punches his chest again, again, as he tries to restrain her fists, to smother her rage with kisses.

You wanna know about commitment? his voicemail said. Nokia, I've had Nokia for twelve years, her voice said. I've called about sixty lovers in that time. Are you receiving me? Nokia will be here after I'm dead, she said. Think about that. Speak later, love you, bye.

Their furniture lacked a coherent ideology, she said. There needed to be a central plan like Roosevelt's or Stalin's. Something had to sweep into power. His and hers, there was no cohesive unity, there were factions, values were clashing; the 70s orange Formica table surrounded by mock-Victorian chairs.

Are you a Queen or a King? she asked him. Divorced men

often buy Queens or one-and-a-half-sized beds, because they don't want to invite a new partner to share on equal terms, and they also don't want to have a full-sized King space beside them when they're alone. Sofabeds are for the indecisive and the promiscuous, they imply impermanence and someone who is willing to sacrifice comfort to protect her lack of commitment. This is what she said. She said 'her'.

Cerebrate, Phenethylamine, Propranalol, Elevera. These are drugs he has found in a Gucci handbag under the bed. *Sertraline* is an antidepressant. *Temazepam* is for her insomnia. Later he will go online to find what the rest are for.

Stella and Eva make a mother's day card for Stella's Mummy. They are painting houses with red, and gardens with green. He cooks dinner and watches his daughter laughing with Eva. Eva paints whiskers on her own face and Stella wants the same. He says, Maybe it's not such a good idea, her mum might complain, but Eva says, For Christ sake, it'll wash off! After, Eva says, Maybe I'll go to some art classes. A week later, she has decided to fill in an application for The Royal College of Art in London. A week later she decides art is decadent, and she joins Greenpeace.

One night he wakes and finds the bed empty beside him. It is four a.m. He finds her in the front room on her laptop. She jumps, startled, when he speaks. She closes the screen, hiding what she was doing. In the last month she had sent out her CV to three hundred companies and joined twelve professional networking sites, some in the States. The time difference she said, that was why she was up. Go back to bed, she said, I'll just be five. Love you.

Stella sits on the sofabed taking photographs of him with her new iPhone. She photographs the pans, the breakfast bar, the view from the window, the television and herself. Eva will not let Stella photograph her.

I can't believe her mother bought that for her, she whispers.

He tries to calm her; it's just a toy!

After the mother collects the child, Eva shouts – have you any idea how much coercive advertising your kid is absorbing, how much she's bullying you and your ex into buying this crap. Three thousand hours of adverts a year – he was sick of hearing her phoney stats – You could have read her a story, but you sat her in front of the goddamn TV and let her film the fucking screen – it's all breaking up into meaningless shit, how'll she ever know what a story is if you don't teach her?

Don't tell me how to bring up my child, OK? He points at her face. Ever!

The next day the television is gone, there are scrape-marks on the floor where she dragged it out. Eva sits in her pyjamas at seven p.m. at the breakfast bar. She turns to him and smiles as if nothing has happened.

Can you remember what it was like before everything had a camera in it? She asks, staring at her phone, then at her laptop, then at the milk carton, then she breaks into laughter, and holds it up, the milk carton, puts it to her eye and says 'Click'.

60s-style suede retro handbag, Securo laptop carrying case, Witch gentle exfoliating face wash, Nice'n'Easy root touch up, Canesten, Scott's Porage Oats.

She jokes that he and Stella are her 'prefab-unit'. All she'd had to do was move into this ready-made family. No stretch-marks, mastitis, career-years lost to baby training, no weaning, no screaming at straying husband – she'd let the real mother suffer all of that for her. Plus, he only had Stella less than half the time so that made them a 'semi-detached prefab family unit'.

Stella is doing handstands by the edge of a tall harbour pier. He tells her it is dangerous. I'm not stupid Daddy, she huffs, I know exactly what I'm supposed to do, this is how you do it, and she goes up on her hands totters back and before he has even risen to his feet she surges over the edge. He runs screaming and peers over. Her body lies twisted and silent on the rocks a hundred feet below. He sits upright in bed.

Eva, where are you?

I'm here, she says. But his hand cannot find her in the dark.

Outside the Odeon, they have seen a film about freedom. He's fired up – We could just get up and go, he says, Anywhere! Twenty minutes later, stuck in traffic, she hides tears. What? What is it? Come back Evey, where are you? Bodies, she says, but there were no bodies in the movie. What, tell me! The film had reminded her of someone. Who? Who? It's like an addiction, she says, You see the end coming from the start. I don't understand, he shouts. The moment you meet, you weigh them, assess their worth, she says, You use them up, burn them out, move on. Who is this 'you'? he asks.

Fling.com, f-buddy.com, Sex2nite.com. He finds them in her recent History, undeleted. She has a *hotmail* account, a *yahoo* and a *gmail*, all password-protected. She has visited sites called *mycreditrating, schoolbuddies, the coming apocalypse, new-mother, eco-escape* and *burn-the-malls.com.*

It is late when Eva returns, staggering, carrying new heels in her hands. She went for a job interview earlier then bumped into old friends, she had told him in a text. He hears her vomit in the toilet and goes through.

So how did it go?

She screams, Get out, I'm menstruating!

He knows she isn't, he knows her cycle, he tells her so.

Don't get wise, OK? Don't start talking like me, it's not attractive. I liked you better when you were naïve.

He is woken at three a.m. by a heavy falling noise. The bed beside him is empty. Eva! Her searches the rooms. She is not in the kitchen but the light is on. Eva! She sits in the shower, clutching her knees, shivering; there are bruises on her back and lower pelvis, which she tries to hide from him. They seem the size of fingerprints.

Piper-Heidsieck, Martha Wainwright, Pink, Virgin, everywhere-all-the-time pre-payment pack, iMac, iPhone, iPod. Estée Lauder Idealist Dual Action Repair Serum, Ambient Moods Volume 3.

He told his wife he was going to London but he drove West and took Eva to the lochs for a weekend. Wow, these are the bonnie bonnie banks, huh? She apologised, she had difficulty unwinding, she found nature pretty unnatural actually. It was like some needy child or some old dying relative, always wanting validation for existing. Mountains aren't beautiful, she said – you know how many people fall off them each year? Nine thousand, she said, I've got the stats somewhere.

The hotel he'd picked was oldy-worldy but she was freaked out by the hunting trophies. Jeeso, how can we sleep surrounded by moose death, she'd said. So they checked out and drove further north. One place was too tartany, another was too American, so all weekend they drove and drove. They couldn't get it right, the place or the sex. They ended up giggling in bed in a B&B with fake-Victorian landscapes and an ensuite that had pink knitted toilet seats. Oh my God, she said, we aimed for adultery and ended up with Horlicks and slippers!

Converting Your Farmhouse; How to Write Screenplays That Sell; A New Planet; Finding a Job Needn't be a Job; The Quran for Beginners. Unpacked in one of her boxes was *The Female Eunuch*, *The Unabridged Journals of Sylvia Plath*, and *Living with Personality Disorder*. Then a book with the spine concealed. He opened to the turned-down page. 'Do not empty your bank accounts before you go. Leave a job application/poem/list unfinished on your desktop. Disseminate misinformation.' The title was *How to Disappear.*

They met at an IBM conference, a year before IBM left the country. She had their ad contract and he was a copyeditor on technical manuals. Jeez, how the hell can you do that? Spend half your life correcting other people's mistakes. I spend all of mine trying to hide my own! They'd been drinking vodka cocktails on the fifth floor conference suite of the Marriot. She said the place had a unique aroma, somewhere between microwaved fishcake and men after they've played squash. There was a fire escape she said, they could nip out for a fag or maybe just jump. As they climbed the stairs he had a pre-sensation of falling.

He recalls it now.

She finds it sad that she only knows the plough, and not what it means. White wine, outside on a starry night, We used to navigate by the stars, we used to be practical, she says. I hate the way we've turned them into metaphors, 'they gazed at the stars', 'reach for the stars', all that crap. Jesus, look at that fucking moon. We never really landed, she said, They did it in a film studio, camera tricks, wires. Her warm breath in the cold, ice crystals crunching underfoot. The moon so bright, grey on white, craters and shadows. Look, she said pointing, there's forgetting, there's tranquillity – showing him the seas that were not seas.

Me Me Me Advanced Wear Nail Polish, Aussie Aussome Volume Shampoo, US to UK 12V adapter, Holistic Face Mist, Valerian, Clear Blue Home Pregnancy-Test Kit.

Eva is pushing Stella on the swings. His daughter laughing, shouting, Higher, higher. This is the first time Eva and Stella have met. Eva had been anxious for hours in advance. What will I wear, what do five years olds talk about, Play-doh? Pop-Idol? Poop? What if I say something inappropriate and she tells her mom? The very first instant at the door, Stella had leapt into Eva's arms, then they'd gone to the park and talked about dogs. Stella wanted one and Eva had got all memory-lane about her old terrier, Fritz. Stella had not wanted to play with her Dad, only her new best friend. Things could not have been imaginably better. He raised the camera-phone to his eye.

Walking by the river on the day he asked her to move in, he'd bought flowers. Shh, my string section's starting up, she said, and rested her head against his. Can you hear it? She was humming. There was no orchestra in his head, only her humming, but he said, Jeez, fuck I can hear it too! She laughed, she kissed him – Oh my God, my God – No one had ever heard her string section before.

Crofts and barns, roofs of slate and thatch, sheep in fields, some with green in their wool, like punks, she says. My God! We have to live here, maybe get a chicken, it could lay some eggs, but I couldn't bring myself to eat them. We'd let them grow old, the chicken and her eggs – I don't care which comes first. She points out of the car window. Look, isn't this so us!

She's talking about setting up a B&B, growing all the food they need to survive the coming economic apocalypse. Plus, he could commute – he only sees Stella once a week, why keep living in the city? She could make the cottage lovely, throw pots, sew curtains, tend the fire. Daffodils, manure, welly boots, deliveries from the coal man, the egg man, the fish man in the fish van, a stream, a burn, roads with passing places, trees growing fungus, a wood-burning stove. A hearth, that's what it means – hearth and home. Home is where the hearth is. OK, she said, This is it, let's do it. Look at me, she said, This is happiness, record this face.

Where the bloody hell are you?

I'm in living rooms, she said, On the leather sofa.

Jesus, you were supposed to pick up Stella from school, he shouted back.

I called her mother, I cancelled already, sorry, she said.

Jesus, what are you doing, we don't cancel Stella OK, ever,

especially at the last minute, we have to prove we're dependable. And you can't call her mother, directly, OK? Don't give her any ammo to use again us. What the hell, Eva!

I've lost my car keys, can you come and get me, please?

He drove to the old mall in a rage, got stuck in traffic and called the ex to check he'd got the true story. He parked and marched through the masses, working out what the hell to say to Eva. He walked the rows of empty stores and found her in the Closing Down Sale in Habitat, in living rooms on the second floor in sofas. Beside her sat a half-eaten sandwich and a notepad. She was patting the sofa beside herself, I'm sorry, she said, I must have zoned out. Her shoes were off and lying beside her bare feet. C'mon let's get you out of here, he said. Where did you put your shopping bags? She looked surprised, then almost disappointed in herself. There's no... I just bought this, she said, holding up the crusts.

He found her car keys in her bag, but she was in no fit state to drive, so they left her car in the car park. It was free parking anyway, he'd come back by bus or taxi, at the weekend to retrieve it. They didn't need two cars anyway, they had to cut costs.

I wanted to get some cotton pillow slips, she said, for the insomnia, I read – 'cotton breathes'. But then there were two-for-one pillow slips and covers together, and I thought – good idea, but then there's the whole size thing. I know the apartment is really small, but I think we need at least a double bed. So then I went to the bed section, but the first thing was kids' beds and then I thought we've got to sort out where Stella's going to sleep, cos kids need something more fixed, and she's growing, and she needs her own room and I need a study if I'm going to get any kind of serious work cos I can't bear working in the bedroom anymore and I won't be able to if it's taken up by a bloody huge bed, so then I'm thinking, we need a real house, a real garden, if you're going to fight for joint custody, so that's a mortgage. So I'm on the phone screaming at the bank to give us a fucking mortgage, and that's when I just had to go back to sofas and... I'm sorry.

That's it, final, we're getting married.

Let's just get the pillow slips first, she said.

The advert shows a domestic argument in a tiny kitchen; a woman in her thirties tearing up her ID and credit cards and walking out into the night, the screen reads – *Don't Look Back.* A woman throws away her wedding ring, photo albums are torn, furniture is thrown on a pyre – *Go it Alone.* Image of young man giving his corporate bosses the finger and marching out – *Take a Risk.* A woman entering a vast empty white apartment, white curtain billowing in wind – *Begin Again.* A solitary naked figure floats, smiling in a vast perfect lake – *Change is Everything.* A woman stands atop a mountain, surveying the whole world beneath her feet, as if she is about to jump, but she doesn't, she breathes, deep. *Live Life at The Edge.*

On the second day he reports her missing and they send people over. They ask for a physical description, they ask about her personality, if there were signs. They ask to see her things.

I'm in this eagle's nest in Iceland, on this webcam, it's awesome, she called through. I love you so much, plus I think I'm menopausal. He walked through and kissed her shoulder. The light from the screen around her head, aura-like. She clutched his hand. I liked it better when we were naïve, she said, or was it you were naïve? He tries again, to re-picture the scene.

On the seventh day, he gets an email from someone called Jake, who claims to be a friend of Eva's. It says simply – *Eva has moved to Chicago. She is safe. Please do not try to contact her. She is sorry.* He is convinced it is from Eva herself. That it's a lie and a final farewell BCC'd to everyone. Or misinformation sent to throw everyone off the scent. He calls the police again. He sends many messages but gets no reply. Practical questions trying to provoke a response. *Where shall I send her things?*

Ugg boots, Sony BlackBerry, Totalcare vitamin D supplement, La Senza Fishnets, Lancôme Laque Fever. He picks them all from wherever she let them fall, and says their names as he packs them back into the boxes she first moved in with. *Bach Rescue Remedy, Hello Kitty Sleep Socks, Nokia Smartphone, Serenity Face Mask.*

Twenty-Two Simple Innovations
in the Science of Consumer Manipulation

Why is it, you might ask, that every time you enter a mall, you lose all sense of time; you 'let go' to a sense of playfulness; you leave your cynicism and worries behind; you become distracted and 'take your desires for a walk'? This may seem 'natural' but mall developers and corporations, over the last sixty years, have employed behavioural psychologists, psychoanalysts, market researchers and architects in order to construct this psychological state. There is, in fact, a covert and ingenious science of consumer manipulation at work. As Edward Bernays, 'the father of public relations' and the nephew of Sigmund Freud once stated: 'It is now possible to control and regiment the masses according to our will without them knowing it.' The following are examples of innovations in the field:

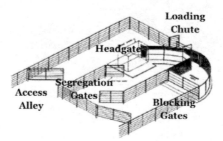

A typical cattle corral

1. *Corralling.* In the old days of the department store, if you ever wanted to get from level one to level four, all you had to do was hop

from one escalator to the next, as they were conveniently placed right next to each other. That all changed with the new architectural layouts of malls that were introduced since the 80s, when retailers discovered that consumers spent more if it was made more difficult for them to get from A to B. To this end, mall architects deployed a structural device first used for the control and manipulation of farm animals.

A *corral* is essentially an arrangement of enclosures, walkways and gates used for redirecting a herd into regulated lines of movement, during times when specific animals need to be segregated, either for sale, for medical reasons, or for 'branding'. The puns and references to cattle do not stop there: market research companies often refer to the importance of 'prodding' consumers. Consumers are onto something when they joke that they are being 'herded like animals'.

In shopping malls, human beings are now corralled into walking greater distances between connecting escalators, so that they will be forced to pass a greater number of stores, and, potentially, get distracted and purchase additional items.

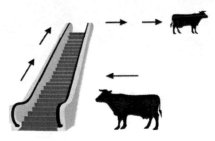

As Michael Niemira, vice president of research for the International Council of Shopping Centers states, '...the longer people stay (in a mall) the more likely they will spend money.' And so architectural devices that further this end have been widely adopted.

A further example of this is food courts and toilets. Since the 80s, these two 'destinations' have been primarily built on the top floor of malls – ensuring that people who have entered to merely use the toilets or grab a quick bite will nonetheless have to walk the entire mall before they arrive at a place where they can satisfy their primal urges.

Corralling also exists within single floor stores. From Marks and Spencers to TK Maxx, it takes the form of constructed queuing lines which use separation fencing (comparable to that which is used at airport immigration) to direct the flow of consumers to shelves conveniently stacked with discounted items. A study by Sales Force shows a 44% increase in sales of such items through strategic placing at queues.

Corralled shoppers in TK Maxx being led past 'impulse' buys as they queue to get to the checkout.

2. *Manufacturing Queues.* Without affecting their profit margin to a great degree, it would be reasonably easy for corporations to employ enough minimum wage staff to ensure that shoppers would rarely need to queue, but these corporations have made it a deliberate policy decisions to understaff their checkout counters so as to manufacture

waiting. As a study from Pakistan shows, 'Crowding usually develops psychological pressure and amplified arousal in consumers who sense a loss of personal space'. Queuing is an important boon for stores as it creates frustration. The longer you have been forced to wait the greater likelihood that you will allow yourself 'a treat' to calm your frustration, and so treats, snacks and special offers are placed strategically at corralled areas. While queuing creates anger (and threatens to expose the fact that consumers ultimately have no, or very little, choice), the opportunity to impulse shop, has a claming effect and gives the illusion of choice and control. Time is subjective, not objective, and perceived time goes much slower if you see other bored people waiting (Underhill 2003). The longer the perceived wait, the more consumers feel internal pressure to turn their passive waiting into identity-affirming action. Their only option available in a corralled area is to shop 'on impulse'. In this way, even impulses are manufactured.

Shoppers killing time with self-affirming 'impulse' buys.

3. *Free or Cheap Parking in City Centre Malls.* City centre malls offer the cheapest by-hour parking of any other car park in any given city. Mall car parks are designed so that those who simply wish to park

cheaply will nonetheless have to exit and enter the car park through the mall in order to get in and out, thus increasing the likelihood of an unplanned purchase. The payment booths for these car parks are also within the mall, not in the car parks, so that even if all you wanted was to park and pay, you will find yourself having to return to the mall forecourt in order to queue, pay, then exit. As with point one, this is a deliberate device intended to make you spend more time in the mall.

The largest Mall in Central London, offering reduced parking rates at 1/5 of the local parking price. During the festive season 2011, parking was free.

4. *Daydreaming in Safety.* Why don't you look at your own feet in malls? Whether it be linoleum or fake marble, you can trust that there is a uniform surface below, safe from irregularities. You won't trip or fall, you also know that there will be no dangerous people, no spitters, no muggers, no litterbugs, no dog shit, no dark corners, nowhere for pickpockets to run, no bicycle messengers to run you over and no bad weather. The high security and the clinical uniformity of the mall allows your mind to drift out of concern for you body, assured that it is safe. It allows you to daydream and fantasise, and that is important, because the mall is all about psychological regression.

5. *Mirror, Mirror on the Mall.* Malls are covered in mirrors and semi-reflective glass, this is not just to reflect light and make space appear larger, neither is it merely a modern style; mirrors create psychological effects. Being surrounded by mirrors makes us feel as if everyone is watching us; it makes us feel ugly and lacking. This is enforced by advertisements with attractive celebrities and by the constant parade of other shoppers, assessing each other and themselves by their own appearances. Ego insecurity stimulates the desire for a 'new me' and encourages purchases of clothing, fashion and signifiers of status. This is not 'superficial' – as Marcuse pointed out, modern retail activates psychological triggers on a deep level, taking us back to a state close to early infancy, before the ego forced its rules upon us to make us civilised. This mirrored world encourages us to regress to the 'Id' and the needy 'mirror stage' of infancy. When the Id is in control of a person, that person becomes like a child, seeking the immediate gratification of the pleasure principle, grabbing things, running from mirror to mirror like an infant, asking 'is this me?' This narcissistic state of mind is encouraged in malls by the use of mirrors. This is what Marcuse means by 'It is the Id that goes shopping'.

6. *Free Samples and Promotions stimulate buying by 28% (Marketing Science N3, vol. 23)*. Women's cosmetics in department stores are a prime example of how this works, with lipstick and perfume samples, free trials and demonstrations.

7. *Window-licking*. As far back as the 1930s, the plan has been to move consumers away from rational behaviour. *'We must shift America from a needs to a desires culture. People must be trained to desire, to want new things, even before the old has been entirely consumed. We must shape a new mentality in America. Man's desires must overshadow his needs.'* (Paul Mazer, Lehman Bros banker.) The perverse result of this has been the progressive sexualisation of retail. Since the 1960s, the pleasures of mall shopping have been mixed with flirtation and sexual parade. The French phrase for window shopping embodies this graphically: 'lèche-vitrine' or 'window-licking.' Part of the pleasure of mall flirtation is the fact that people rarely stop to speak to each other, as they are kept in constant motion; therefore it is flirtation without contact or consequence; a game with the eyes – 'look but don't touch'. It is no coincidence that the phrase 'window-shopping' is used in both retail and dating. Over the last decade malls have seen a rapid lowering of taboos around sexual explicitness, with the opening of lingerie stores and sex shops such as Anne Summers; a process which, in some malls, has led to protests and vandalism by 'concerned communities' and 'family groups', as people protest the intrusion of explicit sexuality into what was formerly the 'family space' of the mall. Women and young men now dress-up to shop in malls in a way which was previously unseen in the era of local shopping. The sexualisation of retail boosts profits, not by making people want to immediately gratify sexual urges, but by increasing

ego insecurity and interpersonal competitiveness.

A display of lingerie in the rotating doors at Silverburn Mall.

8. *Hunger for Hunger.* In an attempt to boost profits many malls are renovating to expand food courts. The logic is simple – if people aren't rushing home for lunch or can get a snack for a screaming child by staying in the mall, they'll stick around longer. Arun Sharma, Marketing Professor at Miami School of Business, claims that shoppers spend almost 20% more at a mall with a 'good food court'.

However, mall food doesn't satiate. Monosodium Glutamate is a central ingredient of most mall food and MSG leaves you hungry even after you've consumed foods that contain it. As with point 5, irrational urges can be rechannelled.

9. *'Desire desires desire'.* As Lacan stated, desire does not have an object or a specific goal, or an end in sight. Psychology has shown us that there is no clear demarcation between desires, and that they can be easily confused with one another: the desire for food, for warmth, for sex, for attention, or for status recognition can be channelled very easily into the desire for product consumption. In the 'Starvation'

experiment (1989), libido was observed to rise as participants craved food; the longer the wait, the greater the arousal. Conversely in the 'Soup experiment' (2002), it was demonstrated that libido in those previously exposed to erotic imagery dropped drastically after food intake (Jameson, 2001). Experiments by Rucker and Galinsky (2009) show that acquiring status-signifying products diminished distress and libido.

The mall interior, with its mixture of ego-objects, visual and aural sensations, tastes and smells, creates a sensorium in which desires become mixed-up, and amplify each other to the point of overload. Malls then offer the confused, hungry, libidinous shopper a solution to their distress – satiation through a purchase. It is no accident that retail therapy is offered as a solution to a state of mental anguish that was first invented by psychologists.

10. *Music*. In the 1970s, music in malls was bland middle-aged, family-based 'muzak', consisting of popular songs with the vocals removed. Mall music is now exactly the same as the music played in nightclubs and lapdancing clubs. A heightened heartbeat, caused by beats of over 60 BPM, creates excitement close to levels of sexual arousal. In turn, through the fusion of retail and pop culture since the 90s, contemporary pop music is all about turning oneself into a commodity. With lyrics like 'Don't you wish your girlfriend was hot like me' and 'All dem boys are lookin at me', the idea of shopping for sexual status is doubly reinforced.

The connection between music and mall retail has now gone full circle, closing a loop: with pop stars now selling their own brands of perfume, lingerie and even bedding. In this way, you can wear Beyoncé, sleep on a Bieber pillow and smell like Britney, as you drift around with their music in your head. Leading teen pop stars now promote themselves in malls, performing mini-gigs to crowds of tens of thousands.

Jedward sing for ten minutes and turn on the Xmas lights at Braehead Mall (2010), Glasgow, while in 2011, Justin Bieber did exactly the same thing at London's immense Westfield mall.

11. *Danger and Sport.* Malls which include skiing, rock climbing, swimming, diving, and competitive sports make up to 12% more profit. Over and above the draw of crowds to public spectacles, a rise in adrenaline level increases desire. See Dutton and Aaron's 'suspension bridge experiment' (1974).

12. *Nose and Toes.* The most prosperous space in any mall is in a department store in the space next to women's shoes. This is because shoe shopping takes a long time and as the customer is waiting for pair after pair of shoes to be tried on, her eye wanders to whatever is in the adjacent space. High-end sellers vie to be near women's shoes and the most popular and profitable business, which exploits this proximity, is cosmetics. Hence, while shopping for shoes, according to retail anthropologist Paco Underhill, a typical female shopper will also buy lipstick, foundation and blusher – powdering her nose while she waits for the arrival of her toes.

13. *Never on Sale.* The one thing in a mall that is never reduced for sale is women's cosmetics. Psychologically, it is the one commodity which has been sold as so integral to the construction of self, that buying it at discount seems 'cheap and nasty'. Instead, to entice buyers to consume more, other offers are made, such as two for one, or 50% off with next purchase, maintaining the illusion of product integrity.

14. *Deliberate Confusion.* Customers buy 14% more if they have spoken to a member of staff (Application of Systematic Layout Planning in Hypermarkets, Bangladesh, 2010). Several leading clothes stores have taken advantage of this insight to create store layouts that create confusion between ladies' and gents' clothing, and by limiting the sizes that are available, thus encouraging the customer to ask for assistance. Customers rarely buy high end clothing, over £100, for example, without having been helped. To this end, stores make it as difficult as possible to pick anything without staff assistance. Beyond this, mall layouts are often deliberately confusing, with mall maps hidden away in corners. Curiously, mall maps in locations as far apart as Florida and East Kilbride omit one very important piece of information – the YOU ARE HERE spot. This again, leads to aimless wandering, which in turn leads to unplanned purchases.

15. *Mall as Babysitter.* Malls now include adventure areas, with bowling alleys, bouncy castles, miniature golf, fun rides, and climbing walls with trained supervision. In this way, malls present themselves as places where parents can have what appears to be cheap babysitting. Malls also often have kiddie safe-drop-off areas such as ballpits, and they host children's events such as birthday parties at discounted

prices. The time when the kids are 'off your hands' then becomes empty time, which parents, since they are stuck in the mall till the babysitting is over, fill with more shopping.

16. *The Cost of Loyalty*. Loyalty cards and Gift cards boost profits. People perceive the value on a gift or a loyalty card as 'found money' or 'free money' and this is encouraged through the naming of such cards 'Reward card', 'Club Card' etc. This creates a psychological effect similar to that of a credit card, only more powerful since the gift/loyalty cardholder doesn't seem to have to pay anything back. However, studies show that customers with gift/loyalty cards spend a lot more than regular customers and that 58% of gift/loyalty card receivers spend 40% more than the 'free' value stored on the card. A typical example from retail clothing is when a gift/loyalty card holder has £15 on their card, rather than purchase £15 worth of good for free, he/she will then splurge on a product that is £15 more expensive than they would usually spend. Gift/Loyalty cards also increase the frequency of visits, generate repeat traffic and, rather unexpectedly, 48% of pre-paid card owners never even bother to redeem the value on their cards (Stats – Vital Cash Flow).

Beyond this loyalty cards give stores the added ability to log their customers retail histories and create detailed customer profiles which allow them to target market which gives them an edge over competitors. Such data, which customers consent to handing over, includes the following: customer age and sex, home address, frequency and brands purchased, transaction value, medical information from pharmacy purchases, demographic basket analysis and customer response to promotions and reductions. Although stores are not permitted to sell this data onto third parties, they can remove customers IDs and pass on aggregated information and 'insights' about consumer behaviour to their suppliers. Data-surveillance through loyalty cards is currently under scrutiny by the UK and Australian government, with respect to breaches of privacy laws.

To date out of the 22 million households in the UK, half own a Nectar card, 15 million people have a Boots Advantage cards, while Tesco owns data on 13 million households. (Australian centre for Retail Studies.)

When you sign for a loyalty card, ask yourself, who is being loyal to who.

17. *Artificial Daylight-Simulation Lighting*. Daylight simulation lights encourage customers to 'lose track of time'. This device has also been used in casinos, encouraging gamblers to lose entire days in pursuit of their addiction.

18. *No Clocks*. The first designs for malls included central clocks in much the same way that Victorian railway stations did, to provide a focus and community meeting point – 'meet me under the clock'. Clocks have been systematically removed from malls and mall design since the 80s for two reasons: (1) Malls are now concerned with keeping people moving and congregation areas slow the flow; (2) As

with point 10, the lack of clocks assists in helping customers 'lose track of time'.

Victor Gruen's 'Clock of Nations' from Midtown Plaza, Rochester, NY. (1962-2008). The clock is now housed in Richmond Airport.

19. *A Safe Haven from the Urban Poor.* Suburban and out-of-town malls are located in places that deter the urban poor; they were in fact first designed as part of the middle class move away from the 'dangerous' inner cities. In most cases, malls can be reached only by motorways ensuring that only those who can afford cars can access them, i.e. the law-abiding middle classes. At all costs, gangs of teenagers and

ethnics from low income backgrounds, must be kept out. This is why malls in most cases have very poor public transport connections to inner cities, and in some cases prohibit bus services entirely. This has resulted in unforeseen and tragic consequences, as in the case of an African American teenager in Buffalo, New York, who died while crossing a seven lane freeway in the attempt to reach a mall.

In the UK, this 'problem' is compounded by the fact that many outer city malls are now located very close to satellite housing schemes which were originally designed as overspill housing for the inner city poor, and which now house people suffering from high degrees of poverty, third-generation unemployment, substance abuse and drug crime. As a result, urban planners have had to use structural devices to deter the urban poor, as in the case of The Fort, Glasgow, located 3/4 km from Easterhouse.

Ease of access by car at The Glasgow Fort, Easterhouse.

Here there is no direct bus link, and the housing estate is only connected to the mall by a patchwork of paths and roadsides. The most direct form of access to the mall, for those from the housing scheme, is to walk beside the slip road from the motorway, where there is no path and walking is prohibited. Families are often seen on the roadside verge with their bags of shopping. Meanwhile, those with cars experience ease of 'access to the latest brands' from the largest motorway in the country.

20. *BYOB*: Be Your Own Brand. In the last decade, mall advertising has gone beyond the idea of simply advertising products, towards a 'holistic' idea of selling you back to yourself. Being your own brand 'Helps you uncover your personal brand and articulate it verbally and visually. Connecting "who" you are to your own unique image.' This is what Marcuse called Pseudo Choice. For example, a female shopper may be told that she has the choice of several colours of nail varnish, and in being convinced of this, she is blinded to the one real choice, which is to decide not to use nail varnish at all. This is an old trick used by salesmen. A salesman will not say 'I will see you on Wednesday', he will give the client a pseudo choice and say: 'I can see you on Tuesday or Thursday'. As with all pseudo choices there is a contradiction lurking within the very structure and the meaning of the words used. Given that malls, by definition, sell only mass-produced globally manufactured and distributed goods which enforce cultural uniformity, the invitation to be unique by being your own brand can barely conceal the dormant and more logical proposition that the best way to be unique would be to refuse to consume all and any brands. The real choice is to *choose not to choose* from what is available.

21. *Shop Alone*. Malls were originally constructed with the nuclear family in mind, and the mother as the ideal consumer, but since the 80s, malls have seen an influx of teenage males, young men

and single people, reflecting changing demographics in society and changing gender roles. The number of one-person households in the UK has increased significantly over the last 30 years – from 18 per cent of all households in 1971 to 30 per cent in 2001. Experts believe that the figure will rise to 38 per cent – more than a third of all households – by 2026. Mall advertising and products have quickly shifted away from the family as ideal consumption unit towards the individual. This makes economic sense. To encourage people to split up shared consumption arrangements, such as the family unit, in favour of 'individual' consumption, results in a growth in duplicate commodities (one broken family requires two homes). According to the UCL Bartlett School of Planning, solitary people now constitute 33% of the population and singles are the largest growth market segment – they consume 38% per cent more products and 42% more packaging than four person households. Advertisers are increasing the visibility of singles in their campaigns and create messages which extol the freedoms of singledom; and companies like Ikea and Habitat are creating products for the single market. Being single was once, for some, a form of rebellion against bourgeois conformism, but is fast becoming the new status quo, and one that better fits the consumerist ethos of infinite choice and accelerating change – 'if you don't like your partner, get a new one'. In the attempt to win over singles, malls now go so far as to have singles nights and speed dating events tied in with food courts.

No matter how much malls try to convince singles to shop inside them, ultimately, this structure will no longer suit modern needs. Already online shopping is causing a collapse in profits, as shopping from home better suits the desires of the new generations of solitary consumers.

22. *No Other Choice.* Finally, no matter how much we protest that we know all of these facts already and that we're not dumb, easily-manipulated consumers, we still shop in malls, precisely because malls and the corporations they house are monopolistic, and aggressively put all other competitors out of business. As with the example of pseudo choice, a dormant question is not being asked. Why do we have so many malls, or for that matter, any malls, at all?

Incident in a Mall # 36.

The Three Degrees and a Non-Event

Two incidents were logged on the daily report sheet of Goldbridge Mall on September 15th 2009. Goldbridge occupies over a million square feet and is located on the edge of a newly expanded motorway intersection that links it to the ring road and centre of the country's largest city. The site is on the edge of a housing scheme and was once that of a council-run shopping centre that was demolished in 2002.

The first incident involved one Betty McAlpine, eighty-three years old, a local resident and 'old worthy'. Betty and two others, Yvonne and Edith, were affectionately known to the staff of the old shopping centre as 'the three degrees'. They were so named, legend has it, not because they sang or danced, or were people of colour, which they weren't, but because they were infamous local gossips, always huddled together, never seen apart; and if you crossed them, they were likely to give you 'the third degree'. Every morning they would arrive at the old centre with flasks of tea and homemade sandwiches and sit all day on the centrally-placed benches discussing the merits and failings of everyone that passed: babies, extra-marital affairs, police arrests; nothing escaped their detection, judgement and caustic wit. The three degrees were pillars of what was becoming an increasingly unstable community.

Throughout the 60s and 70s, the shopping centre had been owned by the council. According to the ethos of cradle-to-grave social planning of the time, it had been permitted to run at a loss in order to attempt to fulfil the essential social functions of nutrition, health, and community cohesion. But during the Thatcher years it had its funding frozen and sank into decline. The bigger stores moved out, leaving vacant lots, which were then barely occupied with passing discount stores, selling low quality – and often stolen – goods. Fresh fruit and veg stores, quality meat, and the latest fashions vanished, although the off-license did a booming trade. Policing then became more difficult as vandalism, shoplifting, vagrancy, and the presence of addicts and street gangs grew. None of which, it has to be said, had been a problem for the three degrees, as they'd lived through worse. Even the junkies didn't scare Betty. Get home and stop yer begging Robert Macfee, she'd once shouted, or I'll tell yer granny and she'll smack yer arse!

Betty had not witnessed the final days of the old shopping centre as she had moved to live with her daughter, Joan, on the other side of the city, due to hip problems. For years she'd been away from her council flat and she missed the place, but Joan had wanted her to move out for good and go into care. There's nothing there for you now, Mum, she'd said, and in a way it was true as Yvonne and Edith had been lost to Alzheimer's and cancer in the intervening years. You'll not steal my house, ya bloody parasite, Betty had shouted.

On the day in question, Betty had been back at her old home for only one day. She had been baffled and disorientated by the sight of the new mall, and a little daunted at the prospect of shopping alone. So she returned to her old routine: she prepared sandwiches of cheese and coleslaw with Mothers Pride and a flask of PG Tips with eight sugars, Tate and Lyle.

The cars seemed faster, though, and greater in number, and

she was cursing her hip replacement as she stumbled through the car park. Her walking stick bashed a car door and set off an alarm. She wondered where all these thousands of people had come from.

The mall seemed to her like some huge ship, bigger than any she'd seen on the Clyde of her youth. Anxiety turned to awe as she was overwhelmed by the bright lights and the lovely smells; the new clothes and happy young faces. As she trod the curving central walkway, she tried to work out what the ground she was standing on had been. The place where H&M was might have been the post office; the place with all the bras (she didn't like even looking at it) would have been where Sammie's baker shop had been.

Her legs were tiring and she wondered if she had missed the benches; she'd walked the length of the mall twice now and had been unable to find any. She finally had to take a seat in a fenced-off area beside a posh-looking coffee place. She sat and unwrapped her sandwiches.

I'm sorry madam, but you can't eat that here.

Betty looked up and a young lass was staring down at her.

Can I drink my tea then? Betty asked, and gave the lass a wink, I won't tell if you don't.

Only if you buy it here, the girl replied.

Well, if I buy some of your tea, will you let me sit here and eat my sandwich? You can only eat what you've bought on the premises, the lass repeated.

She had very poor attitude, Betty thought, and a lot of make-up that made her look like she'd been under a sun lamp too long. She was certainly not from round here.

Alright then, how much is it for a cuppa then? Betty asked.

Earl Grey, herbal or...

Just normal, luv.

One ninety-eight.

Betty said she could buy a bloody box of eighty PG tips for that price, but the girl obviously had no sense of humour.

Fine, said Betty, indignant. Give us a glass of tap water.

We only sell bottled water, the lass said.

At which point Betty picked up her walking stick, sandwich, flask and bag, and headed off, muttering about water: water is free, it's a free country, and such things.

Her search for a bench was futile. On the way she noticed that it was mostly young women here, teenagers really, and there were no old folk. None of the familiar faces. Everyone shipped in from somewhere new. By the main doors, she finally saw an old woman, but the face was strange; the old dear passed her by in an electric buggy. Betty thought the thing looked silly, speeding about like that – a motorbike for cripples – she wouldn't be seen dead in such a thing.

She trudged on, hips aching, to where the pound shop might once have been and discovered an indoor fountain – quite lovely. There was a wee bridge and a pretend stream and water jets shooting high then low, as if in time to some music. There was a little wall and some ceramic dogs or maybe they were concrete. The wall was just the right height. She plonked herself down on it, and unwrapped her sandwiches again.

Excuse me, Madam.

A security man with an earpiece stood before her.

For God's sake, can I not eat ma sandwich in peace! She could tell he was about to repeat the same line as the lass so she asked: Are you a Mackay? You look like a Mackay. You Jennie's lad?

I'm going to have to ask you to move on, he said.

Well, son, my hip's playing up and I'm stuck here like bloody glue, so if you just let me drink my tea I'm sure I'll un-stick in a minute.

He stepped back, talking into some technology fastened to his face. I'll get you some assistance, he said.

She thought them all very rude; a smile would probably kill them.

She looked around and there in a café a woman was breast feeding and a naughty idea came to her. She called out to the young man, and pointed. See, ye see that, what you do about that, eh? Didn't buy that milk on the premises did she?

No reply.

Ach, yer no fun, Betty shouted, yer a waste o' space.

Within a matter of minutes, a young lady had arrived with an electric wheely buggy and was asking Betty to take a seat on it. Shoppers were staring now. My God, what a palaver! She pictured what she must have seemed like to the passers-by: a criminal!

Are ye throwin' me out? Betty shouted. Cos let me tell you, I was here long afore ye were born and yer mither too.

The smiling shop-mobility woman informed her that she was merely here to provide mobility assistance.

Well, Betty shouted, I'm quite happy where I am, so off you go and assist yer own mobility.

I'm going to have to ask you to move on madam, the security man repeated.

She whispered to the shop mobility woman: He's a mummy's boy, he thinks he's tough but he's a big baby.

Meanwhile, at the other end of the mall, the second parallel incident was unfolding. Two feminist activists had staged a protest about the lingerie display in La Senza with flyers which described the store display as 'demeaning to women'. The plan, as they conceived it, was for one of them to chain herself to the metal window shutters – a form of protest with a proud lineage.

When Security informed the women that their protest could not take place, they argued that similar events had taken place outside Anne Summers in Birmingham, London and Edinburgh; that it was their democratic right.

The Operations Manager was called and his explanation, on arrival, was simple, calm and well-informed.

Yes, such protests happen in town centres, he said, but I regret to inform you that this isn't common land, so isn't covered by common law. The forecourt, on which you are standing, the walls and roof are owned by Girelle Services Limited – a corporation with over thirty shopping malls, and well known on the FTSE 100. If you want to protest about La Senza, you will have to either enter the shop, in which case you will probably be ejected by La Senza's security staff, or else apply in writing to Girelle for permission to use their walkway.

Protestor one argued that they knew their rights. They were free to roam anywhere in the country. They couldn't be arrested.

And the operations manager explained patiently that nonetheless, they would probably get sued by the mall owners for a number of small, non-criminal but potentially extremely costly infractions of commercial and property laws. In fact, the flyers they were handing out could be seen as advertising, and they would have to apply for a permit and buy a license to advertise, and hire space to do it. Failing to do so would leave them open to charges of unlawful trading. The price of floor space, by the square metre, was something like five hundred pounds per month.

This is not advertising, that's exactly what we're protesting about! protested the first woman, thrusting a flyer of a naked woman into the man's face. Protestor two tried to remain calm.

OK, so where can we protest? She asked. The Operations Manager, politely, offered to personally show the two women to an appropriate space, which would fall under common law and on which their protest would be perfectly legal and free from further disturbance.

At the other end of the mall, Betty finally gave a sigh of surrender and allowed the mobility people to help her into the shopping buggy, and to give her a lesson in driving it. She thanked them and said she would be on her way. The buggy was surprisingly zippy and it had a convenient basket fastened to the handlebars. It was here that Betty placed her bag with flask and sandwiches, as with one hand she steered, and with the other she ate.

Security pursued her, but her steering was not at all reliable, and so after several bruising encounters they kept at a safe distance, calling out to her once again the endless refrains on the consumption of forbidden foodstuffs in non-food areas.

I'm not on your bloody areas, she called back, with a mouthful of cheese and coleslaw, I'm moving, see!

Betty sped on and then stopped by the toilets to pour some tea. Security tried to corner her and so she accelerated back towards the fountain. This erratic and unpredictable stopping and starting went on for some time, and security were powerless to stop it, as they had become an object of mirth for passing shoppers who were now pointing and laughing at their attempts to restrain the speeding geriatric.

Finally, after Betty had consumed her sandwiches and spilled her tea, she allowed security to escort her away. The spot they led her to was beyond Tesco, beyond the car park, to the rear of and about three hundred yards from the mall, beyond a twelve foot wall with razor wire and CCTV, which protected the trade entrance with its 40ft long lorries and the recycling bins – on a piece of public pathway on the edge of the turn-off to the motorway. She heard shouting, and looked up and saw two young women arguing.

The protestors had been there half an hour and not a soul had passed. They had been fiercely debating the fundamental futility of resistance and still had a large stack of flyers when they saw Betty. One moved over to hand her a flyer.

Betty cut her off before she could explain.

I'm no wanting your bloody adverts, she shouted. The woman shrugged and mumbled and let the flyer fall to the ground. Betty was in a rage. She looked down at the image and it was all boobs and bums and a lass with her mouth blacked-out. Horrible. What the hell was it all about, young women these days! She wanted to shout at the lasses but both had headed off in separate directions, all of their bits of paper dumped and flying around in the wind. These people, they came to her place and threw about nudey boobies. Bloody litter-bugs!

Betty looked round and tried to place herself. There used to be a bus stop round here, next to old Hardy's the bakers. But there was no sight of either. They must've plonked her out on the wrong side, so she was all back to front. Bloody hell! The fastest way would have to be a short-cut over the motorway. But there was no pelican crossing in sight and the nearest one was probably all the way back through the car park to where she'd started, so she decided to stay just where she was and wait for a gap in the traffic. Then she would make a dash for it.

BABY CARE

There are, it has been said, eighty-two types of person in the world. But people are not types, you might protest; they cannot be numbered – such an idea is contemptible to any free-thinking person; a pseudo-scientific lie cooked up by market research companies to put people into boxes, to hide the radical fact that each and every individual is unique and free to forge their own future. This was certainly what Les' parents believed in the spring of 1970, when they celebrated the gift of her birth, and named her in a non-gender specific way as an expression of their belief in social change and sexual equality. In demographic terms, Les' parents would have been seen as a fairly permissive middle-class college-educated couple with a single child – *Edgy Bluecollar Suburbs*, type D22 – also known as *Financially-Limited New Hopers*. But they would have scorned such reductive caricatures.

Les' mother, Kath, was a complex mix of many things: a feminist and a wild-child, a would-be poetess and a part-time office worker (PR). Les' father, John, was a high school Modern Studies teacher who listened to Dylan and Johnny Cash and smoked a lot of pot. They were liberal and progressive and they bought handmade pots and fabrics from Marimeko. Les' first toys were made of wood and came from a radical new store called the Early Learning Centre, because John and Kath were opposed to mass-produced plastic.

As the responsibilities of childrearing and the debts of the 80s started to replace the freedoms of the 60s, both Kath and John sought to re-ignite the old fires with secret lovers. Les' dawning awareness of her parents' infidelities grew as their own mutual antipathy increased. The usual tirades featured blaming each other for missing the boat, tying each other down, selling out, and smashing the handmade crockery. Kath started to drink, secretly, but not secretly enough for her ten-year-old daughter, who found the many bottles her mother had stashed under the sink and behind the bookshelves.

Les went to a state school – which was typical of her demographic – and went on to study for a BA in liberal arts. Later, her parents became *Empty Nesters* after having stayed together 'for the sake of the child' – which was typical of D22s – and divorced to reconnect with their own 'personal voyages', leaving Les with feelings of guilt and anguish and with a profound desire for escape. She vowed she would never 'become like those selfish bloody losers' and so, after graduating and with very little money, she took a year out and explored Europe, experimented with recreational drugs and tried out many new tongues. She fell in love with Jose and Ivan, learned some guitar chords so she could sing along to Alanis Morisette and had an abortion. When the money was exhausted, she returned to her original city and got a flexi-time job in market research, as a stopgap fallback thing, and became one of the newly emerging group of people who worked in call centres and phoned total strangers to ask questions like 'how often in a week do you use a microwave?' and 'do you have a cat, a dog, a pet rodent or none of the above?'. Indeed, at this time Les wrote a story entitled *None of the Above*, about a girl who didn't fit into any of the human categories that she was rapidly learning about.

She found the 82 types at first disturbing. Things like: L76s are *Multi-Ethnic Crowded Non-residents. They live in Third World shanty towns, work illegally and live with high infant mortality and diseases such as AIDS and Cholera: they are the world's largest growth market for pay-as-you-go mobile telephones.* This was so sad and cynical that you had to laugh or you'd go mad. Others were just straight-out weird. Her favourite was B14s or *Happy Families Living in Military Enclosures – a reliable market for self-help books, Disney toys and Anne Summers Products.*

These were actually 'facts', and all written down in the staff 'bible'. Some weeks she'd have to do nothing but phone B14 women and ask questions about bikini-wax or floor polish. Other days it was J51s, or *Grey Perspective Sepia Memories*. She liked asking them about brands of chocolates and painkillers and gifts for their grandchildren from Argos, and they liked chatting to her because they were lonely, because 71% of J51s had lost a partner.

Work paid the rent, which was in an apartment in the edgy mixed student slash immigrant area (E28). Les was disturbed by the fact that her flatmates did listen to indie rock and did watch *Will and Grace* like their demographic profile predicted. There were other things that disturbed her: like how a lot of research info was 'harvested' without anyone's consent from direct debit, credit and loyalty cards, and even dating agency records. She didn't like any of this, but after many false starts at finding other kinds of work, she decided – in her mid to late twenties – that it was an easy regular source of income that gave her freedom to experiment with alternative ways of living in her spare time. She then went through an 'excited and dizzying' period, dating many people from different places, in the search for someone, like herself, who didn't fit any of the boxes. There was Taz (F35), Sheena (A8), and Flack (G42). She slummed it with immigrants and had a brief 'amore' with a *Symbols of Success/Global Connector* who, with his pied-à-terre penthouses in several countries, BMWs, and share portfolios, was a complete caricature of the Type A1 slash 2 that he aspired to be. But he'd kept an old Play-doh model of Kermit he'd made when he was four, and Les found that redemptive. For a while.

Her ability to empathise with and adapt to other people was unique. Her faces and moods, like her wardrobe, changed weekly, if not daily. Flared jeans for one date, an Armani suit jacket for the next; a D&G dress for one, then Nikes and slacks for another. And when she talked to people from different backgrounds, although she did not like to admit this to herself, her market research experience helped in discussing the things they liked. She knew, for example, that E34s used Ecover washing powder and supported Greenpeace, and that F41s liked *Star Trek: the Next Generation* and read *Harry Potter* even though they didn't have kids. It wasn't that she was two-faced; if anything she was 82-faced, or 34-faced, that being the number of lovers she had in her twenties, as was fairly normal for people of her type at this point in time.

Les had a small breakdown in her thirties as her freedom experiment ran out of energy, leaving a great many discarded lovers and friends in its wake. And some of those partners she was just plain scared of. Like the G41s — *brands include Lacoste, Burberry, Buckfast, Farmfoods, Embassy Regal, Nike, Nintendo — a growth market for credit services.* Others, like the B9s, had used her in ways she should have been able to predict in advance. After a late termination, her sixth morning-after pill and a case of Chlamydia, she was told that she may have damaged her ovaries and might not be able to conceive. At this time, it must be said, she had amassed an encyclopedia of disappointments, traumas and personal tragedies, which included the death of her mother, having her stomach pumped, a mugging, and an HIV test.

Safety, Security, Family: these became the words she projected forward to meet in her future. Luckily for her, each fell into place, like steps on the way. She got offered a full-time post (which at that time was rare and to be coveted) and at thirty-six she became a Market Researcher proper, with her own team and glass-walled office. Shortly after, as if prompted, Jason drifted into her life. Unlike Sal (F23) he had emotional and financial stability, and unlike Hector (C16), he was without the burden of unattainable aspirations. Jason was a promising artist with a gentle disposition who did a bit of teaching and had come from a family of Bs before drifting south to settle somewhere among the Ds. They listened to Kooks by David Bowie, ate Doritos together in the bath, and joked about spawning a generation of soggy tortilla-eating little misfits.

To Les's joy, her first pregnancy test revealed that her years of experimentation had not left her barren. She wanted to call the child a creative, original girl's name like Saffron or Jocasta, but Jason suggested a name less loaded class-wise; something simple and easy to say that might give the baby a head start in speech. And as they had chosen, at the scan, not to be told if it was male or female, a unisex name would be ideal. They settled for Sam.

Les and Jason wanted baby Sam's life to be uncluttered and they planned to buy simple wooden toys. The closest they could find were some from the Early Learning Centre; although they were now mass-manufactured– they had an 'authentic feel'.

The financial pressures of impending parenthood forced Jason to retrain as a high school teacher and for them to move to the fringes of the suburbs, so they could have a garden for their newly-born daughter. But baby Sam was colicky and screamy and would not wean, and Les and Jason began to fight as chronic sleep deprivation overtook their new home. Les was prescribed sleeping pills which made her even more drowsy and lethargic during the day and resentful in the evenings. She felt isolated in the suburbs and to calm herself she took to secretly drinking. Her depression was exacerbated by having to return to work, and by political developments which her company was involved in. It was around this time that statistics revealed the 'social ladder' concept had collapsed; that there was only 7% social mobility and that 93% of the population, in spite of all promises to the contrary, would never escape their demographic box.

At work, while doing a demographic study for a controversial proposed 'inner city regeneration' mall development in conjunction with the newly elected council planning department, Les oversaw research on the shopping patterns and values of the target market – D22. On screen she saw the stats map the lives of her parents exactly. During a phone survey of D22s, she then saw her own postcode come up as the most representative segment, then her own name and phone number.

Alone at night as her child and husband slept, an empty bottle of wine beside her, Les counted out her sleeping pills and held in her hand the only means she could see that could set her and her child free from their demographic destiny. She wept and put the pills back in the jar and set the jar back in its place. She tiptoed through to the nursery and stared down at the little empty face. Above the child's whisper of hair were metal safety bars and above that, a colourful poster. There was a picture of an Antelope and then a big letter A. Then B was for Bear, C was for Cat, D...

She could not see what D was for.

Dead Malls, Ghost Malls

In 2010, *Deadmalls.com* celebrated its tenth anniversary; featuring a list of the three hundred dead and dying malls in the US, with site histories, maps, old adverts, photos, retro T-shirts, and links. On the site there are photographs of abandoned walkways covered in the broken glass from a hundred store-fronts; of central play-areas that have become swimming pools due to roof leakage; there are images of escalators covered in moss and creepers that have burst through broken tiles; images of charred store fronts; all accompanied by heartfelt blog reminiscences:

They had Target and Foot Locker and Jollies Arcade. My mom used to drop me there and I'd play Pac-Man for hours – one time this big kid fleeced me over at the fountain.

I just can't believe it's gone, it's like someone stole my past.

Deadmall Tours have become a 'cult' activity for Generation Xers and connoisseurs of decay, who pay money to photograph the gutted shells of the malls where they spent their youth, in much the same way that nature buffs tour and 'bag' mountains. In some cases tours are conducted by torchlight around the interiors of structurally unsound buildings. The phrase that always comes up is 'end of the world'. Dead malls are an image of apocalypse. They are also deeply ingrained in the conflicted memories of Gen X, being both objects of adoration and satire (see George A Romero's classic 1978 *Dawn of the Dead* which portrayed zombies as shopaholics, swarming to the mall because 'it's all they have known'.) Deadmalls.com pays respect to the needs of a generation to mourn its own past.

A dead mall has devastating effects on the community it serves. Over and above the loss of employment, the fall in local property values and tax revenues, changes in population and traffic, and the stigmatisation of an area as 'failed', a closed mall becomes a liability. The abandoned building and empty parking lots become magnets for crime (drugs, prostitution, gang fights) till the only viable option ultimately becomes demolition. (See Eastland Mall, North Versailles; Greengate Mall, Hempfield; Richland Mall, Johnstown.)

Reasons why malls close:

(1) *Recession.* Of the 1,118 recognised 'enclosed malls' (out of 48,000 shopping centres) in the US, over a hundred have closed since 2005. The recession of 2008-10 brought a 7% decline in mall retail and 200,000 store bankruptcies including that of one of the US's largest mall owners (General Growth Properties – 200 properties in 44 states).

(2) *Demographic.* 'Free markets' and short-term employment lead to rapid migratory and spending changes. The movement of women into the workplace has also dramatically cut into daytime profits, as female shoppers were the target market for which the mall was originally built.

(3) *Traffic.* Changes in road networks reroute consumers.

(4) *Online and Big Box.* Since the 90s, malls have lost an estimated 33% of their revenue to online shopping, and to single discount stores such as Walmart.

(5) *Anchor Stores Relocate.* When big department stores, like JC Penney Co, Macy's and John Lewis, relocate to a newer or bigger mall, it triggers panic among shoppers, killing business and prompting mass evacuation of smaller stores. Once the 40% occupancy mark has been breached, mall closure is inevitable.

(6) *Security.* Store vacancies eat into profits for site owners – who are responsible for upkeep and security. Cutbacks in security lead to increased vandalism and crime, which in turn affect retail in a vicious cycle. See Banister Mall, Kansas.

(7) *Overdevelopment.* The US has already reached consumption saturation point, with too much shopping space per American (a condition parts of the UK are fast approaching). It is simply impossible for a household with two cars and four TVs, with PCs, stereos and game systems in every room, with every family member in seasonal fashions, to consume more. The only way for malls to survive in a saturated market is to 'eat each other'.

(8) *White Flight.* When the racial demographic of an area changes, with an increase in the ethnic population, it is common for the white middle classes to take flight and move to another area, taking their spending power with them.

(9) *Killed by a Newer Mall.* Developers build new malls within the catchment area of existing older malls, deliberately intending to 'leak' away customers.

Dead Malls and Cinema

Sherman Oaks Mall (Cal) location for Hollywood the 'Mall Rat' movies, *Valley Girls* (starring Nicholas Cage) and *Fast Times at Ridgmont High*, closed its doors in 1999. The mall in *Dawn of the Dead* (Monroeville, Pittsburgh) which put two competitors into closure since it was built, lost twenty key stores in 2009, placing it 'in danger'.

Bannister Mall, Kansas City (1980-2007), one of the candidates from Kevin Smith film *Mall Rats* and the focus of regional retail in Kansas within the 80s and 90s. When Banninster Mall was demolished (below), the four miles of ribbon retail development that had spread out from it became a 'dead zone'. The mall was put out of business by bigger mall developments in the south of the region and by 'White Flight'.

Two abandoned supermalls in Malaysia.

SHOW ROOMS

It started with Paris. Jane had just moved into Carla's flat and was a little worried about seeming to intrude in the former matrimonial home, so she proposed they take a cheap weekend away to defuse any possible tension. She wanted it to be somewhere they could hold hands and no one would know them or care and Carla could come out of her shell.

Paris was only sixty-five pounds with Easy Jet and she'd put it on her credit card. It had worked out just fine: a big, sunlit-lovers scenario in a place with real culture; all those winding streets and dusty bookshops, and all that fresh coffee and tarte tatin, and all the places where Simone de Beauvoir maybe once sipped absinthe and discussed revolution with singers and artists. Jane led Carla up the many steps to the Sacré Coeur, and together they posed for photographs with their arms around each other and the floodlit church behind. They walked the boulevards and Jane pointed out other women holding hands and they kissed by the Seine and made their tentative love on a creaky old bed in a down-at-heel bodega in the 13th arrondissement. And Carla grew and blossomed and dragged Jane around, French dictionary and street map in hand, searching out places with unpronounceable names, laughing as they lost their way in ancient alleyways.

It happened on the second last night. There had been this couple they'd met in Les Deux Maggots: Philippe and Sandrine, arty and in their early twenties – their English was good. After Pernods, Sandrine invited them both back to her flat to listen to a Carla Bruni CD, as she was amazed that Carla had never heard her namesake before. Carla took Jane's hand and said OK. As soon as they were inside however, Jane sensed Carla's unease. Carla sat upright, uptight, almost scared-looking, on the sofa and hardly said a word all night.

On the walk home she would not take Jane's hand. Carla had to take a sleeping pill and an aspirin that night because of a headache, and curled herself into a protective ball, with her back to Jane. It was only in the departures lounge, the next morning, that Jane managed to prise it from her.

It was just the... their kitchen, that whole raw wood effect, and the rugs too, even the CD rack and that sofa, sorry, I used to have one with Colin. I mean... Sorry, I just have this phobia about... Ikea, Carla said.

You're serious?

Jane tried to joke that maybe there was an upside to it all. It was kind of cool too, didn't Carla think? You know, like that song by U2, like how we're one race, one people, all the same the world over.

Just promise me we won't go there, Carla said, Ever.

Well, if it don't kill ya, it'll make ya stronger.

Jane had no choice but to make a joke of it, there in the car park as they stared out at the big blue walls and the yellow logo. Every weekend for the past month they'd trawled round store after store, Habitat, Bed Bath and Beyond, John Lewis, Debenhams, even Argos, with Carla finding fault with this and that bed in every place. Ikea was the only place left.

Consider it a cathartic experience, Jane said, confront that trauma!

Carla took her hands from the wheel.

OK, so we go in and don't get distracted. We go straight to Beds and Bedding, dodge the crowds and make a quick decision. OK?

That hurt a little: Carla's tone and the insistence on speed, when all Jane wanted to do was defuse the bomb, to goof-out and follow the winding path and sing *Follow-The-Yellow-Brick-Road* and fill the trolley with bits and bobs of this and that, that were probably not really solutions to modern living but just cheap things, brightly coloured: blue and red glasses, incense burners and a bottle opener and some funky swirly bowls, and maybe some flowers, potted of course, because, well, Carla's place was more than a little austere as her ex had pretty much gutted it when he left, and Carla had been remarkably reluctant to restock it with essentials. And his goddamn faux retro yuppie wallpaper had to come down, and that was probably a trip to Homebase, and of course the two single mattresses pushed together on the floor were conspiring to become almost some metaphor for the whole situation.

OK babe, she said, leaning to kiss Carla's cheek, let's get this show on the road. When Carla went silent, Jane often said goofy things to fill the silences; she reminded herself to try to stop that. Carla took a deep breath and reached for the door handle.

Walking across the car park, Jane glimpsed a family of four struggling to squeeze some immense package into a four-by-four and she hoped Carla hadn't noticed. She saw a single straight-looking woman in heels wandering around with some kind of Chinese lamp in a trolley, mobile phone to ear, car fob in the other hand, clicking obsessively, trying no doubt, to trigger the flashing lights of her lost car. Jane wanted to take Carla's hand.

In the spinning door a black kid was messing around with the sensors and the thing kept stopping and starting. They were stuck halfway in and out and the mother was shouting – Jesus, Limal, you stop that or I'll show you my hand. Jane wanted to joke with

Carla about kids and how you just had to love what a pain in the butt they were, but reminded herself that the whole issue was a no-go for Carla.

Inside, the music was 'Do it to me one more time'. And Jane wanted to make a joke but thought better of it. Carla headed to the floor map.

OK, upstairs, and to the right. We can take a shortcut through Kitchens.

She watched Carla's back as she climbed the steps. Her hips swaying in that office suit of hers. It was some weird thing Carla did, putting on her suit on a Saturday, maybe because they didn't have a wardrobe yet or a washing machine. Jane made a mental note to address wardrobes while they were doing beds and to offer to split the cost. Of course Carla would insist on paying for it all herself, but she couldn't keep letting Carla pay for everything. Jane would put it on the credit card.

They were on the display floor and Carla was many feet ahead, as if shopping alone. She moved swiftly past the cuddly toys and climbing frames, on through lighting and lamps.

Hey, Sonic the Hedgehog, slow down, Jane called, then wondered if Carla got the reference.

A young couple blocked their way. The guy was squeezing the girl's ass; she was a peroxide blonde with hipster shorts, fishnets and shiny high-heeled boots. Carla stared as the guy patted the girl's ass in front of the living-room showrooms.

Jeeso, what is this – Neanderthal open-day? Jane said.

We have to go through Kitchens, Carla said, where the hell is Kitchens?

Minutes then, just following Carla and many anxieties and

possibilities as they passed Kitchens and Home Offices, as Jane thought maybe if she finally got down to getting a job it would put less pressure on Carla, and maybe a desk would help, if Carla let her use the front room as makeshift office.

Jane tried to lighten the mood, Hey Carla, why is it that men think beds are for sex and women think they're for sleeping?

Sorry? Carla said, I don't know, why? Carla had thought it a joke with a punch-line. Jane was halfway through explaining that it wasn't when Carla pushed through the double doors.

Eureka, Jane shouted.

Carla got out her notepad with the pre-written dimensions and started assessing. The bed signs said Malm, Hemnes, Lillehammer. Aneboden was 70% off. Jane sat down on the nearest bed and bounced on it. Hey what, about this one? It was wide and had a 70s-style headboard.

No, it's pine veneer; anyway it's too expensive.

But, we're going halfers.

No, save your money, you need it.

Jane looked around to find a bed that was more 'them'. There was a really big one, Bauhaus-looking, beyond the tacky and discounted ones. It had a kind of functional no-frills feel. She moved to it, sat and patted the mattress.

C'mon, it's bouncy, give it a try.

Carla stood there. It's a Hopen, she said.

Yeah, And I'm hopen you'll like it! C'mon, live a little, give it a try.

Carla sat down tentatively, on the edge. Her fingers on the mattress, just by her thigh, testing the tension.

Jane lay back. Snow Patrol were playing on the in-house

radio station.

Hey, she said, 'Will you lie with me and just forget the world?' But Carla didn't get it. So Jane started telling her about her Ikea dream. How once she'd gone to sleep and woken to find herself in a display unit, thousands of people passing as she sat there in her knickers, covering her breasts with her hands. Probably lots of people had that dream now, like the one from school, when you're naked in the swimming pool.

Carla, stood, eyes fixed on something beyond. Twenty feet away there was a three-year-old in a red stripy top, trying to tuck himself into a display bed, the sign above said it was a Hemnes. The kid tried again and again to tuck himself in, failing to grasp that it was a display model, the bed sheets probably stapled on. It was funny but his parents, young, studenty-looking, were too distracted to notice.

Carla was staring. Jane, tried to think of ways to divert her. Babe, how about we try those Lillehammers? Carla seemed not to hear.

The parents moved on and the kid climbed onto the next bed, monkey-like, a muscular little chap. The father was testing a mattress. The mother smiling at the child, playing peek-a-boo round the edge of a wardrobe unit. Peek-a-boo again, peek-a-boo, peek-a-boo, then she stopped and went back to her notepad. The kid feeling neglected, maybe, pretended to be asleep as if in his own bed.

Ok, Babe, you want to move on? Jane said and got to her feet.

The father leaned over and tickled the kid, growling RARRR!!! He picked up the kid, hoisted him onto his shoulder – RARRR! The kid roaring with laughter as his father swung him round.

Carla turned to her. We had a Hemnes before, she said.

And Jane was confused because they were sitting on a Hopen.

Anyway, Carla said, it's all made of chipwood and veneer and it goes to bits if you try and move it around...

OK, look, Jane said, let's have a coffee then... give it a second try once we're refreshed.

Before them, in another bedroom showroom, a single woman in heels with greying roots, stared for a long time into an empty wardrobe, then closed the door, lowering her gaze as its mirrored surface slid before her face. The music was Duran Duran, *Say a Prayer.* Behind her head was a large framed reproduction of a sunset. She opened one drawer, then the next, then the next, then stood back and photographed the empty drawers with her cell-phone.

Carla started walking to the exit.

I'm getting a migraine, she whispered, Sorry, can we do this another time?

This one simple, fucking thing! If we can't...

I know, I know.

Am I talking to myself? Am I mad, what is it with you?

Will you just not... *do that?* OK?

What, what am I doing?

I can't find the car.

Carla was sorry, really sorry, the headache wasn't her fault. And Jane was going on and on, almost shouting at her there in front of so many people.

Jane marched ahead and walked each line till she found it, a hundred yards and two lanes away, making signs with her hands and calling out: PUGG, Pugg! Jane had to turn every thing in the world into some personal nickname-thing; the car registration was P379 UGG, so Jane called it Pugg. Carla had had this car for five years and it had never had a name before, and it was her car, not Jane's. As she walked towards it, it came to her that although Jane had said she'd lived with eighteen different women in half as many years, it was doubtful that Jane had ever bought furniture with a partner.

And Colin on his knees with his toolkit, taking their bed apart and it all breaking into wood chips. And him shouting that it was fucking trash and kicking it, breaking it into ever smaller pieces, and the never-ending processes of physical proximity to a man that you now fear, a now-new stranger. Then holding a bin bag so this stranger can put the broken wood-chips in, and worrying about whether the council would collect it from your door, and all the neighbours, who no doubt heard the fight, staring at those rubbish bags out front, week after week, that are filled with your bed.

She found the car and wanted it all to be over but Jane was just starting.

Like the bloody carpet's rolled up and we need to varnish the floor and get some fucking wallpaper and some paint!

I'm sorry. Just not today, OK?

She was opening the car door. Poor Jane. Lovely Jane. Her friends said Jane was some kind of understandable but symptomatic reaction, and she should stop reading Self Help and Kate Millett.

You know what? You can sit there all you like in your empty house and…

Jane, Please.

No, I mean, there's some things you need, really basic, and I'm not talking existentially, I mean, like a plug for the bath and maybe some hand towels!

Carla couldn't focus, there was this mother and kid getting into a car with a hotdog. Her pulling him in, impatient, the hotdog falling to the ground. The child crying. The mother bending then picking up the meat not knowing what to do with it, looking round to see if anyone had seen, then handing the crying child the soiled sausage to eat.

Carla would have thrown it away, she would have gone back to the store and bought another one, she would have wiped the hotdog on her sleeve and taken a bite herself first, to show the kid that everything was safe and OK.

Carla climbed into the car. Alone for a second she felt the presence of the headless Jane by the passenger door, dreading that click as it opened. Jane had no right, she didn't know what it felt like to be abandoned by a man who had promised you a child, a man who had postponed and promised and postponed till you had sacrificed your years of fertility.

Jane pulled the door. You know what…

Carla reached to turn the keys in the ignition.

No, stop. Hear me out. Jesus, fuck Ikea, you know, you're not the only one, I've had more than a few lovers on a goddamn Hemnes bed before. OK?

Just get in, OK?

Seriously Carla, if you're so freaked out, then let's never buy a bed, let's wait for one to fall out of the sky, no, let's… let's make one. I'm serious. Yeah, no, like buy some wood and fucking… I mean how hard can it be? I mean like carving, what's it called? For Christ's sake, we have to be able to do something for ourselves, it's not like men have the monopoly on everything, right? Give me a hammer and I'll do it. Did people a hundred years ago go to fucking Ikea? A thousand? Homebase! Jane was shouting. Look, right over there. We go in, we buy some goddamn wood.

Jane couldn't be serious, Carla said.

Damn right, Jane was shouting – there were plans online for building just about anything – this DIY show on YouTube. Trust me, Jane said, I know how to do a dovetail joint, my dad taught me, I mean when he wasn't stealing my panties.

This thing Jane did, making her laugh at these horrible things.

I shit you not! Homebase – c'mon. I'll walk home alone by the motorway if you don't come in with me. Fuck it, you drive away and I'll still buy the wood – build a bivouac in the car park!

Her funny angry Jane with all her radical impossible plans that were really just youth pushing against its own limits. Carla reached to squeeze her hand but Jane was out the door shouting, C'mon!

Power tools and nuts and bolts and saws and rakes and hoes and shovels and bags of concrete and sheets of perspex and formica and cornicing and paint and varnish and brushes and ladders.

Jane was pushing the trolley and doing her best to lead Carla around under the pretence that she knew what she was doing, hoping to hell Carla wouldn't chicken out and pull a Barbie on her.

C'mon, we need pine, it should be somewhere at the back.

Carla looked lost, allowing herself to be led. A man passed with what seemed to be the wall of a garden shed in a trolley. If Carla worked out that she was freaked-out then the whole thing would backfire. Did she know how to make a bed or a dovetail joint? Did she hell! She put on a voice.

So my dear, I'm thinking we need some screws, pardon the pun.

Surprisingly, Carla laughed, then Shh'd her, then took over the pushing of the trolley.

As they moved through the aisles, Jane made comments in whispers, pointing out all the middle-aged balding chino-wearers handling hammers and chisels with something resembling intimacy. She had to keep Carla laughing.

You know DIY has always sounded like masturbation to me. Seriously, if you dump me I'm going to have to buy some power tools, they have this vibrate function on drills.

Stop it! Carla's fingers beside hers on the trolley rail as they pushed past bolts and rivets and things she didn't know the name for. And men studying little things made of metal, as if searching for some long lost part of their DNA.

My God! Carla whispered.

I think it's over there, c'mon.

So then it was this weird world of wood and the bluff had to go on. She led Carla round the vast enclosed outdoor space with wood sections as big as a house, through lanes of rough hewn and sanded oak and beams sealed with creosote, past men with spirit levels and measuring tapes. They were lost in ladders when out of the corner of her eye she glimpsed some simple lengths of pine.

Timber!

Carla laughed and she wheeled the trolley towards the stack. They were about two metres long, three inches by three in width, and they had a name. UDF industrial. Reduced price. One ninety-five a length.

Jane picked one from the pile and made a dumb-show of feeling its weight. Carla was behind her. So, this is our bed?

Yer darn tootin', Jane said with her best Southern Hick accent. A lady needs a bed to get her beauty sleep, damn right, I'll cut it and sand it and you betcha, this is gonna be a bed fit for a queen.

This was good. Carla's laughter continued with stacking the lengths of pine.

Is four enough? Carla asked.

And sure enough, she was having to draw up this imaginary schema of some craftsman's plan, and there had to be legs, and there would be mistakes, which would mean more wood.

Hell no, we need another four, ma lady. She was doing her best John Wayne.

You sure you know what you're doing? This is crazy.

Lady, she replied, you wanna go back to Ikea, then more fool you, I's gonna make you a four poster built with lurve!

They had to wait till they got through the sliding doors to laugh at that moment when the checkout girl had done a double-take at the sight of two women buying industrial timber.

They laughed at the trolley that had a bent wheel, which they had to push together because it went sideways, because of the weight. Laughing all the way back to the car, across the many lanes. Carla got her keys out and her breath back and opened the boot.

But would they fit? Goddamn it, she was saying, still with her cowboy accent. Carla was trying to squeeze them in and they

271

were going all the way to the front windscreen and still poking out a foot at the back. They don't bloody fit! Shit, what are we even doing? Carla said. Then she broke a nail in shifting, sucked it and fell silent.

Jane saw how this could easily be their final moment: two women shouting at each other in the space between Homebase and Ikea.

A saw! That was what she said. I'll go back in and buy a saw, OK? It was desperate but seemed the only option. Yup, I'll buy a saw an' I'll cut them an' they'll fit. You wait an' see.

You're crazy.

Trust me, sweetheart.

Going back through the sliding doors she pictured Carla left alone with the pile of wood as couples stared. It led her on quickly into the aisle of tools and there were maybe forty saws there, all with different teeth and gauges.

A saw, I see a saw, she joked to herself, but playing with words seemed childish and empty when Carla was not beside her.

The eight lengths of pine had been stacked against the bedroom wall for three weeks and Jane was out again, at another job interview, or so she said. Jane's joke of the other day had troubled Carla. She'd asked when the building of the bed would actually start and Jane said: To be honest, the only kind of joints I've ever made are the ones you roll!

She looked over at Jane's stack of things in the corner – a bag of clothes, some books, an iPod, a pair of hiking boots. How much more of an effort it had been to move the wood in than it had been for Jane to move in with her few bags.

She touched a section of pine. It was rough and no doubt would need to be sanded. Making this bed, if the whole thing hadn't been a joke, would require many other tools, many of which Colin had maybe once had and had maybe taken with him, but Jane had not bought or thought of buying any. Carla stepped back from the stack and gazed out the window at the trees. They had moved here because of the park, they had planned to watch their children playing beneath the trees, the cherry blossoms falling snow-like in spring.

The scent of pine, as she shifted a beam, and the sense memory of a splinter and of a mouth sucking it out from her finger, lips and teeth on her skin – her father?

She and Jane had become friends now. Just friends. No sex, not that she'd ever got good at it. Her friends had been right, a phase was all it had been. Jane had never intended to build a bed. That was clear now.

Something had to be salvaged. The pine had to be dealt with one way or another. It seemed to be laughing at her in its mute innate state. If she threw it out then she and Jane would split. Not immediately, of course, it would take time, a slow decline. Carla had never been good at ending things; she always waited for the other to strike first, even though for months, years, she could sense the end coming. They were like flatmates now, and soon Jane would pay rent, and then even the kisses would stop.

The wood in her hands, she heard herself saying, Take it into your own hands.

She went online and searched for 'pine bed plans'. She found many sites selling Ikea-type prefabricated assembly packages, then one: a hippy designer in Des Moignes, with pictures of his finished structures with plans, with diagrams of joints and instructions. For free.

Ridiculous – she'd never made anything in her life. But it was Saturday and she was alone and damn it. Crazy, but she was out and on the expressway and turning off to the retail park and parking with a list in her head: sander, screwdriver, chisel, three-inch screws, spirit level and some tool she couldn't find the name for, but she was sure she could locate it on the shelves without the humiliation of having to ask a man.

So there I was with this saw in this car park, with all this stupid wood.

I can so see you, all butch, Beth giggled, sipping her wine, touching Jane's knee.

Right, and she's looking about like this desperate housewife, and I'm saying if you hold one end and prop it up against the boot, then I'll saw. Seriously, and I've never sawed anything in my life and it keeps snagging every time I try. And there's all these macho jerk-offs staring at us from their four-by-fours… we'd parked just in the middle, between Homebase and Ikea and that other… I forget.

Carpetworld? Bed Bath and Beyond?

Yeah… whatever, and one guy even asks, Can I help ladies? Like, fat and fifty, and I give him the finger. So then, this takes a whole forty-five minutes and you should see her face, and I'm thinking this is beyond Laurel and Hardy and I'm getting blisters anyway so I say, Your turn madam.

No! Does she…?

Come on – Barbie sawing wood in a car park? So, she's sitting in the car, like in denial, in a rage, and it hits me that things aren't going to work out between us. I mean, what was I even thinking?

Poor Barbie, Beth said, setting down her wine. Kind of romantic though, Would you make a bed for me? Jane lifted her arm and let Beth snuggle under.

Jane was about to say, Sweetheart, I'll make you a four-poster built with lurve, but then recalled she'd said the very same words to Carla. Many things were like this now: repetitions with different faces, jokes retold. People became stories you used to amuse or seduce others. The energy spent. The law of diminishing returns. She could almost grasp now why Carla's face had often seemed so haunted.

But then the warmth of Beth's lips on her neck, tracing a whispered line to her ear; the tingling glow; the spreading ache; the forgetting that is touch. Bed, she said.

She searched with her fingers for flaws and just by the top edge there was a roughness. She put on her mask and picked up the sander, revving it, then feeling its bite and hunger as it took. She pulled back, just there, like you have to, before it digs in and leaves its mark. It must serve you. Respect the power in your hands.

The four sides were complete. With the help of the mallet, the dovetails joined, as if falling into some secret alignment behind all things. Nine weeks, every night after work, little by little, till it had become all-consuming. The many return trips to Homebase, the mistakes made, the online videos watched, the purchase of the essential tools, the practice cuts, the trying again, for there was nothing else for it.

She stood back and stared again at the frame. There was this moment with the empty square sitting vertically against the wall, when she feared the instant it would be laid down, when the plan would have to face the reality of inherited floorboards and bevels, bends and miscalculations.

The cross-slats were prepared, three inches wide and half an inch thick, not less, because they could snap under human weight, not more because they had to be supple and bend and give and accommodate.

She checked the printout instructions again and saw that her work was good. He saw his work and saw it was good, she heard herself saying, and it was from the Bible and that made her laugh. She took off her mask and turned the sander off at the wall. The trigger was sensitive, you could set if off by nudging it with your foot, it could wrap around your leg and take off your skin. This had almost happened last week.

All was nearly ready. The frame was heavy, built to last, it would have to be given three coats of varnish as per instructions with sanding between coats and measured drying times, but all that could wait, it needed its test, to see if it sat right.

A double bed, even though there was no longer any need. She couldn't face the possibility of broken bits in bin bags.

She took a breath and laid it down. It sat right, almost, apart from the bottom left leg but then she had an idea. She went into her back pocket, took out a Homebase receipt, folded it a few times then stuck it under the leg. It sat just right. Then she got the slats, and there was a moment when she feared she'd got the measurements wrong, but they sat snug; one just needed a bit of weight to make it sit just right.

She stood there, woodchips and tools all around and silently stared. Some moment needed to be acknowledged, celebrated, a bottle opened maybe, something had to be said. The wood would not talk to her. She could maybe call Jane. No.

There was no point putting the single mattress on top. A solitary single on a king-size would look ridiculous. And she didn't want to cover it, wanted to keep staring at the wood that she had cut, measured, sanded.

She sat on the edge and it took her weight, creaking slightly in its joints. She ran her hand along the wood, and it was warm and strong and soft. She tested the cross slats with her weight and they did not snap or creak or shift. She went down on her elbow and moved her pelvis onto the slats, pulling up her feet. It was wide, as wide as she could reach. She pulled herself along the slats and into the centre holding onto the edges. The slats dug slightly but not painfully into her back. She thought of vertebrae, the ribs of the wooden frame.

She closed her eyes and felt it beneath her, supporting her, taking her weight.

A bed, she whispered in wonder at the sound of the word. As if it was the first time she had heard or said it. I have made a bed.

Incident in a Mall # 33

The Daily Terrorist

She comes every day at nine-thirty and leaves at eleven. She comes again at seven p.m. and leaves at eight-thirty, just before the doors close. She never shops, or slows her stride – she walks. She starts at the south entrance by M&S and walks past H&M and Starbucks, towards the north wing. She walks with focused intensity and does not stop to talk to anyone or gaze in windows; sometimes she has to dodge those that do and they stare at her. Some of their faces register alarm, though there have been no official complaints. She reaches the utmost north tip by Debenhams, and follows the wall as it bends round past Accessorize, then heads back south again, past Gap to reach her entry point, then she starts again. In her three daily hours of walking, she circles the entire mall maybe fifty times. Then she leaves, with no purchase, not even a coffee.

It is not only her presence that has troubled the security staff, it is her appearance: she looks like women they've only seen in the news, from Iraq, from Palestine – those things they wear over their head.

Security have had many discussions about her. Perhaps she was casing the place, some said. There had been suicide bombings in malls in Germany and Turkey at the time. Sally, whose brother had lost two of his mates to a car bomb in Baghdad, said that with that Burka the woman could only have one thing in mind. Sadiq, a Muslim, if somewhat lapsed, from Pakistan, took objection to such wild speculations and clarified that it was not a Burka, but a 'Hijab' or head scarf – the head and body must be entirely covered, as is the way, but the face is permitted to be exposed.

It was decided to place the woman under surveillance and to, at the first opportunity, confront her and lead her into the back for questioning. Every day for weeks, her actions were recorded on CCTV. She always entered at the same door and always did fifty rounds of the mall. On one occasion, she stopped to buy some water from WHSmith, but that was all. You could set your watch by her time of departure.

As the months went by, the suspicion grew. The mall had recently been put on alert because a notorious local family who made a living as professional shoplifters had, on one of their last operations, taken to wearing Burkas, exploiting the ample room within the garment for concealing stolen goods and also exploiting the security staff's fear of confronting women of the Islamic faith. There had been one hilarious arrest in a competing mall, when the 'woman' in question was apprehended with three designer suits, and many blouses stashed under a Burka. After a struggle to remove it, the thief had been revealed as none other than the Godfather of the infamous crime family. There had also been news stories about a bank robbery, down south, with sawn-off shotguns concealed under Burkas. The image created fear. Sally said France was quite right, making the veil illegal. We should stop any more of them coming into our country.

It was noted with nervous laughter, by another member of staff, Tony, that beneath the robes of the 'terrorist' he'd glimpsed a pair of trainers, a bit worn down at the heel. Air Jordans.

On the day that the terrorist threat level had been raised – due to a failed bombing attempt at a local airport – it was decided at the morning staff meeting that someone should intercept the woman. Sally forcefully volunteered but Sadiq proposed himself to try to de-escalate the situation.

The event was of such interest that even the Operations Manager joined the staff at the chosen time to watch from a good viewpoint at a safe distance (near the staff elevator). The place of interception was chosen as Debenhams, before the woman turned for her second lap. This spot was far enough away from the doors for an escape to be difficult if she tried to make a run for it. All of these details had been worked out with military precision. They staff were on edge, joking with Sadiq to try to hide their mounting anxiety. Sadiq checked the time, took a deep breath and headed off to engage.

The staff watched as the woman made it to the spot and Sadiq strode up to her and raised a hand to stop. Many other hand signs were exchanged and it seemed Sadiq was drawing symbols in the air, which might have been religious; then he stroked his beard and nodded, and shook his head. Sally said they should get the police on standby. But then the woman started nodding her head or maybe even bowing to Sadiq. Sadiq, then, unexpectedly, pointed out the crowd of staff to the woman. The crowd immediately separated and pretended to be busy, while each, individually sneaked peeks at the action. To their surprise, the woman did not leave the building but returned to her walking.

The crowd re-amassed as they waited for Sadiq's return; he was taking his time, smiling to himself, it seemed,

What? Tell us? Said Sally.

He looked at all the expectant faces and broke into laughter. Tell us?

OK, Sadiq said, she has seen this on telly.

What? C'mon don't take the piss. Tell us.

Old ladies do this in Nebraska, he said, old men too.

What, for fuck's sake, tell us, Sadiq.

She is from Syria, and is a family woman, her children go to the local school, her English is not so good.

Aye, and c'mon.

She drops them off at school then she comes here. She feeds them their supper then she comes here. The father puts them to bed. He is Lebanese, owns a very good store in town.

So, so?

She likes to be fit of mind and body, as is the way. She lives in the scheme and does not like to walk in the streets because they shout and throw things. She comes here because she thinks it safe, and likes the temperature.

But why, for fuck sake?

It is called mall-walking, it is very popular in California, she has seen it on Oprah, it is a kind of keep-fit.

And the staff laughed and laughed but then the woman walked past them, her eyes to the ground, her Nikes kicking up the back of her robe, and so the staff dispersed, somewhat shamed of face.

But what was to be done? At the staff meeting the next morning they had one of their most heated debates. Sadiq proposed that if it made customers uncomfortable then he must ask the mall-walker to do this elsewhere. But then Sally interjected – For fuck's sake, no, if she lives in the scheme then I know what she means, those bastards'll throw shite at you even if you're no wearing a fucking Burka.

A Hijab, more than one of the staff corrected.

Aye, whatever, fine, I say let her stay.

And so they did and they did not interrupt her routine again. And Sally even had to resist the impulse, on a few occasions, to go up to the woman for a chat. And Sally came to say, several times, that she thought the big black dress and the scarf were not such a bad idea – I mean look at the young lassies these days, c'mon, dressed like bloody tarts! Maybe I'll start walking round here myself, she said, Cos I could do with losing a bit off my thighs… and I mean, it's cheaper than a gym, right?

And the woman, whose name Sadiq never asked, because it is not the way, walks still, for three hours, every day, apart from times of religious festivals particular to her faith, in which she is absent, and on those days the staff miss her like one would miss an hour from the clock.

Sign from a shopping centre in Iran, promoting the wearing of the Hijab.

'Don't Get Malled'

Prof. James Anderson (65) has yet to go down in world history, perhaps because what he did was to stop something from happening rather than creating something new, and this is rarely seen as progress. Nonetheless, in 1977 in the town of X, Jim and a group of only twenty local activists were the first people in history to take a leading American mall-developer to high court and win their case. As a result, the proposed 500,000 sq ft regional mall in the Michigan region was never built. (For legal reasons the name of the corporation, hereafter referred to as The Corporation, cannot be included in this account, as dictated by Prof. Anderson and recounted here by the author).

Back in the 70s, Jim was an untenured lecturer in American History, in X – a fairly prosperous town with a large student population. Jim had a history as a civil rights activist and had once received death threats as a result of his vocal opposition to compulsory military service during the Vietnam war, but he was by no means a Red or a hippy. He was, and still is, a practicing Quaker, a responsible family man and a scholar. Jim's concern over the proposed mall was initially somewhat abstract, perhaps even academic. Over the years, he had developed a concern over how the US had thrown away its railway network infrastructure in favour of poorly-planned road networks, and he was alarmed at the ease with which urban planning had been handed over to real estate developers. The year before the action, Jim had 'cut his teeth' with the bureaucracy and lingo of city planning in contesting the widening of a small local road, and although he had failed to stop the development he had learned a lot about 'zoning'.

In the Spring of '77, the local council Planning Commission granted The Corporation permission to go ahead with the construction of their regional mall on land which had previously been zoned for the construction of a research park. Jim claims the proposal was met with a 'hallelujah chorus' among the council, with the promise of vastly increased local tax revenue. Jim saw the flip-side and so intervened at the monthly planning meeting, using his right under state law, as a concerned citizen, to request that a full environmental impact study be commissioned before the deal was signed.

This was where, Jim claims, the intrigues started. The Planning Commission refused to do an environmental study and passed the proposal with their recommendations to the local council, who voted four-to-one to accept the mall. Everyone thought this was the end of the story, apart from Jim.

Jim was no stranger to hard study, so he dug into the laws of local government. He realised that since there was a local election coming in the fall of '78, he had the opportunity to put the issue on the ballot for the city-wide election, for the populace to vote on. The legal grounds were that the mall permission was in violation of the city master plan, which had been laid out a decade before. Jim started a petition drive. He needed 5,500 signatures and 108 days clear of the elections to get the issue on the ballot. With a group of only twenty people calling themselves *Citizens for a Liveable Community,* Jim set about doing fundraisers and getting the signatures. It's like Jesus said, Jim states, Give me twelve good people, we don't need a cast of thousands. The 5,500 signatures had to be verified, and this was tricky because of the large transitory student population, so they aimed for 7,000 to be on the safe side. With 6,000 verified signatures the mall issue was requested to be put on the ballot.

The city council and The Corporation were thoroughly upset and baffled. The Corporation took the proposed ballot to court, trying to place an injunction against the election. The claim they made was that 'zoning issues are not subject to a vote of the people'. Such a contentious and apparently undemocratic claim only inflamed the activists and locals.

At this point Jim and his team felt legally confident and went out of town to consult other city and town planners and to hire a nationally renowned attorney to help in training them on presenting their own legal briefs. Jim put a large proportion of his savings and salary into the case.

In turn, The Corporation hired one of the biggest lawyers in the US – a man who would go on to serve on the sixth circuit court of appeals: one step below the supreme court. However, while the preparations for the court hearing were underway, The Corporation found themselves in stalemate; unable to proceed with the construction, and caught up in growing controversy.

Jim quotes American basketball hero Magic Johnson in describing the spirit of their work for the court case – 'If you're gonna go, go all out. Leave it all on the court.' Jim gave everything he had, and to the surprise of locals and the media, the judge ruled in favour of the citizens: The mall proposal would be on the ballot papers at the next election. The judge, a conservative, also declared that in his twenty-five years on the bench, the case had been the best presented that he had presided over. Mall construction was blocked until after the election in the fall of 1978. The Corporation then decided to take the decision to the court of appeals – another slow process which also may have caused the public to turn against them, but their lawyer advised that they sit it out. They also decided to put pressure on the local community by claiming that they might move the mall to a neighbouring town, thus depriving town X of retail and revenue.

While locals became increasingly divided, Jim played what might have been his ace card. He started early on the election campaign and did more research on The Corporation, discovering that they had opened a mall on the outskirts of a town in North Dakota. Jim, hired a local photographer, very cheaply, to walk around the town, photographing the impact the mall had had on the centre. It was only when he saw the pictures that he knew he'd struck gold; the photographs showed abandoned stores and deserted streets. With these shocking images he then started a print campaign. 'What malls do to your town'. His slogan was 'DON'T GET MALLED'.

In face of the fierce and growing opposition, The Corporation's lawyer then advised that they negotiate. They would agree to an election on one condition: That the YES vote be worded for the Mall, and the NO – against it. This might seem like a shrewd idea: historically, in the US, there is a stigma against voting negatively and psychologists have proven that people prefer to vote for a YES. However, Jim and his team felt their case was strong enough to survive, regardless of the wording, and drove a fierce NO campaign. In turn, perhaps because of their witty, catchy, almost advertising-style slogan, *Don't Get Malled* became a national news story.

The populace of town X in the fall election of November 1978 voted, by a 15,000 vote margin, against the mall, and it was never built.

As for town X, it was another fifteen years before any mall

was built on its soil. The one now located there is considerably smaller than The Corporation's proposal and at a different location; its anchor is a Myers store, and all-in-all it's fairly modest. Nonetheless, the downtown of town X has struggled over the years to fight for custom with the suburban mall.

As for The Corporation, their ambitions to be mall developers were given a setback and they focused more on retail and less on construction in the years that followed.

These days few people know of Jim's actions in the 70s, and he rarely tells this tale. He is now a senior lecturer in American History and has kept on working past retirement age because he loves his subject, his country and the energy of young people. He has also become a grandfather and his son continues his community-based political work through the medium of photography, citing his father as an inspiration, documenting the rebuilding of New Orleans in the aftermath of Hurricane Katrina. Jim describes his relations with the people from either side of the mall campaign as 'neighbourly', although he reports that now and again he still gets 'dirty looks' from affluent old ladies who would have just loved to have had a shopping mall on their doorstep.

BORDERS

It is 1989, Harry is eighteen, and something momentous is occurring. Not the fall of the Berlin wall, although he does watch it on telly with his flatmates, but the opening of Princes Gate in the town centre. The papers say proudly that it is – *the largest glass-walled retail structure in Europe – built to last three hundred years*. Margaret Thatcher, it is said, is performing the opening ceremony, and she'd been in power since Harry was eight, so he turns up with his mates to catch a glimpse and maybe laugh at her ugly face. Harry can't see her from where he's sitting; protestors are obscuring his view with their fists and banners and slogans: CAPITALIST SCUM. HOMES FOR THE POOR NOT SHOPS FOR THE RICH. Harry isn't into politics or shopping; he's just sitting on the railing with his mates, the taste of hash on his breath, listening to a tape on his new Walkman, watching the protestors throwing eggs and the police arresting them. It's amusing for a bit, a laugh. This is the first time that he sees her; the flash of her dyed-red hair as she is thrown into a police van. He finds it kind of crazy, demonstrating against a building that was already there and the size of an Olympic stadium, but her screams seem to sync up with the music in his ears and that is cool and ironic.

Back home Harry sits in his window, lights a Marlboro and tries to write a poem about the girl, in the style of Ginsberg: *Glass-light, scream-fight, red-head, red or dead* – it has a rhythm and could be a song. He could join a band, Tony played bass. One day the world would listen to what he felt inside, when he worked out what it was. Everyone is now free in the newly freed market. One day, he might do the States, drive Route 66. The first George Bush has just been elected and Harry is teaching himself how to do the three main chords behind all the great rock and punk classics. Stairway to Heaven is kind of naff, but he's sure he'll get there eventually. He pauses between chords to try to blow smoke rings, his mates all did smoke rings and chicks think they're retro and hip. He fails at the smoke rings and the chords and laughs at himself.

The communist ceilidh must be the second time he sees the girl. It is maybe nine months later and Harry has grown his hair long and dyed it red; he's into grunge and Bukowski; he's getting through an eighth of hash a week and is rarely attending lectures at uni. He's with Tommy and some other mates in an old man's pub off Grand Street and they're arguing as they've spent all their money on ecstasy and don't have the price of admission to a nightclub. An old woman, hippy-looking, grey haired, hands them a flyer: FINAL FLING – CPBG. It doesn't register at this point that the CPBG is the Communist Party of Great Britain; that in the last two months the Soviet Union has collapsed; that hundreds of thousands of former soviets are running into the open arms of the West. He notices only that the flyer says *Free Admission* and *Band* and *Whisky shots – 50p*.

The place is down a dark alley, across from a 70s multi-storey car park. The room is large and almost empty, the walls nicotine-stained with plastic hospital-like seats, fluorescent lights and lino. The members of the former Communist Party of Great Britain are only ten in number and all of retirement age. An old crooked man is on stage playing highland dance music on an accordion. There's a table of white bread sandwiches, with the crusts cut off; another with old books and pamphlets; there's no bar, just an old fat guy with a 40 oz whisky bottle, filling plastic cups, a look of surprise in his eyes at seeing new faces.

See man, Harry yells to Tommy, it's time-warp, it's *The Twilight Zone* and he hums the tune. Some old guy is trying to explain why the CPGB are disbanding but he and the lads are too stoned and joking about *Terminator*, putting on Schwarzenegger voices. *Ze world vill end in ze year 2011.* Harry is good at voices.

Harry buys his 50p shot and throws it back, buys another two as it's only a pound. Some ancient old dame asks if he and his mates would like a dance. It's daft and weird so he says, Sure, what the hell.

They are put in formation by the old crow as the man at the mic announces a Dashing White Sergeant. The guys are in hysterics as the old folk line up and the dame shouts instructions: Clockwise, three beats, forward then backwards then a turn. The old Stalinist is leading them round by the arm, trying to teach them, but they're falling about laughing. It's another tune then, Strip the Willow and the old folks are clapping and stamping their feet, happy to have the young lads spinning in their arms. Maybe it's the tabs kicking in or the twirling and birling, but Harry is so high he could fly. Tommy is beside him then grinning, ranting. Wow, it's like fucking *Twin Peaks*, man.

A moment then, Harry glimpses an old couple, in a dark corner, holding hands; the man shaking his bald head, staring at the floor, the old wife stroking his brow. It's like some movie he hasn't seen before. The old man is crying. He thinks maybe someone has died, then realises, it was maybe the Communist thing. It wasn't right being there, like laughing at a funeral.

C'mon, he says to Tommy, fuck this for a laugh.

They Strip the Willow through puddles heading for the subway, and this is when he sees her again. Her red hair is now blue and she stands alone in the underpass clutching newspapers as clubbers stream past through the rain. Her voice piercing the dense dark, calling out again, again, 'This week's Workers News'. He stands staring at her, transfixed as his mates dance on. Her stoic stance, her cheekbones skull-like under the fluorescent light, the perfect proportions of Faye Dunaway; the speeding taxis like a soundtrack rising around her. He could speak to her, but does nothing. He lets his mates drag him away.

It is six months later when he stumbles across her again in a small struggling independent bookshop, called Smith and Sons, five blocks from the new mall. She is behind the counter in the Sociology and Self Help section. Her hair is bleached white. She looks punkish or lesbian, Doc Martins and dungarees. He likes a challenge. He has confidence now in chatting-up girls after having bedded seven or so and he has a girlfriend, Jane, who he's splitting up with. He looks around for an opening line and sees a petition on her counter, saying SAVE THE BOOKSHOP.

Hey, he says, is this like a Save the Whale kind of thing?

She does not laugh and explains that Smith and Sons has been here a hundred years and has important collections of work by local authors and scholars not found elsewhere, that it is going to be bought over by a national chain store, Ottakar's. If he isn't going to buy anything he should at least sign the petition – right there on the counter. There's this way she has of sweeping the hair from her eyes, like she's annoyed with her own body. Harry thinks this cool. She says many things he cannot grasp, like how the *Net Book Agreement* has just come in; how all the independents will go bust when the supermarkets are flooded with cheap paperbacks.

That's progress, huh? Books are way too expensive anyway.

Are you joking? She asks.

I suppose.

Fine, enjoy your *shopping.* Her tone at that word, so full of venom.

He fumbles and mumbles and says lots of sorries and laughs nervously and signs her petition but what he wants is to see her again so he says he'll come to the meeting.

She writes down her number with a pencil on the back of a till receipt. It is her landline, the number for the place where she lives. Her name is Zoe. Zoe Spence.

They meet in a small rented Boy Scout hall each Friday. Harry finds it boring when the old folk debate local politics. They say that since Princes Gate opened, Jensen's, the old department store has gone bust. And how many bakeries, butchers, clothes and book shops have closed down. It is only when Zoe shouts that they must think bigger, globally, that Harry wakes. He loves it when she rants about CIA coups and assassinations: Guatemala, Chile, Peru. She has been loaning him her Chomsky and Debord, her Althusser and Marcuse. He's got through seven books with her help and sometimes she comes round to his to debate details; she sits on his floor, cross-legged with her boots kicked off and underlines sentences for him.

We accept the myth of the self-made man, but cannot grasp that the opportunities for the individual are determined by forces we cannot see. We live in an invisible prison.

As she rants, he finds himself just staring at her face. Love, she says, is a patriarchal construct. Women aren't property. She thinks relationships are a bourgeois distraction. He has never met any of her friends.

They walk the new mall together pretending to be shoppers.

She is always two steps ahead, decoding, teaching him how to see.

She despises the new Ottakar's but leads him inside. She curses the women's magazines, the slim smiling made-up faces, the top tips for a better you. *The planned obsolescence of the female body,* she calls it. Pornography, she says, at least exposes the true power dynamic. Her own outfit is three years out of date: flat soled shoes, baggy jeans and jacket; all unflattering. He has a theory that Zoe's commitment to the cause is an inverted hatred of her own natural beauty – her DNA is that of a winner. She must hide her form, her legs, her slender neck from even herself. In the store she pulls over a rack of magazines with pictures of pouting lips and breasts and they scatter the floor. And so they run.

Outside, by the bins, he tells her she is amazing, but she is silent and he feels a fool for trying to flatter.

Another day at the mall. Look at them, she spits as they walk past Gap. Children in military fatigues. She is convinced that Gap are in league with the war mongers. The clothing companies and TV channels and CD manufacturers are owned by conglomerates that have shares in weapons manufacture. Wake up! She shouts, but the masses do not wake from their slumbers. She whispers to him: They walk like sleepwalkers, in manufactured dreams. Millions, sleeping.

There is a new lingerie store and Zoe targets it. Sex is taking over, she says, We use the petty conquests of seduction to make up for our political impotence – fucking is our only permitted illusion of power. In every passing female form, in the season's ever more revealing fashions, he sees the truth of her words, but still he wants only to touch her.

They walk the aisles of lingerie and she takes gum from her mouth and sticks it inside a brassiere; she tears off a shoulder strap; she knocks panties to the ground and dirties them with her boots; she drags a permanent marker over a row of twenty chemises, destroying the pink silks.

Again they run for cover and hide by the bins. He tells her this is the most radical thing ever, being her comrade. No, she says, we've done nothing, we are worse than nothing. Still, at least she he has said 'we'.

The protest group in the Boy Scout hut disbands, there is no mass rising, no riot or insurrection. A pile of her radical papers lie, for weeks, where she left them on the floor of his bedsit. She grows frustrated with reading. Knowing is not enough, she shouts. Critique without action is impotent. Months pass and still they have not touched. Always they walk the mall, like she is drawn there in some negative mirroring of the shoppers. In The Body Shop, she sneers at the better-world fair-trade stickers. How can they all fall for the lie, she whispers, do they really think they're making the world a better place with Holistic Facial Scrub. It makes her sick, so sick she could kill herself.

On that day she does not want to drop coins in the escalator, or seem to believe, as she did before, that if many were to do this, every day, all the escalators in the world would grind a halt. The week before, he'd made a joke about it. Small, change, he'd said, dropping his tuppence, big change starts with small change – geddit? She did not laugh and does not now; she keeps her hands in her pockets as they ascend and descend.

It happens outside Toys R Us, she has just shaken his hand by way of a comrade's goodbye but he holds on and she does not pull away. She tells him of the protests she plans to go to: against McDonald's, Proctor and Gamble, GAP, Unilever, Nike, the IMF;

she will hitchhike to Birmingham, London, Paris. We have to move to direct action, she says. He can resist no longer. He closes his eyes and offers her the only radical act he can imagine. She accepts his lips and pulls him closer.

The day after they have sex she buys him a cigarette lighter. It has a communist insignia on it, it's authentic, from the fall of the wall. A week later she shouts at him.

I can't believe you light your capitalist fags with that lighter!

Hey, welcome to Marlboro country, comrade. He jokes, making the peace sign.

Whose side are you on Harry?

I'm a Libran, he says, making the sign of the scales with his hands, then cupping her breasts, You gotta weigh all the possibilities!

She laughs then hits him. He senses she is tormented by his goofing over serious matters, his adoption of contrary positions for a cheap joke, his inability to make choices, good/bad, left /right, his fence-sitting, procrastination, lack of integrity.

Why can't I just despise you? She groans.

De spies, he says, shh, don't move, he puts his hand to her mouth. De spies are everywhere!

She laughs and that laugh of hers, he thinks, is something she seems to hate about herself, as if it were a sign of weakness.

Her head is not clear anymore, she sounds like her mother, she says and she fucking hates that and then they're always sleeping late and then she forgets even what year it is. It must be 1990 because they argue about the internet, she thinks it a distraction, that it will amount to nothing. They stink, she says, they wear each other's clothes and stink of patchouli and sex and sweat and fried eggs and they must buy washing powder, not biological but ecological, but they can't afford it. Harry has given up his studies to be closer to her. A stupid bloody idea, Zoe says, because of her situation at work.

In the hours when Zoe is not at the bookshop she is out on the streets with her petition and Harry is beside her. She does mail-outs and the petition is signed by many of the leading authors in the country. In an independent paper she has an article published damning the takeover by Ottakar's. It passes, however, without complications, and most of the staff are told they must re-apply for jobs with the new owner. Most apart from Zoe. There is a Fire Sale, Zoe weeps, when she tells them that they sold everything, even the tables.

In sleep she claws his back, she whispers in the dark, tells him over and over that this is now, that we are we, but what are we to do? We must do something. They fight daily, they make love, she cries and tries to leave him then wakes in his arms, and always it is the need, clawing, the silences after, the shared breath, slowing together.

Then it is the burst condom and the skipped period. It's like it's his fault. How can she protest now? Who would bring a child into this world?

Hey, no worries, Harry tells her, I'll get a job. Hey, maybe even in Ottakar's.

You think that's funny? You're completely fucking amoral. What do you actually believe in, Harry?

The joke comes to him and he can't help himself, so he starts singing – Hari Krishna, Hari Krishna, Hari, Hari, Hari, Hari.

That's it, fuck it, fuck you.

You babe, I believe in you. C'mere.

He gets the job in Ottakar's in the mall, stacking shelves. She will not speak to him. She is making lists, charts of actions to take. *Smash the thing that smashes you.* He cooks for her, cares for her.

OK, so I'm the enemy and you're sleeping with him, he says, C'mon, even revolutionaries have to eat. Here, I made a yuppie salad, seriously, with avocado – you gonna eat it or critique it?

At work, one of the bestsellers is called *The End of History and the Last Man,* she has to read it so asks him to steal it for her. Nights, she sleeps in the kitchen, on the floor, so she can keep studying, and in the days she is a silent, wandering, sleepwalker without sleep. It makes her mad with rage, the author claims that capitalism is utopia achieved. She asks Harry to steal more, she wants to read Milton Friedman, all the right wing economists, she has to know. One morning he wakes to find her, still in her clothes at the kitchen table, book open before her, manic notes scrawled over the text.

She starts reading about the Baader-Meinhoff and revolutionary terrorism in the 70s. He sneaks a look at a page and finds that Baader's first revolutionary act was to firebomb a shopping centre. On another he reads that Meinhoff abandoned her two children to join the armed struggle and was murdered by the German state. Zoe is nearly two months pregnant and they have to make a choice.

Mornings, she retches in the sink and he hovers behind her, her bloodshot eyes shooting back. What? What?

We could actually… he finds himself saying, I make enough and there's child benefit. In some way he cannot grasp, some clench in his gut, he feels the child and cannot agree to a termination. Confrontation, however, never works with Zoe.

Think about it, we could be like white-trash, teenage moms, join the proletariat.

She is wearied by his every utterance.

He offers to go with her to the clinic; he thinks they might talk her out of it, but she insists on going alone. Back home she is in tears; they lectured her, made her fill in a questionnaire, they said she needed an AIDS test, they questioned her about her sexual history and drug use and took notes; there had been a dozen Barbie doll bitches there queuing up for abortions. Drugs and surgeons, she couldn't bear the thought; these cancerous American poisons.
She had walked out.

Babe, he says, It's great, we'll keep it... or maybe we could just wait a week and...

What do you want? She shouts, Make up your mind for once in your fucking life.

I want what *you want.*

He wakes in dark. She stands naked by the window, her face reflected, ghost in the glass, the sounds from night clubbers outside, chanting, drunken in the streets.

Zoe, come back to bed, it's cold, he whispers. She talks as if to herself. What I hate, she says, What I hate is not the secret wars or the toxins or the burned corpses of children in Nicaragua or the babies born without eyes in Indonesia, but the happy faces, here, right here in the mall – the people who wear Che Guevara T-shirts made in sweatshops, who give money to charity and do nothing. It's this, just this, exactly, here, the people, everyone.

He comes to her, skin on skin.

Even us?

There is the clutch, the need, the pulse through them both,

like blood.

I hate you, she whispers.

I hate you too, he says, For ever and ever, in sickness and health, till death do us part.

Explosions in blue and red light in the sky on his way home from work, it is bonfire night and he's bought her some discounted carnations from Tesco and stolen a book on parenting. Through the door he calls her name. The flat is empty. All she has left behind are some old pamphlets, a pair of laddered tights and a single red Doctor Martin Boot. He stands in her window and sees the fire beyond the fireworks, hears the sirens scream. He follows the many running, towards, not away from the fire. It is Jensen's, the old department store, and for eight blocks he runs. The flames bursting out through window frames. He forces himself closer, feels the scorch on his face as fire engines spend themselves and the streets run red with reflections. Police push him back, shouting, Not safe, gas, Go back! In the crowd the many voices talk of vandals, of an insurance job, of the shame and the waste. An old woman says she can remember the toy section from when she was child. Forgotten mannequins drip from exploding windows. Harry stares into the empty eye sockets of the smoking shell and takes it as a sign.

He tries to find Zoe through friends and friends of her friends; he reports her disappearance to the police but no one knows or cares. Seven months pass and he is sure she is alive, that she has kept the child. What street is she sleeping on in Paris, Brussels, Moscow, Seattle, the child to her breast?

There is a recurring dream at this time, images from the fire at Jensen's mix with news reports on the LA riots. The streets are on fire and thousands smash the windows and run, snatching video recorders, computers. He stands before the windows of a large technology store, a stack of TVs, twelve or more mounted one atop another, three by four. The footage is from his city, the fires, the petrol bombs, the looting. He cannot hear the reportage from CNN, but all around he feels the rage of the streets, people running behind him, screaming, chanting. A helicopter breaks the air and lights scan the streets, police megaphones, smoke, tear gas, but he does not turn, he focuses on the screens. As the first of the looters breaks out into the streets, the sight of them dragging their TVs ignites hysteria in the crowd that has come to watch; hundreds then engulf the doors of the mall overpowering the security staff. The TV cameras arrive before the police reinforcements and their footage is broadcast live around the world. The spark ignites in Paris, Chicago, LA, in Singapore, in Lodz and Birmingham. Blacks run the streets, hurl bricks through the windows of speeding SUVs; police in gasmasks spray teargas and water canon as hundreds swarm past overturned flaming cars to snatch goods.

Then he sees her, running wild with the others, a baby strapped to her back, as she throws a flaming thing. He forces his face to the glass to see better, but the view changes, it is from above now, a view of the mall, then it zooms in. It shows a man standing before a window of TV screens. He turns to try to locate the camera; the angle is from above. He looks up and in that split-second of delay from simultaneous live broadcast, he catches his own face on the screens.

Sometimes in the dream he smashes the window, other times he breaks into a run, to escape the camera in the sky. One time, he tries to carry home the TV, running through alleyways, his screen face cradled in his arms, watching it fade as the cord snaps and the power dies.

He stacks the shelves, and in his solitary way tells himself that Zoe was wrong, on many things. It is 1993, there is new corporate lingo to learn, team building exercises. *Thank you for shopping at Ottakar's.* He gets back into music again, all the bands are angry, trippy, psychedelic. There are drugs and clubs and distractions dancing before the eyes. Days he stands there at the till, after a night of no sleep, coming down or still high. They are selling the same books in the supermarkets for half the price, but he doesn't care. Madonna's sex book is a bestseller, they are selling black plastic bondage gear in Dorothy Perkins. Everywhere, every image is of sex. And Zoe was right.

He gets into the net, the cost of processing chips has come down to such a degree that he, like millions of others, can afford his first PC and printer. Dell and Hewlett Packard. Days at work and nights alone and he has to do something, and he always thought he could be creative, so he tries to write the story of Zoe.

He thinks it might make a good film and so he reads one of the new how-to- write-screenplay manuals. He applies to go back to uni, to study creative writing. Girls have come and gone, he is twenty-three and the job in Ottakar's is steady income and helps keep him sane. One night, he finishes a litre of cider and starts to print out the script about Zoe, but the printer cartridge he bought only last week is empty. Drunk, he calls the 24 hour helpline and the jingle is some kind of corporate hip-hop. The voice is a recording, the system is automated, he has ten touch pad choices and follows the maze. Finally – Jesus, thank fuck, there are people on this planet.

So sir, if you'd just like to give me your name and address. He does what he's told. If you'd like to hold sir. After ten minutes of on-loop jingles, the line goes dead. He redials and starts at the start again. To the next human he complains about what happened, he now has two complaints to make, can I please please please complain to someone, if that's not too much to ask? He follows the touch pad commands and gets put through to what he thinks is customer complaints, it has been forty-five minutes, paying premium rate. That same chirpy recorded voice he first heard when he started says, hello and welcome, this is an automated service, please listen to the following options. He puts his fist and feet to the PC and printer. The phone too finds itself on the floor among the wreckage, staring back at him, as if laughing.

It also happens with food. Ready-made meals snigger on supermarket shelves. And clothes; the heels were going out of his boots and so he had to go to TK Maxx in the mall to buy a new pair. Five hundred choices, seventy styles. A Russian couple behind him, smiling at a pair of trainers, and the rage, again.

Zoe's voice in whisper: *It is a greater sickness to be well-adjusted to a sick system.* Black is back. Forty-five new ways to be sexy. I lost ten pounds in thirty days. How to thrill your partner in bed. Change, change and nothing changes. IBM, Ciba-Geigy, Microsoft, CNN, destroy the thing that destroys you, Disney, Bechtel, PepsiCo, Tesco, SONY, Time Warner.

He studies in libraries, he steals every book he can, every radical critique, continuing her work in her absence. Everything is connected in the conspiracy and everyone is blind. He is in Tesco's. He needs milk, bread, cheese, he needs to learn how to eat again, but everything is full of the poison. He has a packet of prawns in his hand and sees industrial effluent pumped into rivers, dead fish floating in Indonesia. Exxon Mobil, Nestle, Unilever, Halliburton, Monsanto. Shoppers, standing in line smiling, and the song on the speakers is about being sexy. A child has a DVD of an American action movie with heroes with guns on the cover and he is going to grab the stupid mother and scream, Wake up, Wake up!

He's drunk on the third floor atrium, staring down at them all. He sees women dressed like pop stars; kids in Disney-branded clothes; Che Guevara T-shirts in lime and peach. A man with the Nike logo cut into his hair. He's clutching the atrium railings. Kill them all and start again, from day one. Or himself. Yes, to see their faces down there by Starbucks sprayed with his entrails.

Excuse me, sir. Can I help you? A security guard.

Me? Great, absolutely fine, fabbydoo. Just holding onto this railing like a ballerina, doing some leg-stretching exercises.

He lets the security man guide him down the escalators to the doors and twitters all the way: Thanks so much, really, I think you saved my life, good for you, it's a wonderful place, don't worry, I won't be back. On the way out he passes two girls in fluorescent fashion tights from the 80s. Fine, he tells himself, don't judge, they're just like me, manky little hypocritical survivors. *The future will be about forgetting, they will make us consume the same dreams again and again.* Fine, so be it. The air he breathes, he tells himself is OK – forgivable that it's synthetic oxygen, pumped with bread smells, with perfumes – this is the way it is, and look at the faces, they seem happy, happy enough, and who am I to judge? Perhaps a certain kind of person has to feel oppressed to feel virtuous. Zoe's apocalyptic desires are ego, not politics, she didn't want to make anything better but for everyone to feel her pain. Yes, that is it. People have never been happier, look at them. A mother in slut-pink and a baby in a pink buggy in pink clothes sucking on a pink dummy passes. It's going to be tough, he tells himself, every day it's going to be the same and anything will set him off, but he must stop judging and accept, accept, even if that means forgetting all he's learned. Yes, he will kill, not them or himself but Zoe. If he is to survive, he will have to kill the voice of Zoe.

Every day he walks past the vast new construction site to the north of the city centre. The scale is daunting, as large as two football stadiums; there are dozens of earth movers, diggers, razor wire and surveillance cameras around the perimeter wall. It makes no sense: how could a city centre sustain two competing malls? He walks the walls and notes that the graffiti now imitates that of black American gangs. He stands beneath a hoarding that announces the mall's name in bold bright font – *Northfields*. An architect's computer simulation shows the futuristic metal structure, walls of dark mirrors, images of people photo-montaged as if from other images, laughing as they carry shopping bags. Among the coming stores they advertise is Borders, an American company. Harry has read that in the last year, they have opened fifty stores in the UK.

Within six months of Northfields opening, Princes Gate goes into decline. There is graffiti on the doors and windows have been smashed. It would last three hundred years, they said, three hundred years.

Waterstones buy out Ottakar's and Harry is once again unemployed. After a six month wait to see a therapist on the NHS, Harry is given his first appointment. The doctor does not analyse him in any way but simply prescribes him antidepressants, which have just recently become widely available. He kills the thought of what Zoe would say, the image of millions sedated. He is started out on Prozac. The doctor explains that the side effects may temporarily include an increase in suicidal feelings and possibly an inability to achieve sexual climax. Great, Harry jokes, Finally a cure for premature ejaculation, awesome!

Harry experiences all of the sides effects but takes the pills and waits, staring at the walls, counting the time till the end of a working day, till sleep, no music in his room, his guitar long neglected. He tries to masturbate, and at first images of Zoe come to him, but the enthusiasm required seems impossible to muster.

He attempts to mix with alcohol just to see what happens. He takes an armful of Zoe's books and makes a bonfire out the back. As he places his hand in the flame the reaction is delayed, almost two seconds, like with the live broadcasts on the smart bombs in the middle east. He heads out to what will be the first of many nightclubs to test the limits of his medication. Zoe is fading, he is learning how to fuck and forget, to shop without panic; he gets his first credit card and buys his first pair of designer jeans.

He moves to London in '99 then back, then to Manchester in 2002, then back north. He works for Waterstones then Foyles, and takes odd jobs between in IT, data entry, secretarial work and call centres. He tries to teach himself the guitar five times and gives up smoking maybe nine times. There is Becky, the IT geek – she is on antidepressants too and they can't come. Charlie is married, she has a rottweiler. Debbie has three other guys he knows of. She's Manager of the Hard rock café franchise, incredible nipples but a bit of an alchie, and needy, sends him ten text messages a day. Internet dating – he finds it hard to recall a time that existed before it. And Carlotta, from Napoli, the trip when she says, Why you no love your city? Why you so sarcastico? And Wendy from California who finds him so funny, thinks he looks like Ewan McGregor. She makes him say everything twice so as to hear his 'sexy' accent.

Perhaps he is happy in this time, perhaps happiness, as they say, has no story to tell. There are times though when the déjà vu of one lover shines through the skin of the next, and he dreads the ghosting. As Joan says – when things get samey and cuddly the game's up, sunshine. Joan has many lovers in rotation, like the way they employ staff at Borders. Three hours stacking shelves, three hours front of house, three hours admin. Cyclical Rotation. And Cheryl the stalker, and the TEFL girl, Denise, and night classes in cookery, and the Open University in Business Management and Gloria and the abortion. Ella called him 'Amore'. Don't you think my thighs are too fat? She asked, every day.

And changing from Prozac to Sertraline to Detocoline back to Sertraline. And health pills and the morning-after pill, five times with different women; once he even hid it in a girl's salad. Sonya.

Every birthday he catches himself thinking – My kid would be seven now, or nine or twelve. The clawing in his gut diminishes, becomes abstract, disembodied. One day a call comes through telling him Tommy has died in a road accident, and it takes him a while to remember – Tommy.

So then there's reading sci-fi 'for pleasure' and a period of exercise and health food. The vegetarian diet, then the vegan, then no-carbs, then the Jamie Oliver cookery course and his first seared squid. And finally, almost mastering Stairway to Heaven, and how to tell a good wine. And Elise and Yvonne, and seeing U2 in the stadium with clingy Carol, and getting into Eminem and rave music five years too late and The Smiths – ten years. And he buys his first mobile phone, a Motorola, then changes to Nokia, then his first iPhone. And two gulf wars and two presidents Bush, but he studiously avoids all politics. And Denise is a hairdresser and likes The Spice Girls and keeps her heels on when they fuck. And this is change and change is good, everyone says. He joins a gym, then Facebook arrives and he has two hundred and twelve friends. He has a Ford then a VW then a Volvo. He gets a tattoo of a dragon to match Sharon's, then regrets it almost immediately. His mother has a mastectomy, then dies. Time is like this now, fragmented, episodic, the only thing that seems to have a future is work. He finally gets a foothold on the corporate ladder at Borders and decides to come off the antidepressants and get married.

He's thirty-four and Sarah is very unlike him, but he thinks this good. She has an extensive collection of Clarins facial creams, drives an SUV, has a bookshelf of self-help and do-better-in-business manuals; she works in PR for the company that manage Northfields; she likes him because he is arty and funny and she thinks herself too square; she listens to Mariah Carey and Whitney; her flat in the West End is worth two hundred and eighty thousand; she has a sister in New York who works for Goldman Sachs, and she has a facial and bikini wax once a month. It is the afternoon of September 11th when she calls him from work in tears, she has been trying to get through to her sister in Manhattan and the lines are down. At night, at hers, they watch the repeated footage of the impacts and the tiny black figures falling and she grips his hand. Goldmann Sachs were on the twenty-third floor. The phone rings then, and her sister is safe.

She weeps, My God, it could all just end, just like that. She asks him to please give up smoking. He asks her to marry him. He will no longer resist becoming a normal well-adapted person, or procrastinate, or see both sides anymore, or let situations decide for him, so that he can fatalistically blame them later. He will believe in marriage and the company and will make a new family to erase all trace of the past. At work, he fights for the post of buyer, and gets promotion.

The wedding is a traditional affair. Sarah wears white and insists he allow her to buy an Armani suit for him. She is surprised by how few of his friends and family are on the reception list. Throughout the procedures he tells himself that, finally, this will kill off Zoe. *Love is a patriarchal construct, no one owns anyone.* He finds himself weeping during the vows, for reasons he can never explain to Sarah.

In sickness and in health.

After the ceremony, they pose for photographs and everyone, it seems, has one of the new digital cameras. Flashes in their faces as they hold hands, as she smiles for the cameras and he looks at her. On some level, he knows he doesn't even love her, but that he can, through an effort of will, make himself, finally, get a life.

There are dinner parties and aspirations and he gets promotion to assistant manager. Northfields Mall has boomed and they are trying to conceive a child. She buys vaginal thermometers and how-to-make-baby-manuals, she buys relaxing Body Shop massage oils and has her monthly cycle written up on the kitchen calendar.

He comes across the book by accident at work: *Finding the Light,* by Zoe Grove. It is not her second name and there must be many Zoes. He flips the back cover open and there is the author photo. She is dressed in white, with white grey hair. It cannot be her.

But the eyes.

Zoe Grove was twenty-seven when a profound spiritual transformation virtually dissolved her old identity. She is now a counsellor and spiritual teacher, and author of The Power of Now *and* The Heart in Time. *She lives with her partner and son in Los Angeles.*

He could laugh out loud – what a sell-out, a hypocrite, two steps away from fucking Hari Krishna. But then the son. There is no further information on the web search he conducts in his locked office. Still, he cannot stop reading.

Every individual has the power to transform and rebuild their own world.

My God, Zoe.

His insomnia disturbs Sarah, she protests that he has become needy, always trying to make love to her in his sleep, he talks in whispers, paws at her. Each night as she struggles to sleep beside him, he reads and measures the changed contours of the face on the book cover. There are many references to children.

We must dig into the dark soil and hold and nurture it, like an innocent child at play; only then can we become one with others and join the light in the darkening world.

Days, months, and Sarah cannot get pregnant. She does tests and it is his fault. She says deep down he doesn't want the child. They fight more and more.

He is haunted by the Battle of Seattle on TV, anarchists and water-canons. He swears at the news. Fucking hippies, why can't they leave us alone?

It is the night of a dinner party with a couple Sarah knows from work: Tony is in PR and Debbie is Regional Manager for Starbucks, she is four months pregnant and talks of the baby's room, the birth with water tank and pelvic massage and how you can bring your own music to the birthing room. They've chosen U2 and Vivaldi. There are quiet words to Sarah about conception tips. Harry tries to keep busy in the newly-designed kitchen as they talk, muffled beyond the serving hatch. He is sure they're attempting to talk politics. My God, they have no idea. He buries it in the mixing of sauces, the cutting of coriander with the Sabatier knives Sarah bought for his thirty-fifth birthday; he follows the recipe from the River Café Cookbook, but can't help but hear.

This Tony thinks the world is in a terrible state, something has to change, he calls himself a Liberal-Socialist, he gives money to this child in Angola.

Debbie says they receive a photo in the post once a month, her name is Tolla, this beautiful girl, seven years old, such deep dark eyes and such a radiant smile.

And Sarah, says, How wonderful.

And Zoe will not let him alone. *Charity perpetuates a system of colonial oppression.* He stirs the sauces and throws back some cooking wine. *If there was no charity then the extent of our complicity in oppression would be revealed.*

Actually, the guy says, the work that Nike are doing in local schools, sponsoring children, not that he's for multinationals… Yes, it complex, he hears Sarah saying, But, good for you, let's see her again, and she must be looking at the photo of the child.

Harry pictures the consequences of what he is about to do and say in advance, but the force is too great to resist. He marches through, actually brandishing a wooden spoon. Wow, it's wonderful the 'good work' you're doing, he jeers, And y'know the best thing about charity is that it changes nothing, so you can keep on giving

311

and giving again, and it's, of course, tax deductible, as it is for Nike. Actually, he says, sweatshops are a fine thing and it's really wonderful that people in the Third World are getting the opportunity to earn two dollars a week and have access to so much excellent Western culture, and so many wonderful products. That, actually, Tony, is an idiot, that Socialism is a terrible and terrifying thing. Have you ever stopped to think what the logical outcome of your rather sentimental views are? To build the world anew you first have to destroy the old, that's Mao, by the way, and Mao was a genocidal maniac. In fact, he'd once been a revolutionary socialist himself, but saw the error of his ways, and nothing fucked him off more than squeaky-clean liberals who lacked the education to grasp that Neoconservatism was the only answer, and if they wanted to keep feeding their fat fucking SUV they'd better pray for a new invasion of Iraq.

Silence then. C'mon, for fuck sake, what's wrong with you people? I'm joking, have a sense of fucking humour.

In bed Sarah cries, her back to him, flinching at his touch. He offers to go back on the antidepressants, but still she is cold. So he starts his confession; he tells of Zoe and the child.

... and you did nothing? Who are you? Who the hell are you?

I'm fucking Elvis, I'm Jesus, he says, I'm anyone you want me to be. C'mon, I'm sorry, OK, OK? I've said sorry, what more do you want? Hand puppets? I can stand on my head.

Harry lets the divorce take its course, as if it were a force of nature. Time passes slowly in the following year. He is promoted to Regional Acquisitions Manager. He downloads pirated music, while online sites like Amazon start to eat into his company's profits.

Northfields, finally, after a decade, causes Princess Gate to close for 'refurbishment'. Harry dates Liz, a divorcee with two kids: Jason and Emma. Emma likes to play hide-and-seek behind the plastic animals in the park. Jason is suspicious of Harry and walks everywhere with his iPod, earphones in his ears while playing a portable Nintendo DS. Harry tells Liz he'd like to get to know her kids more, and proposes she move in to his bachelor bedsit. She stops returning his calls. Harry subscribes to another dating site and posts four new identities for himself, two are just for a laugh. One identity is a lesbian called Shazsquirts, another is a gay man called Superchunk. He gets hundreds of replies but soon tires of it. He takes up the guitar again with the help of YouTube, gives up smoking again and the US invades Pakistan.

It is the 21st of November 2009 and Harry has just received notice that Borders will be filing for bankruptcy. He has taken a day of sick leave and is on the Virgin high-speed train, seated in First Class, heading south. The country speeds past as if it were some old tape on auto-rewind, he reflects, then laughs at himself. He's no writer, he's maybe not had a creative thought in decade. He is on his way to see Zoe Grove, author and guru, reading at Borders, Piccadilly Circus, as part of her tour to promote her new book *A New World*. He plans to meet her face-to-face, to ask about the child.

He has to get out at Carlisle, during the five-minute stop, to have his first cigarette in five years. To calm the panic in his chest. He has kept her lighter all this time.

Over a hundred miles, he scans *A New World* for traces. But all signs of himself have been erased; her past is a web of fictions and jargon. *We must embrace the child within, if we are to give*

313

birth to a New World.

Manchester, Wolverhampton. How many times had he travelled this route? It had been British Rail once, now it was Virgin. Seventeen years, but there seems no logic to the fragments, no straight through-line. At Birmingham New Street he has palpitations and considers getting off and finding the first train back home. He forces himself to sit and endure. If he does not confront her this once, he will never know for sure.

How old would his son be now, if the son is his? A teenager. My God, how many of those years were about forgetting Zoe?

The neon ads of Piccadilly flash. Zoe's book launch is at seven-thirty but Harry's nerves undo him; he has to find a chemist to buy some valerian or something stronger. Then he's just wandering and needs a drink and another cigarette. By the time he gets to Borders, Zoe has already started her reading and the auditorium seems full; he doesn't want to draw attention by walking in, interrupting. He lights a fag outside, and watches her through the gap between the three-for-two window displays.

She sits in a long white dress of simple cotton, microphone at her mouth. She has a slow graciousness about her moves, a way of looking up at her fans with a quiet smile. She is full of face, her long flowing white hair; that same way of brushing the hair from her eyes.

How can he enter now? He should go. No. Breathe, be calm.

He cranes his neck and, through the window, in the front row he sees a teenage boy in retro hippy clothes, holding the hand of a girl the same age. They stand out from the others and Zoe smiles over at them.

His chest tightens; no more cigarettes.

There is applause and people are standing, and he must go

now, either inside or away. This same old swithering. *What do you believe in Harry, what do you want? I want what you want.*

He has to do something, really do something, just for once. He stashes his fags, takes a breath and steps inside.

The usual procedures are observed; from fifty feet away he watches Zoe being led to the signing table and the stack of books, the queue forming. He breathes, he waits, he looks for his son, but has lost him momentarily, then is thrown as another teenager appears in line, and maybe he has been wrong.

Hipsters and hippies everywhere; an old dreadlocked man with a struggling infant; girls in sandals; thirty in the queue before him. Zoe is calm before the adoring who reach to hold her hand and kiss her; she gets them to lean in close, perhaps asking them to spell their names then signing with a swift flow of the hand. The queue inches forward. He counts his breaths.

Hey, Harry, that you?

He turns and a guy in a Borders shirt is standing beside him. Northfields? Right?

Harry apologises, the guy was HR or PR, met him before, a real loudmouth. The guy talk and talks, Hey, what you heard about the bankruptcy shit? Folk are getting scared here, leaving the sinking ship, the rats!

Sorry, Harry says, I'm just here to get my book signed.

You're a blast, Harry. Hey, come and talk when this is done, in the back, we've got a couple of bottles.

The guy has set him on edge. There are twenty more fans ahead of him. Time ticking, inching forward.

What if he was to get to the signing desk and Zoe was to look up at him and her face go cold? Maybe she'll set down her pen and say, You should leave.

No, she will greet him and locate the boy in the room and she'll call out Evan or Jacob or... she will say come and meet your father.

Breathe.

Later they will walk together, all three, through the flashing advertisements of Piccadilly and then Zoe will tell him that his son is learning to play the guitar, and she will ask, did you finally learn Stairway to Heaven?

What if she doesn't recognise him? It would be better to go now. She has her faith. *The past is a sore which we pick again and again until we learn to let it heal.*

But now he's confused because the kid is getting his book signed and Zoe is clearly asking the kid to spell his name. So she aborted and this whole thing has been some idiotic fantasy. The teenager and his girlfriend are leaving. Now he wants to run but he's next in line after the big woman with many bangles who bends forward and kisses Zoe and tells her that her books saved her life.

And look, her hands, her neck, the way her hair falls over her face and she brushes it away. He has to be brave, just for once.

He inches forward, it is his turn now.

Hi, thanks for coming, she says and barely meets his eye, and her voice has an American twang. Would you like a dedication?

And he is dumb, mute and stupid.

Well, how about I just write your name? She says, she is maybe used to people freezing before her. Some kid at the back is crying.

Harry, he says.

Well, thanks for coming Harry, and her eyes are down and

she has seen a thousand like him. I hope you enjoy *A New World*, and already she's leaning to the side to smile at the next in line, as she starts to write.

It's Harry, with a Y, he says, the old joke, not with an 'i', not like Hari Krishna.

She looks confused, something trying to register. Just then the old dreadlocked man arrives carrying a crying kid, three or four years old.

Sorry to butt in, he says. Hey babe, Tomo wants to go, we heading soon?

Harry steps back and witnesses Zoe take the child in her arms, Oh baby, what's wrong? Momma won't be long. Harry edges backwards and turns to go.

Harry Mackay, the loudmouth shouts, Hey Harry, where you going? C'mon in the back!

Zoe stands. Harry?

Harry shrugs. Yup, suppose so, he says. And Zoe laughs, My God, Harry, how are you… you work here… in Borders?

The father butts in again, he whispers in her ear, she nods, puts on a polite smile to Harry, apologetic, as he tries to read what is being whispered through her face.

Well, she says, Harry, we have to go now, but we should absolutely stay in touch, definitely. It's so good to see you again. I can't believe it… I…

And he is silent and she is too, and she struggles to contain a smile, a smile something like the one she once struggled so hard to destroy.

Goddammit, she beams, Are you on Facebook? Here… She takes her pen and writes her Facebook ID and email on the page. Send me a friend request, OK? It'll be great to catch up… so amazing to see you again, really. She is so close, he could touch her, slap her, kiss her. He turns to walk away, but her hand is on his shoulder. Harry, no, wait! He stands there as she stares at him, shaking her head, I can't believe it, I really really can't. She leans forward and kisses his cheek. He tries in turn to kiss hers but she pulls away. As he nods and turns to go, she says something he does not quite catch, it might be Peace to you, or some such thing. It might have been Sorry.

It is the final day of the Fire Sale at Borders in Northfields. On YouTube, all around the country, employees have posted videos of themselves, dressed up in party hats and superhero costumes; one of the counter staff in Birmingham performed a funeral service for a stack of bestsellers then handed them out for free. They have turned it all into a joke, they are young, after all, and have no allegiances. They will move on and start again.

He walks into work to say goodbye and good luck to all of his colleagues and friends, but most have already gone and the junior staff in their zombie masks and red wigs do not want to share their laughter with him as he is a manager and culpable.

He walks the floors and there are random stickers on everything: £1, 20p, 10p; everywhere people are grabbing books and magazines; shelves stripped bare to the wall fasteners; lighting fixtures hanging empty from the ceiling; a fluorescent strip light lies smashed on the carpet, glass crushed to white powder. There is this one guy with a bin bag grabbing all the paperbacks he can; folk are fighting over the remaining celebrity biographies; all the display tables stacked to one side in the place where the bestsellers used to be with price tags on them – 'Table 50p'. Harry needs to be alone and climbs up to the abandoned top floor; he walks through the piles of packing boxes and forgotten classics to the access door for the offices.

He laughs to himself – There had been twenty bookshops in this city and now there were only three. And did he care? Twenty years and four different stores and never, not for one moment, had he said 'this is me', 'this is what I do', or even 'I love books'; it must have been years since he'd even read one. His job had been no different from selling widgets, jeans, trainers.

Last week he applied for a late shift baking bread in Tesco's, then in Asda in the fish section. Loaves and fishes. You had to laugh. Or there was work in telesales – opportunities, they said, looking for young energetic and ambitious individuals. They asked him to describe his top ten qualities. Sell yourself to us, they said. Point one: I have a sense of humour. He had to laugh. He'd long since given up on being anything – to be mediocre, that had been his goal: a mortgage, a family, some friends, a neighbourhood, a car; these things would have been outstanding, but oh no, they had to take that away too, had to make you fight tooth-and-nail for every last scrap. It was a twenty-year running gag, a bum deal, they'd sapped even the energy required to be angry.

He heads towards the office doors, intending to go out back to the fire-escape for his fag, like he used to, but when he tries his pass code it has been changed. He takes out his Marlboros and Zoe's lighter, it is nearly worn smooth now, another few years and the insignia would vanish. No one is around so he decides to light up there and then – this solitary copy of *Crime and Punishment* staring back at him. He inhales deeply and tries to blow a smoke ring and fails. Even that, for fuck sake. He'll go and sign on tomorrow, then throw the fags away, give up for good. How many times has he told himself the same damned thing? How many years spent just giving up? Tomorrow, he will, this time, for real. He'll go through the week of shivering and craving and not blame anyone or anything. Maybe three weeks it'll take to get the poison out of his system. That, small goal as it seems, will be something. That's what he'll do.

He stares down at a pile of memoirs, some reality TV star, who's faded already, who looks exactly like one or two others. Faces come and go and hemlines rise and fall. Punk and grunge and reggae and every movie you've ever seen, all repackaged. Everything returns so nothing dies, so nothing will ever be truly loved or mourned.

A life story, eh? What would his be? Shite, served him right for never making up his mind. But, seriously, how could you have a life when they kept shifting the goals? Work, relationships, everything, they'd broken it all down into such tiny pieces, it took a superhuman effort to try to forge it all into anything that lasted more than a few months. A lot of bloody effort for a pish in the wind.

He takes what he thinks will be his last puff, then feels foolish, as there's nowhere to stub out the butt. He looks around and decides on the edge of a shelf, but as he does it, the red ember falls onto cardboard packaging. He tries to stamp it out but there is smouldering, then a small flash as plastic wrapping takes light. By the time he's gone to find a fire extinguisher and discovered they've been removed, flames have started climbing the shelves.

Even as it grows Harry can't help but laugh. This comedy show, this Charlie Chaplin slapstick. Yup, the joke's finally on you, smarty-pants. It wasn't like he'd wanted it, or tried to achieve this ridiculous event. Maybe huge accidents were the fate of the useless.

He stands back and watches as the flames tear through the abandoned books, stands back and lets the flame do what it wants, laughing at its willfulness. Hell, maybe Borders would be happy, they could do an insurance job for fire damage. And he doesn't run, or try to put it out; others could do that, if they really had to. The alarms scream round him, people running in panic, he can hear them on the floors below. Smoke is in his lungs, and the sprinklers wet his face, but the flames fight on, and he thinks them quite beautiful and does not run. Maybe the mall will burn to the ground and they'll come and arrest him, maybe they'll lock him in jail, call him a terrorist. What a laugh, the old Zoe would have been proud of him. He would scream at them all, I did it, it is I, returned from retail. Lord of fire and revolution. There are millions of us, sleeping!

The flames reach their fingers for him, but he remains, feeling the test of heat on his face. And as the sirens wail and the voices scream, he does what he has always done – nothing. But this time, for once, he knows, it is really something.

A Brief History of the Mall
Part 8, 1990s onwards.

8. Dead Malls and Live-in Malls, 1990s to the Present Day

From 1994 onwards, retail in the US moves away from malls to retail parks and discount outlet centres such as Walmart and TK Maxx. This, along with a shift toward e-commerce (Amazon, eBay), further eats into declining mall revenues. The log-jam of market saturation in Western Europe and North America begins in 1995. All of the largest malls in the world are thereafter built in 'developing' and 'expanding' countries.

Eastern European and former Soviet countries rush to develop western-style economies, selling off local land to private developers, rapidly and on a vast scale. Wenceslas Square is eclipsed as Prague's main tourist destination by two new malls which attract more tourists than the historic centre; while GUM in Moscow – once turned into State offices by Stalin – becomes a high end shopping mall. From 2004, Bulgaria, Croatia, Romania and Belgium race each other towards the western-standard retail goal of 100 sq m of retail space per 1,000 people. In the second quarter of 2009 there is an 85% increase in investment in malls in Eastern and Central Europe, at a value of two billion Euros.

The first Asian mega malls, such as SM Mega Mall in the Philippines (2002), confirm a movement in global finances to the east. The South China Mall, Dongguan, (9.6 million sq ft) opens in 2005 and has 1,500 stores, boasting an 85 ft replica of the Arc de Triomphe, a replica of the bell tower of St Mark's Square in Venice, gondolas, bumper cars, and a 553 ft indoor-outdoor roller coaster known as Kua Yue Shi Kong or 'Moving Through Time and Space'. Although it is reported to be 'stillborn', 'deserted', 'the largest white elephant in the world', it demonstrates Chinese ambition, resilience and the power (and well-funded folly) of its newly unleashed capitalism.

The second largest mall, as of 2011, is the Golden Resources Shopping mall outside Beijing. The third is the SM Mall of Asia in the Philippines and the fourth is the Dubai Mall, in the United Arab Emirates (part of a much larger lifestyle centre featuring one of the world's largest aquariums – with 41,000 fish – a view of the Burj Khalifa, the world's tallest building; the 'SEGA Republic' indoor theme park, an Olympic size skating rink and a 5-star hotel). Other new malls in Malaysia have also eclipsed US malls in terms of scale and ambition, and future developments such as the mall in Doha, Qatar, scheduled for completion 2012, will become one of the biggest structures in the world – the size of 110 football pitches. Even East Timor, one of the world's poorest countries (after a twenty-four year war with Indonesia) is to have its first mall, the Timor Plaza, in 2013. While Fiji constructs its first water park 'Mega Mall: Fun World Centre' – a 10-acre themed water park with a 'real beach' – projecting an annual future income of $40 million. In 2010, US based investors JSM (who already own $1.5 billion worth of US shopping malls) announce plans to invest up to $600 million in malls in Cambodia and Vietnam.

In India, the rise in mall construction is astonishing: with only three malls in 2003, there are three hundred and twenty by 2010. From 2004 to '09, China builds 500 new malls while at this same time, according to the ICSC, only one new enclosed mall was built in the US (2006). In Canada only two malls have been built since 1992. From 2008 on, Western European cities such as Glasgow, Angers, Hamburg, Leeds and Bristol, place moratoriums which prohibit future suburban mall developments and all focus is shifted to 'urban regeneration' with city-centre malls attempting to reverse the drift away from the city to the suburbs. In 2010, 93% of all retail developments in the UK are in town centres. The great majority of these are either supermarkets or malls with supermarkets as anchors. In 2010/11, over three hundred community groups in the UK take action to block Tesco developments in their areas, as part of the 'Tescopoly' movement. A few, like the anti-Tesco protestors in Partick, Glasgow, achieve their goals and force the developers to look elsewhere. The recession of 2008-2011 hits American malls hard as 200,000 individual stores close with almost 50% loss in mall revenue across the board. The Dead Mall becomes not only a symbol, but a material indicator of the decline of the US dollar. It also vividly demonstrates the unsustainability of the consumerist project, built, as it is, on the belief in infinite economic expansion and on the idea that new 'needs' can be artificially manufactured and manipulated indefinitely, in a world with finite resources. The failure to satisfy essential human needs, in many developed countries, throughout the 'austerity measures' of 2009/2011, initiates a backlash against laissez-faire capitalism and malls and the multi-national brands they house become targets for demonstration, vandalism and looting (Ireland, Spain, Greece).

In the US, from 2005 onwards, dying malls are saved through redesign, conversion or through going 'hybrid' with outdoor promenades, street markets, park areas, and a 'back to the past' aesthetic. There is a desire on behalf of the consumer to reclaim malls as 'social areas', and malls in California are for the first time in history legally redesignated as 'public places' – which permit the right to congregate and to freedom of speech.

From 2006 on, several 'saved' US malls are rezoned for mixed usage such as 'housing'. In Europe, large superstores start to build housing as part of supermall development deals, as a way to appease local opposition and 'give something back to the community'. Tesco plans to build nearly 4,000 homes in the UK in 2012. The projects for the future are 'branded homes' and 'live-in malls'.

In the US, the Mall of Georgia is emblematic of the new hybrid 'living' mall. It has a redesign built around an open-air streetscape, with a community centre, a Greek-style amphitheatre and a local farmers' market. The glass ceilings are broken open, the car parks planted with grass, the linoleum floors paved. The architects claim that the concept behind the redesign is the Greek 'Agora'.

Incident in a Mall # 52

Chalkmarks

There are chalk marks on the grey walls; they stretch on and on, down through featureless passages cut off from natural light; scoring the many floors which mirror each other only in anonymity.

Here, behind the scenes, there are almost two kilometres of service corridors. They connect the rear entrances of every retail outlet via elevator and stair to the subterranean service entrance where the tons of daily goods arrive in vast trucks that appear mostly in the dark of night. None of the light or sound from the mall enters these corridors; it is like walking through an old black and white photograph. Walls, floor and roof are grey concrete, the neon lights illuminate sewage pipes and electrical wires, which give the corridors their only colour – save for the chalk marks, in shades of pastel peach and blue, weathering to white on the walls. These are not drawings: there are no scrawled images of faces or genitals, no words, dates, names or jokes. They are not graffiti as was first thought, but simple lines, stretching hundreds of yards; it took time till the reason for their existence was revealed.

Unlike the mall proper where the brand names are spot-lit and bright, here in the dark, the rear doors of the stores can be located only by tiny generic numbers that it might take a torch to read; there are no logos. For security reasons, the stores do not advertise their names; perhaps they do not trust the delivery men who service their competitors. The only way then to locate the rear door for Gap, or H&M, or Starbucks, is to follow the numbers till you find the one that corresponds, on some list, to their name.

You rarely meet another human in this place, and if you do, you would not stop and talk. Some hold their breath, most try to retrace their way to the exit as soon as they have deposited their crates and boxes of shirts, coffee, shoes, bras, party hats.

As the corridors have no windows or features, there is no way, unless you were to bring a compass, that you could orientate. The only thing for certain in the labyrinth is that the smell rises from the sub-basement. It lingers on the clothes of those sometimes met in the service elevators, whose job it is to deal with the twelve daily tons of waste and recycling. The smell has been compared to soured-milk, burnt meat, dust, fish, cat piss, house fire and candyfloss.

The mall designers must only have thought of the bright-lit stores and not of how they would be served, or maybe something must remain dark and secret about the stocking of storerooms. Many delivery workers get lost, and perhaps this happens because they drive to and serve many malls each week, and all are variations of the same grey edifice. Tales are told of voices heard screaming, of men kicking walls, of a Gap man, found asleep in a dead-end. There is no signal for mobile phones in the lower two floors. Some joke of what would happen if you had a heart attack; how long it would take for them to find you. The CCTV is sparse, one camera at each of the four corners, so the majority of corridor space is blind.

There is a story of two mall cleaners, who, for a joke, camped out, beneath a lower stairwell, building a home of packing boxes. They slept there for one night, then two; after four days they had still gone unnoticed and their joke turned cold.

Sounds can sometimes be heard from inside the locked

storerooms: one was of a child repeating the same word over and over, hour after hour – Mommy, Mommy, Mommy. Another was a drum beating. Toys in the storeroom of the Early Learning Centre sometimes fall from shelves and turn themselves on. Senior staff play pranks on juniors; they send them on pointless errands; they tell them that the place is haunted and creep up on them in the dark. They joke about this only outside at the service entrance, as they gulp in huge breaths of sunlight and cigarette smoke.

There is one floor, beneath the sub-basement, which is out-of-bounds; it is something to do with security and emergency, they say, but will say no more. Perhaps it is a lie concocted to scare. The empty floor beneath all floors, as long and wide as the whole mall above, but with no shop or sign or window, all dark, in dust.

Many fear getting lost and so the chalk marks are, it is said, the ingenious solution to this problem. Each line like a ball of twine in a maze. No one knows who first came up with the idea, or how it spread. Perhaps one person followed the first line and found it led to a delivery point, then went home and got his or her own chalk to, next time, mark the journey to their required door, so as to save time. Other lines then followed in different colours, some in staccato or dots to distinguish themselves from others. Many paths joining then separating to different destinations.

Some may have bought chalk for this purpose, others maybe used what was at hand. The yellow and pink could only have come from a children's blackboard. The blue chalk, perhaps, for a snooker cue or from a long-forgotten art box.

The miles of service corridors are now covered with so many chalk lines that they blend with one another, erasing their original purpose. Some say they look like cave paintings, but they are a strange art, devoid of images; mere lines that map the lives of those who drew them. The mall owners insisted that the lines be cleaned off, but the cleaners eventually gave up. The lines they were too numerous and wound their way round the entire structure. They were scored in too deeply.

The lines have already lasted twenty years and outlived the millions of advertising images that have flashed by in the brightly-lit mall beyond. The lines, no doubt, will remain etched on the walls till the mall itself reaches the end of its life.

And one day amidst the rubble of the ruins, in daylight and dust, someone might see those chalk lines and wonder who drew them, and what they were once supposed to mean.

YOU ARE HERE

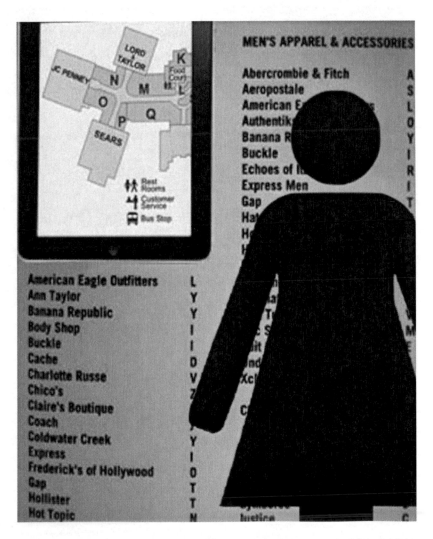

They are due to arrive at 2.45. You have whisked round the space, making sure there are no accidental remnants from the last viewers. Someone dropped a receipt one time and it looked like litter, and your supervisor saw it and you were reprimanded. You have taken the dead flowers from the vase by the window and put in the new ones, the same as the last, irises, as per instruction, and sprayed the rooms with lavender air freshener. You have straightened the paintings, which did not need straightening in the first place, which you do not like, which are so obviously photographic reproductions of what once might have been real paintings. Landscapes. Abstract.

You have told yourself not to be anxious but this only made things worse. You are paid on commission and are new to this. 'Real estate' is a strange phrase, nothing real about it at all. But you have to make your first sale. You have to put yourself in their place, they said. You have to feel and feed their excitement.

A new exclusive development in a former retail space.

But you do, you feel for them and it's hard for people to invest in a place that no one has lived in before. They want to see signs of habitation, of a past, to assess themselves against others, to see things they can improve upon or erase, they look for flaws, marks on walls, dampness. They knock the walls and the kick the skirting, they make plans. But all is new. The white, white walls and the untouched, unscuffed laminate flooring. Perfect is only a word, not threatening in itself. But still, you have only ever lived in places that had traces. People are imperfect, perhaps that is why you are single again. Stop it before you start. Run over the words.

Easy access to the very best shopping the city can offer.

You walk the empty rooms to kill time, to memorise the things you must say, to put on your face for greeting them at the door. The dimensions are impressive, your heels echo in the air. But there is something clinical about the placement of the magazines on the glass-top table, about the potpourri in the bowls designed to look like they were handcrafted.

A secure environment with gated security.

You stand by the window and look down. There are the trees, the new trees in lines, there is the fountain, and the metal sculpture of the woman rising from flame-like flowers. They come here, they look around the space, they marvel at the size, the light from the bay windows, then they come to this window and they look out. They often take a step back, as if from an electric shock. They ask strange questions, like: When the centre closes, does that mean we're locked inside? Do we get a discount in all the stores? They laugh together, because it is always couples. They have trouble getting away from what it was before, they can't see the potential, the hope in forgetting. The men sometimes say, It's like Disney World.

Ideal for upmarket first time buyers.

You have to make this sale. You have your own debts. You had no idea when you bought that first flat with him, with that tracker mortgage, that after two years it would revert to the base rate. Hope and gratitude erased the small print and you signed too swiftly. You were ambitious together – you thought things would only get better, as everyone said they would. After selling up, after he left, and the mortgage men typed in their numbers and quadrupled your monthly payments, you had no choice but to sell and take the final blow. A thing called negative equity. Twelve thousand. You had to ask your mother for help, and when it came, so too came the phone calls, not once a month, like before, but once a week, and the tone, asking you about how you were, about your diet and relationships. Asking for names. Anyone new? This is what debt is.

Real estate... Say it with a smile. Be glad for that opportunity. It's not your career, just a way to get by until things go back to normal again. You'll do this for a few years, keep yourself to yourself, make some serious money, then move on, move back to where and what you wanted to do, to be.

You're staring at the immense wall-mounted flat screen TV. They never gave you the remote, for that you are glad. You have stopped watching the news. They are rioting in the cities. Some of them mere children.

Run over the words.

Within driving distance of the city's artistic West End.

You look down on the heads of the shoppers below. You're wondering about their debts and their smiles. How the two things could ever be reconciled. Children run around the fountain, laughing, playing hide-and-seek. How will you ever be secure enough to have children? The poor have it easy, ignorance is bliss. You should have had a child when you were twenty, thirty.

Easy, fast access to the central belt motorway system. With free parking in the mall itself.

You will never make the sale if you keep on like this. You have to believe in it to sell it. You have to want to live here yourself. This is what they say. You will, you will will it upon yourself, to believe in this space, this condo apartment in a mall. If you could afford it, you would want to live here yourself. Yes, it's true. Maybe belief is like that these days, something you suspend till the deal is done. To buy you time to find out again, or maybe for the first time, what it is you believe in.

The open plan space is what you want it to be.

The view – yes, it's hard to understand how a shopping centre could be a home, but maybe this is the way it will be from now on. Forty-five identical units. Last time you rambled nervously with that couple, the woman pregnant, you said things you shouldn't have. You made a stupid joke, you said, Well if the city starts to burn you'll be safe here, it's miles away and Security will keep the riff-raff out. Riff-raff, like something you'd say to a child.

The music from the mall is muffled by the reinforced glass. You watch two buskers below with their guitars, but can't hear their music. The man with the dreadlocks seems to be singing with passion, head high, mouth wide open, standing beneath the foliage. There never used to be buskers in malls, perhaps things are changing for the better.

Yes, you would like to live here, would love to be able to shop again, to get a pedicure, down there, to get back in touch with fashion again. You see yourself strolling below, after work, alone, going from shop to shop till it's time to eat. You could buy the food from Tesco at the far end, you could buy a book from Waterstones, everything under one roof. And when the stores are closed and there is nothing on TV you could take a stroll, in perfect safety, past all of the locked facades; window shopping within your own home. And if it gets lonely, there is, you heard, a speed-dating event once a week in Pizza Express. You could meet someone.

A space open to possibility.

Try the smile, untense your shoulders. You must be the face they need to see when they push the buzzer to be let in. Picture them at the door. A couple. Maybe she, like that one before, is pregnant. Nouveau riche, most likely, but you must not judge. Maybe they are scared too and putting on a face. Maybe it's like this for everyone.

335

Run over the words again.

A new exclusive development in a former retail space.

Yes, make yourself believe, it wouldn't cost you so much to dump who you were and be what they want to see, in this flat where a storeroom used to be.

Easy access to the very best shopping the city can offer.

Smile as you greet them. Your real smile. Think of it as a date.

Ideal for upmarket first time buyers.

Walk around the space as if you own it.

Within driving distance of the city's artistic West End.

Make them feel as if they live there already.

Easy, fast access to the central belt motorway system. With free parking in the mall itself.

Yes, you would love to live here. You would leave the walls white to remind yourself that this is your final fresh start.

The open plan space is what you want it to be.

The buzzer is buzzing. They are here.

Focus on your breath, take a second, tell yourself where you are.

A space open to possibility.

Yes, finally, you are here, you are here.

ACKNOWLEDGEMENTS

I would like to thank Creative Scotland, and in particular Gavin Wallace and Aly Barr for their support, feedback and encouragement. I would also like to thank the staff of the many malls within Scotland who, with their generosity of spirit, made this project possible. Thanks also to the international academics who have guided me through the webs of facts and counter-facts. A huge debt of gratitude goes to Mark Buckland, MD of Cargo Publishing, for taking a risk on this project and for investing it with so much energy and imagination. Another big thanks goes to my editor, Anneliese Mackintosh, for her empathy and understanding, and to my fellow Scottish authors, Doug Johnstone and Rodge Glass, who have given invaluable feedback and support. Thanks also to a network of magazines, such as *The List*, *Edinburgh Review*, and websites such as *3:AM* and *Dangerous Minds*, who have taken an active interest and encouraged me to see the project to completion. I would also like to thank Ryan Van Winkle and the Edinburgh International Book Festival for bringing me out of my shell, and pushing me on to face the challenges of a wider audience, and my old friend Dave Anderson, whose photography and faith in the importance of documenting daily life has been a source of inspiration. I would also like to thank the sociologist Zygmunt Bauman for providing me with the tools to understand the world we live in. Last of all I have to thank my wife, Emily Ballou, for her enduring support over the three years in which I have ranted and raved about a subject that to some seems insane or inane, but which has been all-consuming.

'Every epoch, in fact, not only dreams the one to follow but, in dreaming, precipitates its awakening. It bears its end within itself.'

Walter Benjamin.

The Arcades Project.

1939.

Some of the these stories have appeared in *Gutter*, *Edinburgh Review*, *The List* and *Birdville Magazine*.

PICTURE CREDITS

Victor Gruen and Bruce Dayton with a model of Gruen's Southdale Centre, Minneapolis, 1956. Victor Gruen Associates

The Parade of the Contrade in the Piazza del Campo in the Sixteenth Century. Artist Vincenzo Rustici: Comune de Siena.

Galleria Vittorio Emanuele II in Milan, 1867. Unidentified photographer. Sec. XIX terzo quarto Civico Archivio Fotografico, Milano.

Tanks in Red Square mark the 40th anniversary of the Communist rule in Russia, 1957. Photograph: Bettmann/Corbis

Brock Burn, beside Silverburn mall, Glasgow. Photographer: Gerard Blaikie

Braehead © Google maps 2012.

Bannsiter Mall, Kansas. Photographer: Darrel James

Abandoned Malls, Malaysia. Photographer: Raz Talhar

Iranian mall sign. Photographer: Habib Majidi

Mall Still Open. Photographer: Ed Hanson

In all other instances, photomontages are by the author.